Theosis and Religion

Participation in Divine Life in the Eastern and Western Traditions

NORMAN RUSSELL

University of Oxford

T0381692

CAMBRIDGE
UNIVERSITY PRESS

CAMBRIDGE
UNIVERSITY PRESS

Shaftesbury Road, Cambridge CB2 8EA, United Kingdom

One Liberty Plaza, 20th Floor, New York, NY 10006, USA

477 Williamstown Road, Port Melbourne, VIC 3207, Australia

314–321, 3rd Floor, Plot 3, Splendor Forum, Jasola District Centre,
New Delhi – 110025, India

103 Penang Road, #05-06/07, Visioncrest Commercial, Singapore 238467

Cambridge University Press is part of Cambridge University Press & Assessment,
a department of the University of Cambridge.

We share the University's mission to contribute to society through the pursuit of
education, learning and research at the highest international levels of excellence.

www.cambridge.org
Information on this title: www.cambridge.org/9781108418683

DOI: 10.1017/9781108290852

First published 2024

A catalogue record for this publication is available from the British Library

Library of Congress Cataloging-in-Publication Data
NAMES: Russell, Norman, 1945- author.
TITLE: Theosis and religion : participation in divine life in the Eastern and Western traditions /
Norman Russell, Oxford University.
DESCRIPTION: Cambridge : Cambridge University Press, 2024. | Series: Cambridge studies
in religion, philosophy, and society | Includes bibliographical references and index.
IDENTIFIERS: LCCN 2023045651 (print) | LCCN 2023045652 (ebook) |
ISBN 9781108418683 (hardback) | ISBN 9781108406338 (paperback) |
ISBN 9781108290852 (epub)
SUBJECTS: LCSH: Deification (Christianity)–History of doctrines.
CLASSIFICATION: LCC BT767.8 .R885 2024 (print) | LCC BT767.8 (ebook) | DDC 234–
dc23/eng/20231129
LC record available at https://lccn.loc.gov/2023045651
LC ebook record available at https://lccn.loc.gov/2023045652

ISBN 978-1-108-41868-3 Hardback
ISBN 978-1-108-40633-8 Paperback

Theosis and Religion

Theosis, originally a Greek term for Christian divinisation or deification, has become a vogue word in modern theology. Although recent publications have explored its meaning in a selection of different contexts, this is the first book to offer a coherent narrative of how the concept of theosis developed in both its Eastern and Western versions. Norman Russell shows how the role of Dionysius the Areopagite was pivotal not only in Byzantium but also in the late mediaeval West, where it strengthened the turn towards an individualistic interiority. Russell also relates theosis to changing concepts of religion in the modern age. He investigates the Russian version of theosis, introduced in the West by Russian members of the Paris School after the 1917 Revolution. Since then, theosis has undergone additional development through the addition of esoteric elements which have since passed into the mainstream of all theological traditions and even into popular spirituality.

Norman Russell is Honorary Research Fellow at St Stephen's House, University of Oxford, and Professor of Patristics and Byzantine Theology at the Istituto Teologico di Santa Eufemia di Calcedonia of the Orthodox Exarchate of Italy. He is the author of the acclaimed *The Doctrine of Deification in the Greek Patristic Tradition* (2004).

Cambridge Studies in Religion, Philosophy, and Society

Series Editors

Paul K. Moser, *Loyola University, Chicago*
Chad Meister, *Bethel College, Indiana*

This is a series of interdisciplinary texts devoted to major-level courses in religion, philosophy, and related fields. It includes original, current, and wide-spanning contributions by leading scholars from various disciplines that (a) focus on the central academic topics in religion and philosophy, (b) are seminal and up-to-date regarding recent developments in scholarship on the various key topics, and (c) incorporate, with needed precision and depth, the major differing perspectives and backgrounds – the central voices on the major religions and the religious, philosophical, and sociological viewpoints that cover the intellectual landscape today. Cambridge Studies in Religion, Philosophy, and Society is a direct response to this recent and widespread interest and need.

Recent Books in the Series

Roger Trigg
Religious Diversity: Philosophical and Political Dimensions

John Cottingham
Philosophy of Religion: Towards a More Humane Approach

William J. Wainwright
Reason, Revelation, and Devotion: Inference and Argument in Religion

Harry J. Gensler
Ethics and Religion

Fraser Watts
Psychology, Religion, and Spirituality: Concepts and Applications

Gordon Graham
Philosophy, Art, and Religion: Understanding Faith and Creativity

Keith Ward
The Christian Idea of God: A Philosophical Foundation for Faith

Timothy Samuel Shah and Jack Friedman
Homo Religiosus? Exploring the Roots of Religion and Religious Freedom in Human Experience

Sylvia Walsh
Kierkegaard and Religion: Personality, Character, and Virtue

Roger S. Gottlieb
Morality and the Environmental Crisis

J. L. Schellenberg
Religion after Science: The Cultural Consequences of Religious Immaturity

To the memory of
George Russell
1914–1995

Contents

Preface

The title of this book had already been chosen when I was invited by Chad Meister and Paul Moser to contribute a volume to their series. I liked it because I saw that it offered me possibilities for ranging much more widely than in my previous work on deification and perhaps making connections that I had not seen before.

Theosis has become a vogue word in Anglophone theology. Although long familiar to patristic scholars as a Greek term – θέωσις, meaning literally 'becoming god' and signifying deification or participation in the divine life – it was not widely discussed until towards the end of the twentieth century. There appear to be several reasons for this. First, the scholarly foundations needed to be laid through a close examination of the relevant texts. Then, the rise of the Ecumenical Movement (which led to the founding of the World Council of Churches after the Second World War) was necessary in order to bring Western theologians into dialogue with their Eastern counterparts, stimulating the former, initially representatives of Reformed Churches, to take a fresh look at their own soteriology. Anglicans and Roman Catholics in the early days had their own contacts with Orthodox theology through their interaction with the Russian émigré theologians who had settled in Paris after the 1917 Revolution.

At the same time, there was a parallel development in the understanding of 'religion'. Religion was subjected to theological and sociological critiques which sought to deconstruct what was seen as a fundamentally nineteenth-century ideological category. As a result, departments of theology in many universities were renamed departments of religious studies. On a more popular level, in Western Europe and North America there has been a move away from commitment to specific churches ('organised religion') to an interest in 'spirituality'. God is back, as some commentators have said, but not as the God of the traditional Western theological systems. The purpose of this book is to uncover the different meanings of theosis that have emerged in recent years and to relate them to developments in our understanding of religion.

In the course of writing this book, I have incurred a number of debts to friends and colleagues. I am especially grateful to John Gale, whose thoughtful comments on working carefully through the entire manuscript have greatly improved the book; to Matthew Levering, the Press's reader, who likewise made a number of perceptive and very helpful comments that are reflected in the final version; and also to Eduard Borysov, Maria Carlson, Douglas Dales, Paul Gavrilyuk, Pantelis Kalaïtzidis, Daniel Keating, Étienne Leclercq, Andrew Louth, Spyros Petritakis, Raymond Russell, and Antonella Sannino, who answered queries and sent me copies of their articles. I also thank Chad Meister and Paul Moser for their great patience in the face of my long delay in submitting the manuscript. My earliest book on deification was dedicated to the memory of my mother, my first teacher of Greek. This book is dedicated to the memory of my father in grateful recognition of the unfailing support he gave to my studies over many years.

Abbreviations

CCCM	Corpus Christianorum, Continuatio Mediaevalis
CH	Corpus Hermeticum
CWS	Classics of Western Spirituality
Denzinger	H. Denzinger (ed.), *Enchiridion Symbolorum*, Barcelona, 1951
GCS	Die griechischen christlichen Schriftsteller der ersten drei Jahrhunderte, Berlin
JEH	*Journal of Ecclesiastical History*, London
LXX	Septuagint
NRSV	New Revised Standard Version
PG	J.-P. Migne (ed.), Patrologia Graeca, Paris, 1857–66
PL	J.-P. Migne (ed.), Patrologia Latina, Paris, 1844–64
SC	Sources Chrétiennes, Paris
TTB	Translated Texts for Byzantinists
TTH	Translated Texts for Historians
WCC	World Council of Churches

Introduction

The Extraordinary Rise of a Theological Theme

WHAT'S IN A WORD?

Word studies have their limitations but words are important. Without a clear terminology, ideas can become fuzzy, none more so than ideas concerning humanity's relationship with God. The word at the centre of this investigation is 'theosis'. With the accent on the 'o', it more often than not indicates a Protestant mindset. Catholics and Orthodox prefer to speak of 'divinisation' or 'deification', in the Orthodox case also *obozhenie* (обожение), or 'theosis' (θέωσις) with the accent on the 'e'. The word has spread beyond Christian usage to the Mormons and has even appeared in New Age discourse. Its first use can be dated precisely to the year 363, when it was coined by St Gregory of Nazianzus as a synonym for spiritual ascent in his *Fourth Oration*, an invective he delivered on the death of the emperor Julian the Apostate (4, 71; PG 35, 593B; Moreschini, 2000: 132). Subsequently, it was used several times by Gregory, but although taken up by Dionysius the Areopagite, Leontius of Jerusalem, Maximus the Confessor, and John Damascene, it did not become the standard term for deification until the late Byzantine period.[1] The earlier patristic term was *theopoiēsis* (θεοποίησις), rendered into Latin as *deificatio*, 'deification'.[2] It should be noted that the Greek word for god, *theos* (θεός), without the definite article is to be distinguished from *ho theos* (ὁ θεός) with the definite article. Without the article, *theos* is often

---

[1] For detailed references, see Russell, 2004: 341.
[2] According to Souter, 1949, the earliest writers to use *deificatio* belong to the fifth century, Ps.-Rufinus and Ps.-Marius Mercator. Augustine uses the verb *deifico* but not the noun *deificatio*.

used in an adjectival sense. It means 'divine' rather than a particular god, whereas *ho theos* is reserved for the One God. So *theōsis* (the -ωσις ending indicating perhaps a more intimate relationship that the -ποίησις ending) fundamentally means 'becoming divine', or acquiring the attributes of divinity, chiefly those of immortality and goodness.

Several scholars have suggested refinements in the way terms are used to refer to this 'becoming divine'. In 2007, the Evangelical theologian, Roger Olson proposed distinguishing between 'divinisation' and 'deification', reserving that latter for views on participation in God that rely on the Palamite distinction between essence and energies (2007: 199). A few years later, the Baptist New Testament scholar Ben Blackwell discussed Paul's soteriology under the title of 'christosis' (2016: 264–66). A more radical suggestion has recently been made by Eduard Borysov, an Evangelical, who, taking his cue from Blackwell, would like to see the term 'christosis' replaced by 'triadosis' on the grounds that the Christian's 'becoming divine' is not just the result of union with Christ but entails participation in the trinitarian relations of Father, Son and Holy Spirit (2019: 2). These neologisms are intelligent, but it remains to be seen whether either of them will catch on. Greek speakers prefer the linguistically more correct *christopoiēsis* or *enchristōsis* to 'christosis'. By the same token, *entriadōsis* is to be preferred to 'triadosis'. 'Theosis' will probably be with us for some time yet.

THEOSIS IN DIFFERENT CHRISTIAN COMMUNIONS

The meaning of theosis varies in emphasis according to a writer's confessional allegiance. For Reformed theologians, mainly Baptists and Evangelicals (who much prefer 'theosis' to 'deification', perhaps because of the latter's pagan connotations), the term expresses a participatory soteriology – becoming children of God through union with Christ – in both its Pauline and Johannine versions (Blackwell, 2016; Byers, 2017). For Anglicans, it is above all participation in God, 'the goal of God's saving and restoring work in human beings' (R. Williams, 2021: 93). For Roman Catholics, it represents 'the full outworking of grace in the Christian life' (Keating, 2007: 5). For Orthodox, it is a relational term expressing the Christian's ultimate participation in the life of the Trinity, often with reference to the divine energies. While these brief definitions are broadly characteristic of their respective communions, none of them belongs exclusively to any single one. It used to be thought that deification was peculiarly Eastern Orthodox and quite foreign to the West. The prevailing opinion now is that all Christian communions hold some version of theosis as expressive of their soteriology. What has brought this about?

The driving motor has been the Ecumenical Movement. Modern Anglican interest in theosis goes back to meetings in the 1920s between Anglican and Russian theologians that led to the founding of the Fellowship of St Alban and St Sergius.[3] The Russian theologians were members of the so-called Paris School, who a little later also engaged in conversations with sympathetic Roman Catholics of the *ressourcement* movement. It was only after the inauguration of the World Council of Churches in 1948, however, which the Orthodox joined at its inception, that dialogues began between Orthodox and others at the official level. It is not a coincidence that the identification of the theme of theosis in Martin Luther by researchers working at the University of Helsinki under the supervision of Tuomo Mannermaa was made at around the time of theological dialogues conducted between the Russian Orthodox Church and the Finnish Lutheran Church. The findings of the Mannermaa school were communicated to the Anglophone world in 1998 by two American Lutheran scholars, Carl E. Braaten and Robert W. Jenson (1998).[4] Six years later, a well-attended conference on deification was held at the Theological School of Drew University, a Methodist foundation in New Jersey, which resulted in the publication in 2007 of a significant collection of papers on the topic, *Partakers of the Divine Nature* (Christiansen and Wittung, 2007). Another conference, in which the Ecumenical Patriarch, Bartholomew I, participated, was held at the Catholic university of Leuven in Belgium in 2015. Some of the papers on the Western mediaeval and early modern traditions given at Leuven have been published under the title *Mystical Doctrines of Deification* (Arblaster and Faesen, 2019). Since these conferences, books on deification have multiplied. The theology of theosis has been identified in a large number of writers of both the Catholic and Protestant traditions from the early Latin Fathers to modern theologians such as Hans Urs von Balthasar and Thomas Torrance. Books and articles discussing the Orthodox perspective on deification have been fewer but nonetheless significant. What was an

---

[3] Modern Anglican interest in Eastern Orthodoxy in general goes back much further to the visits of William Palmer of Magdalen to Russia in the 1840s and the foundation in 1864 of the Eastern Church Association (now the Anglican and Eastern Churches Association) with support of leading members of the Tractarian movement.

[4] For an overview of the Mannermaa school and its influence, see Kärkkäinen, 2004.

exciting theological novelty two or three decades ago has now become mainstream.

A THEME OR A DOCTRINE?

Are all these writers, however, discussing the same thing? Gösta Hallonsten, in an important contribution to the Drew conference volume, insists that a distinction should be made between deification as a theme and as a doctrine (2007: 283–84, 287). The theme is found widely in the Western tradition, largely through its presence in the Latin liturgy,[5] and refers to participation in the divine life as humanity's final goal. The doctrine is a good deal more comprehensive, 'encompassing the whole economy of salvation' (Hallonsten, 2007: 284). In another important contribution to the same volume, Andrew Louth makes a comparable distinction between a lesser arch in the theology of salvation and a greater arch, the lesser arch 'leading from Fall to redemption, the purpose of which is to restore the function of the greater arch, from creation to deification' (2007: 35). Clearly, in the view of both Hallonsten and Louth, the term 'theosis' should be reserved for the greater arch, reaching from the creation of the world to its eschatological fulfilment. Theosis 'is not some isolated *theologoumenon*,' says Louth, 'but has what one might call structural significance' (2007: 43). This structural significance originates with the creation of humanity in the image and likeness of God and attains its full expression through the incarnation, death, and resurrection of the Word, the intention of which is to reconstitute humanity in the way that God intended. Our true humanity, reconstituted in Christ, is appropriated through our life in the ecclesial body but not without intense ascetic struggle. Louth lays great emphasis on the ascetic commitment of Orthodoxy. Accordingly, he sees the *Philokalia* of St Makarios of Corinth and St Nikodemos of the Holy Mountain, published in Venice in 1782, as a work of 'towering importance', of greater importance than the official doctrinal pronouncements of the same period or even the writings of the Russian émigré theologians of the early twentieth century. The transformatory significance of theosis, a transformation that is not simply eschatological but begins with the ascetic struggle in this life, is to be sought primarily in Orthodox experience. In Louth's view, such a concept of theosis is merely adumbrated in Western texts.

---

[5] On the liturgical aspect, see Ortiz, 2019a.

Louth has not modified his opinion since his Drew lecture. Indeed, in a recent book review he declares: 'Deification, θέωσις, is at home in Greek intellectual culture in a way denied to Latin intellectual culture' (2020: 837). He is clearly referring to the structural significance of deification, to deification as a *doctrine* with cosmic significance integral to a given writer's work rather than as a *theme* reflected occasionally in such phrases as 'image and likeness', 'adoption as children of God', 'participation in God', and 'wonderful exchange'. I think he is right, despite my own effort (in the book that he reviews) to find common themes linking Greek and Latin authors. There is no Latin equivalent in the patristic tradition to Maximus the Confessor or Gregory Palamas, for whom deification provides an all-encompassing doctrinal perspective. It is only in the mystical writers of the later Middle Ages that deification comes to occupy a comparable place.

The exploration of deification as a theme can nevertheless yield interesting results. As he looks 'east in winter' in his book of that title, Rowan Williams considers what it means in the ascetic tradition both to affirm and to deny the 'self', that is to say, to attain an interior awareness of a personal God and at the same time to shed the specific and negate the particular. The imagined individual self must be rejected but not 'the eternal interdependence in giving that constitutes the trinitarian life, and the dependence on eternal gift that constitutes the finite world' (2021: 109). In the case of Fr (now St) Sophrony (Sakharov), the implications of the practice that the *starets* expounds for achieving this, says Williams, reconfigure what the call to solidarity might mean and also 'direct us to a new imagining of Christian ethics' (109). For ordinary non-monastic mortals, the practical laying hold of deification even in this life might look something like this:

The fact that theosis encompasses the whole of the economy of salvation means that it is intended for all believers without exception. To live theosis, then, means to lead our life in an eschatological perspective within the ecclesial community, striving through prayer, participation in the Eucharist, and the moral life to attain the divine likeness, being conformed spiritually and corporeally to the body of Christ until we are brought into Christ's identity and arrive ultimately at union with the Father. (Russell, 2009: 169)

Here certain themes are brought together – Christian solidarity, Eucharistic ecclesiology, ascetic struggle, 'adoption into the relatedness of the Word to the Father' – but within the context of an ontological transformation of the believer that goes beyond the attainment of any metaphysical understanding, although the latter is not to be despised. It is the incorporation of various themes into a coherent and even universal whole that constitutes the doctrine of deification. What is missing in the above definition, however, is any reference to the Holy Spirit. This is rectified in the following definition by Paul Gavrilyuk:

> Deification is a process and goal by which the human being (or in some way creation as a whole) comes to share in or participate in God, Christ, divine life, divine attributes, divine energies, or grows into the likeness of God, while remaining a creature ontologically distinct from the Creator. This process is often also described as divine adoption, regeneration, sanctification, and union with God. Human deification is made possible by the incarnation of the divine Logos in Jesus Christ and is sustained by the Holy Spirit through the sacramental life of the Church, prayer, ascetical discipline, and growth in virtue.[6]

The characterisation of deification as both a process and a goal is significant. It is not simply a theological theme or motif, although it is that as well. It is the path by which the whole of created reality, through the human person, having come from God by the kenotic act of creation, returns to him by incorporation, as Williams has put it, into the relatedness of the Word to the Father. Theosis ultimately is a doctrine in which a number of different themes have their place within a larger structure.

THE BOOK'S RATIONALE

Deification in many of its manifestations is not restricted to Christianity. It is found in Late Antiquity's main philosophical tradition, Platonism, and also more marginally in Judaism and Islam. There is a comparable teaching, too, in the ancient Vedanta schools of India and even in the modern religion of Mormonism. I leave the non-Christian traditions aside, however, except insofar as (in the case of Platonism and Judaism) they impinge on the main Christian traditions of Eastern and Western Europe, not only because of my lack of competence in these fields but also in order to develop a coherent argument on the evolution of the doctrine or theme of deification specifically in the Orthodox and Western Christian traditions.[7] Moreover, I discuss this evolution during the first

---

[6] Paul Gavrilyuk in a personal communication dated 25 November 2020. This definition will be incorporated into the Introduction of the *Oxford Handbook of Deification*, edited by Andrew Hofer, Matthew Levering, and Paul Gavrilyuk, to be published shortly by Oxford University Press.

[7] For an engaging overview that ranges widely over non-Christian versions of deification, see Litwa, 2013. Litwa traces 'the discourse of deification' from the ancient Egyptian pharaohs to Nietzsche's Superman, seeing them all as manifestations, or 'models', of the

thousand years only very briefly simply as a basis for a more detailed consideration of some of the major developments of the last millennium. Two things in particular struck me in the course of my research. The first is the central importance for deification of Dionysius the Areopagite,[8] in both East and West. The second is how the esoteric traditions came back into fashion, particularly in the sixteenth and early twentieth centuries, making their own distinct contributions to the concept of deification. These two facts are not entirely unconnected.

The methodology followed is that of *Ideengeschichte*, the history of ideas. Chapter 1 explores the meaning of religion – which is much broader than the belief-system of any given ecclesial communion – and also the meaning of theosis in its early historical development. Religion is considered up to the modern age, but theosis only to the end of the patristic age as the springboard for the study of later developments. Chapter 2 traces the post-patristic career of theosis in the Byzantine world, with the definition (at the Constantinopolitan Council of 1351) of theosis as participation in the uncreated energies. Chapter 3 looks at the Western reception of Dionysius the Areopagite and the channelling of thinking on theosis, through Dionysius, into the Western mystical tradition. At the time of the Renaissance, this tradition morphs into the esoteric, as is discussed in Chapter 4. In Chapter 5, it is shown how the esoteric contributes to the Russian sophianic versions of theosis. Chapter 6 examines the patristic retrievals of theosis in the twentieth century, and Chapter 7 explores how, through such publications as the *Philokalia* and the *Way of a Pilgrim*, theosis reaches a broad non-churchy audience.

In the book review mentioned above, Andrew Louth regrets the attempt of the book's contributors to make the Greek and Latin Fathers speak in a uniform way. There is a difference of style, he says: 'what would seem to me a real pity would be if Christians felt that there was to be only one theological style' (2020: 837). The difference in style that we can discern by taking a broad perspective lies not only between the Greek and Latin Fathers but also between them and the Western mystics of the

---

same theme. He rightly says that 'we stand on the brink of a new discourse' (ix). Dissenting from his fundamental thesis, however, I hold that the Christian versions (interconnected as they are in various ways) are significantly different from their non-Christian analogues.

[8] I drop the 'pseudo-' because although briefly challenged in 532, Dionysius's identity as Paul's Athenian convert was not exposed as a fiction until the fifteenth century, by the Italian scholar Lorenzo Valla. As it no longer causes confusion, I am happy to call Dionysius by his chosen nom de plume.

late Middle Ages, the esoteric thinkers of the Early Modern Age, the sophianic theologians of nineteenth-century Russia, and the moderns who have retrieved the notion of deification in some form or other and enriched it from a variety of sources. Theosis is a polyseme, a word with more than one meaning. The discussion that follows attempts to explore these meanings in a selection of different contexts, which, while far from being comprehensive,[9] will indicate, I hope, the broad trajectory of the notion of theosis since it first emerged as a theological theme.

---

[9] I particularly regret not having dealt (through lack of space) with the French Oratorians and Spanish Carmelites of the seventeenth century.

I

What Is 'Religion', What Is 'Theosis', and How Are They Related?

During my last year at my London grammar school, I attended a class in Latin poetry conducted by the headmaster. In his book-lined study, a small group of pupils read with him *De rerum natura* – 'On the nature of things' – by the great Epicurean philosopher-poet of the first century BC, Titus Lucretius Carus. Not far into the first book of the poem, after a catalogue of crimes committed, according to Greek mythology, in the name of religion, we came to the line: *tantum potuit religio suadere malorum*, 'to such great evils was religion able to impel people' (1.101).[1] 'Mark this line well', said my headmaster, and I have never forgotten it. At the time, its meaning seemed perfectly clear: the superstitious element in pagan religion could persuade people to undertake evil acts in the mistaken conviction that they were pleasing the gods. Later, I came to see that the point Lucretius was making was more philosophical. What he meant by *religio* included not only superstitious awe but also conscientious conviction, moral obligation, and regard for the sacred.[2] As an Epicurean, Lucretius was a materialist who wanted to free his readers from anxieties such as the fear of death. Any supernatural concern that prevented the mind from attaining a detached state of tranquillity was to be deplored.

---

[1] The Penguin Classics translation by R. E. Latham renders the line: 'Such are the heights of wickedness to which men are driven by superstition.'

[2] These are the primary meanings of *religio* as used by Cicero (who probably edited Lucretius's poem for publication).

In his contempt for religion, Lucretius was in a minority. The dominant philosophy in Late Antiquity was Platonism, and the Platonists took religion and the existence of the gods for granted. For them, the gods occupied a celestial realm remote from human concerns; the cultic side of religion (until the time of Iamblichus) was of little interest. Once when Plotinus (205–270) was asked by one of his senior students to accompany him to the temples on the feasts of the gods, he replied: 'They ought to come to me, not I to them' (Porphyry, *Life of Plotinus*, trans. Armstrong). The spirits (δαίμονες) that lurked in the temples were very inferior beings to a philosopher whose guardian spirit, as an Egyptian priest living in Rome had once declared, was actually a god.

Christian writers sought to distinguish between acceptable and unacceptable aspects of *religio*. The rhetorician Arnobius of Sicca, writing at the end of the third century AD, makes a distinction between *religio* as 'religion' and *religio* as 'superstition' through interiorising the former ('opinion constitutes religion') and relegating the latter (*superstitio*) to external cultic acts (*Adv. nationes*, 7, 37). The etymological origin of the word *religio* was also investigated as a guide to its fundamental meaning. Cicero connected *religio* with the verb *relegere*, 'to read over again', in the sense of 'pondering what pertains to God' (*De deorum natura*, 2, 28). Writing in the first decade of the fourth century, Lactantius, a former student of Arnobius, questions Cicero's etymology, preferring to connect *religio* with *religare*, 'to bind': 'We have said that the name of religion is derived from the bond of piety, because God has tied man to himself, and bound him by piety' (*Divinae institutiones*, 4, 28, trans. Fletcher). Augustine suggests alternative derivations, either (following Lactantius) from *religare*, 'to bind together', in that religion binds human beings to God (*De vera relig.*, 55; *De civ. Dei*, 10, 1; *Retract.* 2, 13, 19), or (following Cicero but interpreting the word differently) from *relegere*, taken to mean 'to re-elect', consciously to make a new choice: 'by our re-election ... we direct our course towards him with love (*dilectio*), so that in reaching him we may find our rest, and attend our happiness because we have achieved our fulfilment in him' (*De civ. Dei*, 10, 3; trans. Bettenson). For Augustine (as for Cicero), religion is therefore closely associated with worship, which in Latin is *cultus*. In this connection, finding the term *cultus* too broad because it can also refer to relations between human beings, Augustine turns to the Greek. The various Greek equivalents for *cultus* seem to him preferable, especially *thrēskeia* (θρησκεία), which he says is the Greek word which Latin translators habitually render as *religio* (*De civ. Dei*, 10, 1).

Biblical use of the word *thrēskeia* is rare, occurring in the Septuagint only in two deuterocanonical works composed originally in Greek, the Wisdom of Solomon and Fourth Maccabees.[3] Both were written in the early first century AD, probably in Alexandria and Antioch, respectively, at a time when the emperor Caligula was demanding worship from the Jews. In the Wisdom of Solomon, *thrēskeia* refers to the worship of the ruler (14.17) or of idols (14.27). In Fourth Maccabees, it is put into the mouth of Antiochus when he refers to the 'religion of the Jews' (5.7, 13). Nor is the word *thrēskeia* commonly used in the New Testament.[4] According to Luke, Paul declares 'I have belonged to the strictest sect of our religion (θρησκεία) and lived as a Pharisee' (Acts 26.5). And in the Letter to the Colossians, Paul (if he is indeed the author) warns his readers, again in a Jewish religious context, against the cult (θρησκεία) of angels (Col 2.18). The only other New Testament text in which 'religion' is mentioned is the little ethical treatise in the wisdom tradition known as the Epistle of James. There the author says: 'Religion (θρησκεία) that is pure and undefiled before God, the Father, is this: to care for orphans and widows in their distress, and to keep oneself unstained in the world' (James 1.27).[5] Thus, in the New Testament, 'religion' refers – not always positively – to a 'cult' or a 'faith' in the modern sense, a defined system of belief, worship, and moral conduct. It is not comparable with the act of faith-trust (πίστις), which is the wholehearted acceptance of the Christian kerygma.

The rather sparse references to religion (θρησκεία) in the Greek literature of the Late Roman Empire are in harmony with the usage of the Septuagint and the New Testament. In the Greek version of the Acts of the second-century Scillitan martyrs, it is Saturninus, the pagan proconsul, not Speratus, the Christian defendant, who describes his own practice of piety as a religion (*Acta Scillit. mart.*; ed. Robinson 1891: 113). Several pagan authors use 'religion' to refer to worship offered to the gods (e.g., CH XII, 23, Schiavoni, 2018: 230; Iamblichus, *De vita Pythagorica*, 3, 6,

---

[3] The early Israelites had no word for 'religion', which in modern Hebrew is *dat*. The word *dat* enters the canon of Scripture for the first time, as a loan-word from Persian, in the Book of Esther, where it is put in the mouth of King Ahasuerus at 1.13 and of his chief minister Haman at 3.8. The Septuagint and the modern English versions translate this as 'laws' (νόμοι), referring to the laws and customs of the Jews as opposed to those of the Persians. *Dat* still signified law (both divine and human) in mediaeval Hebrew.

[4] As K. L. Schmidt says in his article in Kittel, 'This paucity is quite striking in relation to the whole sphere of Gk. literature' (1965: 155).

[5] In all three cases, the Vulgate translates θρησκεία as *religio*.

32). The Christian authors of Late Antiquity and Early Byzantium who speak of 'the Christian religion' (ἡ τῶν Χριστιανῶν θρησκεία) include Clement of Rome, who gives a summary of the Christian faith (with an emphasis on moral conduct) introduced by the words 'the religion defined by him is the following' (*Clem. Hom.*, 7, 8, 1); Cyril of Alexandria, who frequently refers to 'the religion of the Christians' and 'our holy religion', especially in Book VII of his refutation of Julian the Apostate;[6] and Dionysius the Areopagite, who commends 'the more-than-wise truth of our religion' (*Letter* 7, 3: τὴν ὑπέρσοφον τῆς θρησκείας ἡμῶν ἀλήθειαν). By the ninth century, in the context of the Iconoclast Controversy, Theodore the Stoudite is able to speak of 'our religion handed down by our fathers' (*Letter* 71, 63: ἡ πατροπαράδοτος ἡμῶν θρησκεία). But θρησκεία is also applied to other systems of belief, to pagan cults (Athanasius, *Contra Gent.*, 23, 37 and 29, 37; Sozomen, *Hist. eccl.*, 2, 6, 1; John Damascene, *Expos. Fidei*, 77, 29), Judaism (Eusebius, *Demonst. Evangel.*, 6, 3, 4), Islam (John Damascene, *De haeres.*, 100), and even Christian heresies such as Arianism (Socrates, *Hist. eccl.*, 5, 12, 18 and 6, 6, 8). Among Greek speakers, the orthodox Christian faith is described quite often as a 'religion' when it is contrasted with other bodies of doctrine or organised forms of worship but rarely when it is considered in itself as the path to salvation.

In the early mediaeval Latin West, *religio* was used most widely of the cult of a saint. Drawing on the sense of 'binding together', it also signified a religious order. When qualified by *universa*, it indicated Christendom as a whole. These meanings were enriched in the later Middle Ages by Thomas Aquinas (c. 1225–1274). In the second part of Part Two of his *Summae theologiae*, he devotes a section (question 81) specifically to the topic of religion. In the first article, he considers 'whether religion directs man to God alone'. After reviewing the different theories of the etymology of the word and the discussions of *religio* by his predecessors, particularly Augustine, he concludes that it does indeed direct man to God alone. It is therefore a virtue because 'it belongs to religion to pay due honour to someone, namely, to God' (*Summa theol.*, II, iia, q.81, art. 2). Moreover, it is a moral virtue, because unlike a theological virtue, which is focused on the last end, it concerns things that contribute towards that end. Thus, religion is equivalent to sanctity, which 'differs from religion not essentially but only logically' (*Summa theol.*, II, iia, q.81, art. 8).

---

[6] For example, 1, 34; 2, 23; 5, 1; 5, 13; 6, 31; 7, 8; 7, 22; 7, 26; 7, 30; 7, 38.

Knowledge of the Thomist notion of religion as a moral virtue entered the Greek East through the translation of the *Summa theologiae* made in the fourteenth century by the statesman Demetrios Kydones (c. 1324–c. 1398) with the assistance of his brother, the monk Prochoros (c. 1333/ 34–1369/70) of the Great Lavra.[7] Thomas's *religio* was translated as θρησκεία; but although the translations of the Kydones brothers were widely read, the sense of θρησκεία as a virtue did not take root. Among the Greeks, *religio* in the moral sense was, and remained, *theosebeia* (θεοσέβεια), 'religious feeling' or 'reverence for God'.[8] Although only once mentioned in passing in the New Testament (1 Tim 2.10), the use of θεοσέβεια in the Septuagint, especially in Job ('truly, the fear of the Lord [θεοσέβεια], that is wisdom' [Job 28.28, NRSV]) and in Sirach ('but godliness [θεοσέβεια] is an abomination to a sinner' [Sirach 1.24, NRSV]), ensured its prominence in Greek Christian literature. From the second century onwards, θεοσέβεια was commonly regarded as the opposite to pagan superstition or false religion, *deisidaimonia* (δεισιδαιμονία), and indeed became the usual term for the Christian faith when the latter was not being considered in terms of a doctrinal system. Gregory Palamas (c. 1296–1357), for example, in all his voluminous writings never once uses the word 'religion' (θρησκεία) but often refers to 'reverence towards God' (θεοσέβεια).[9] Even though θρησκεία never became a moral virtue among the Orthodox, Thomas's definition of religion in relation to faith, religion being not faith but 'a solemn declaration of faith through certain external signs' (*fidei protestatio per aliqua exteriora signa*: τῆς πίστεως διαμαρτηρία διά τινων ἔξωθεν σημείων, in Kydones's translation), did in fact harmonise well with the Greek tradition (*Summa theol.*, secunda secundae, qu. 94, 1).

By the early fifteenth century, the way Greeks and Latins understood 'religion' had much in common. On the philosophical level, both sides saw 'religion' as referring mainly to the external expression of belief, in the case of Aquinas as a system of signs pointing to faith (*protestatio per aliqua exteriora signa*; *Summa theol.*, secunda secundae, qu. 94, 1), in the

---

[7] For an overview of the influence of Aquinas on Byzantine thinkers, see Plested, 2012: 63–134.

[8] In the fifteenth century, George Gemistos Plethon made θεοσέβεια the first of his 'special virtues' after the four 'general virtues' of prudence, justice, courage, and temperance. On this, see Hladký, 2014: 153.

[9] In the *Letter to His Church* (§ 7, line 14), written while he was in captivity among the Turks, Palamas refers to the Christian religion as τὸ σέβας ('worship' or 'adoration', hence 'religion', 'the Christian religion' being indicated by the definite article).

case of the Greeks as the 'activity' of faith (ἐνέργεια πίστεως).[10] On this level, religion was the system of doctrine and worship that defined a 'faith community'. George Gennadios Scholarios (c. 1405–c. 1472), the first patriarch of Constantinople under Ottoman rule, brings together two of the then current senses of 'religion', that of cult and that of the expression of feeling, with his own definition of θρησκεία: 'worship and reverence of any kind with regard to God' (λατρεία καὶ τὸ ὁποιοῦν σέβας περὶ Θεόν) (*Grammatica, Oeuvres completes*, vol. 2, 456). We thus enter the modern world with a definition that treats religion as an empirical reality and indeed as basically a human phenomenon. This is an approach that would be developed extensively in modernity and beyond.

PHILOSOPHICAL NOTIONS OF RELIGION IN THE MODERN AGE

The fundamental shift of outlook marked by the Reformation, the Enlightenment, Kant's 'critical' revolution in philosophy, the French Revolution, and the rise of scientific disciplines relying on objective methods of investigation created a chasm between the pre-modern and the modern worlds. Some continuities with the older ways of treating the topic of religion did persist, but the new intellectual climate gave rise to a variety of new approaches developed by philosophers and social scientists in the conviction that critical analysis and rational explanations of human phenomena such as religion are the best way to give us insight into whatever truth they contained.

In 1781, Immanuel Kant (1724–1804) published the first edition of the *Critique of Pure Reason*, his epoch-making investigation into the possibility of metaphysics. His reflection on the concept of God caused him to reject traditional proofs of God's existence such as the ontological argument (on the grounds that this argument merely relates two concepts to each other, not a concept to a reality) without, however, denying the reality of religious experience. Although religion (*Religion*) fell outside the scope of theoretical reason, it nevertheless fulfilled a practical need as the path to the highest good. This pragmatic approach to religion was to exercise profound influence throughout the nineteenth century.

Kant's pragmatism was profoundly uncongenial, however, to his younger contemporary, Friedrich Schleiermacher (1768–1834). Coming from a pietistic Moravian background, Schleiermacher developed a

---

[10] George Gennadios Scholarios, *Contra simoniam* II *Oeuvres completes*, vol. 3, 243.

philosophy of religion as 'feeling' (*Gefühl*), specifically a feeling of absolute dependence (*Abhängigheitsgefühl*), understood not as emotion but as
insight or intuition unmediated by any intellectual concept. Such intuitive
'feeling' does not, however, remain a purely inward matter; it is manifested in actions and is thus open to investigation by the natural sciences.
Schleiermacher was strongly opposed by his fellow Berlin professor,
Georg Wilhelm Friedrich Hegel (1770–1831). The intellectual world of
1820s Berlin was polarised between conservative evangelicals and philosophical rationalists. Hegel attempted, from a liberal Lutheran stand-
point, to steer a middle path. He defined religion 'as "a mode of
consciousness" that seeks to establish the truth of the relationship
between man and God'.[11] Religion and speculative philosophy, for
Hegel, were not in opposition. Both dealt with God as the manifestation
of a spiritual principle: religion doing it through images and representations, philosophy in a more developed way through conceptual analysis.
The philosophical system resulting from Hegel's analysis was not a static
one. The spiritual principle, *Geist*, becomes self-conscious in humanity
and evolves towards higher forms through the dialectical process for
which Hegel is celebrated, that of thesis, antithesis, and synthesis. The
higher unity thus achieved emphasises the dynamic immanence of the
divine in human life, an immanence that is realised by a rational process.

Hegelian idealism dominated philosophical thinking on religion for the
rest of the nineteenth century. In Germany, the Old Hegelians developed
the conservative side of Hegel's religious thinking and had no problem
with the official Lutheranism of the Prussian state. The Young (or Left)
Hegelians, who included Ludwig Feuerbach (1804–1872) and Karl Marx
(1818–1883), were altogether more radical. In 1841, Feuerbach published a book which was to be very influential in the second half of the
nineteenth century, *Das Wesen des Christentums*, translated into English
in 1854 (by Marian Evans, five years before her debut as the novelist
George Eliot) under the title *The Essence of Christianity*, in which he
presented what he called 'the true anthropological essence of religion' as
the projection of human qualities on to an imaginary divine being.
Feuerbach's critique of religion was adopted by Karl Marx, who saw
religion as an element in the development of human self-awareness. Marx
famously declared that 'religion is the opiate of the masses', but this must
not be taken as a contemptuous dismissal of religion. He saw religion as

---

[11] Dickey, 1993: 309, citing Hegel's preface to the second edition of *The
Encyclopaedia* (1827).

'the expression of real suffering' and a protest against it. 'Religion', he said, 'is the sigh of the oppressed creature, the heart of a heartless world and the soul of soulless conditions'.[12] Nevertheless, religion remains a human construct, a product of intellection.

A turn away from Hegelian idealism was marked in the early twentieth century by Rudolf Otto (1869–1937), whose *Das Heilige* (1917) was translated into English as *The Idea of the Holy* in 1923 and has never been out of print. Otto claimed that his fundamental insight, namely, that humanity's primary religious experience is the experience of the numinous (a word he coined himself from the Latin *numen*, 'divine power' or 'divine majesty'), came to him during a visit to a Jewish synagogue in Morocco in 1906. Like Schleiermacher, whom he admired, he rejected discursive reasoning as the path to a sense of God. It is the non-rational aspects of religion that have priority, among them the sense of the holy. But the holy is itself associated with moral goodness and is thus the product of conceptual thought. Behind the holy lies the numinous, which is beyond moral concepts, beyond intellection itself – a *mysterium tremendum et fascinans*. This 'wholly other' power or dynamic energy (*mysterium*) that evokes dread (is *tremendum*) and yet at the same time captivates (is *fascinans*) transcends conceptual thought. Otto's claim that this sense of divine awe is a Kantian a priori category has not been found convincing, but it cannot be denied that he brought to the debate on the nature of religion a powerful account of religious consciousness.

Otto impressed Edmund Husserl (1859–1938), the founder of the 'descriptive science' of phenomenology, which sought to treat the object as pure phenomenon by investigating the structures of consciousness and conditions that make experience possible. The topic of religion, however, was 'bracketed' (set to one side) by Husserl and most phenomenologists. The most notable exception was Max Scheler (1874–1928), whose application of the phenomenological approach to the topic of religion has proved very influential. Religious experience for Scheler is a given that cannot be derived reductively from anything else. Nor can its reality be established analytically or by the application of the empiricist's principle of verification. Openness to the divine is simply a fundamental aspect of being human. In his important *Vom Ewigen in Menschen* (1921), translated into English as *On the Eternal in Man* (1960), he argues that what makes religious experience possible is the presence of the eternal in

---

[12] From Karl Marx, 'Critique of Hegel's Philosophy of Right', 171, cited by J. Raines, in Raines, 2002: 5.

humankind. All human beings are theomorphic in their essential structure through the presence of the eternal within them. If prevented from fulfilling this innate reaching out to the absolute through the experience of love, they will latch on to some substitute or other.

A different philosophical approach, but with a similar focus on the human yearning for self-transcendence, arose in France with Émile Boutroux (1845–1921). For Boutroux, the essence of religion (*religion*) lay in the strange human claim to be able to go beyond that which characterises society and the individual (Magnin, 1937: 2261). With this claim as his starting point, Boutroux reflected on the mechanical determinism of the science of his day and found it wanting. The human yearning for self-transcendence, he felt, is not necessarily an illusion. It could be correlative to a capacity capable of fulfilling it. This capacity would enable the human person to co-operate with a higher being and surpass him/herself. Religion advances from the obligation of the human person to surpass him/herself to the power of actually doing so: 'Whoever participates in the life of God is in possession of the power of truly surpassing nature, of creating. Religion is creation, creation that is beautiful and salutary, in God and by God' (Boutroux, 1926: 224–27; cited by Magnin, 1937: 2262). 'Religion, in short', says Boutroux, 'is the effort to enhance, to enlarge and transfigure the very basis of our nature, thanks to this power that enables us to participate in a mode of being other than our own, a mode that wants to embrace infinity itself: love' (Boutroux, 1925: 97; cited by Magnin, 1937: 2264).

Boutroux developed his ideas partly in reaction to William James (1842–1910), whose Gifford Lectures of 1900–1902, published in 1902 as *Varieties of Religious Experience* and translated into French in 1905, have remained very influential.[13] James had expressed the belief (in Lecture 20) that the visible world belongs to a larger spiritual world from which it derives its significance and that the purpose of human life is to attain union or 'harmonious relation' with 'the higher universe'. James's recognition of a personal need in human beings for transcendence resonated with Boutroux's convictions, but his dwelling on psychological states ('I do believe that feeling is the deeper source of religion, and that philosophic and theological formulas are secondary products' [1902: Lecture 18]) was regarded by Boutroux as too individualistic and too

---

[13] For an excellent discussion of James's continuing importance, see Taylor, 2003.

narrow.[14] Boutroux himself believed that there were other paths besides the emotions leading to God, paths that were epistemic (metaphysics), aesthetic (art), and self-transcending (religion).

Boutroux's student, Henri Bergson (1859–1941), was, like his teacher, opposed to scientific determinism. He came to international attention in 1907 with his book *Évolution créatrice*, translated into English in 1911 as *Creative Evolution*, in which he argues that evolution is governed not by a Darwinian mechanism of natural selection but by a life force that he calls the *élan vital*. A living dynamism is also at the heart of his teaching on religion. On this front, he opposes Kant's moral philosophy, which he sees as a stifling closed system limited to a particular society. Against Kant, he sets an 'open' morality not intended, like Kant's 'closed' morality, to ensure social cohesion but to allow for intuition, artistic creation, and mystical ascent. These two moralities reflect two different kinds of religion, a closed morality corresponding to a static religion, and an open morality corresponding to a dynamic religion. In his last book, *Les deux sources de la morale et de la religion*, published in 1932, Bergson sets out a religious version of the *élan vital* ('life force'), which finds its highest expression in mysticism. Some beings have been called into existence, he says, who are destined to love and be loved. They are the creative energy before it is defined by love. They are distinct from God, who is this energy itself. They have arisen in the portion of the universe that is our planet in order to triumph over materiality and finally return to God. These are the mystics, who have opened a path for others to follow (1932: 276). Catholic critics did not approve of this deification of the mystic as the only genuine exemplar of dynamic religion. It is perhaps not coincidental that in 1910, when Bergson was appointed to a chair at the College de France, his first course of lectures was on Plotinus.

Bergson went out of fashion as the next generation of French philosophers turned their attention to the work of Husserl and Heidegger. But in the 1960s, there was a revival of interest in him. Jacques Derrida (1930–2004) claims that, along with Kant's *Religion within the Limits of Reason Alone*, Bergson's *Les deux sources de la morale et de la religion* enables us still 'to think religion in the daylight of today without breaking with the philosophical tradition' (Derrida, 2002: 78; cited by Raschke, 2005: 3). 'Derrida goes on to say that his project for "thinking religion" is

---

[14] James defined religion as 'the feelings, acts, and experiences of individual men in their solitude, so far as they apprehend themselves to stand in relation to whatever they may consider the divine' (1902: 31).

drawn from "the famous conclusion of the *Two Sources*, the memorable words that 'the essential function of the universe … is a machine for the making of gods'" (Raschke, 2005: 12, citing Derrida, 2002: 77).

The way Derrida 'thinks religion' is through textual criticism, or, as he puts it, the 'deconstruction' of texts.[15] The conceptual oppositions that the linguistic structures of texts conceal lead us into meanings beyond those intended by their authors. The 'myth of presence' is the assumption that we gain our most complete understanding of something when it alone is fully present to our minds. In fact, we need to do much more: we need to take into account all the contexts and associations of what it is that we are focusing on. With regard to religion, Derrida rejects Wittgenstein's injunction to silence.[16] *Il faut parler*, 'one must speak', and to speak is to respond to the promise implicit in religion. Derrida plays with the root meanings of *religio* (which he understands in one of the etymological senses given by Augustine, that of 'binding together' or 'reconnecting') and *sacramentum* (in the sense of a 'sworn oath') with the result that he declares that there is no religion without coming into unity (*alliance*) and without promise to bear witness (*promesse de témoigner*). That, he says, is the horizon where *religio* begins.[17] Where it goes from there is not so clear. Some have seen an affinity in Derrida with the apophatic tradition, others have spoken of 'a religion without religion', for Derrida seems to weave together a suggestive 'archive' of images, sounds, and gestures, and yet he rejects all philosophical or theological assertions about the divine. The post-secularist 'resurgence' of religion in which Derrida became interested in the last years of his life is not simply a return to an earlier intellectual stance but is highly subjective and deliberately full of ambiguities.

SOCIOLOGICAL, ANTHROPOLOGICAL, AND CULTURAL NOTIONS OF RELIGION

Late nineteenth-century philosophical reflection on religion, particularly in its French form, led to the scientific study of religion as a human phenomenon. The sociological study of religion goes back to Émile

---

[15] 'Derrida's term alludes, deliberately, to Heidegger's project of the destruction (*Destruktion*) of the history of ontology': Richmond, 1995: 180.

[16] Nault, 1998: 133, with reference to Wittgenstein, *Tractatus Logico-Philosophicus*, proposition 7.

[17] Nault, 1998: 142, citing Derrida, 2002 (in the original French, 'Foi et savoir', 43).

Durkheim (1858–1917), who, like Bergson, had been a student of Émile Boutroux. It was perhaps Durkheim's studies with Boutroux that planted in him the seeds of his conviction that social facts could not be reduced to the sum of individual behaviours. Durkheim's functional definition of religion is set out in his massive study of totemism among one of the indigenous peoples of Australia: 'A religion is an interdependent system of beliefs and practices relating to sacred things, that is to say, things that are set apart, forbidden, beliefs and practices that unite all who adhere to them in a single moral community called Church' (1912: 65).[18] The fundamental distinction for Durkheim is between sacred and profane. The sacred is experienced communally and the communal has priority over the individual. The actual content of belief is secondary, for 'it is the Church of which he is a member that teaches the individual what these personal gods are, what their role is, how one enters into relationship with them, how one must honour them' (64).

By contrast, Durkheim's German contemporary, Max Weber (1864–1920), sought to discover what religion actually meant for those who adhere to it. His key term is *Verstehen*, 'to understand', in the sense of to undertake a participatory and interpretative examination of the various manifestations of religion in order to understand what these signify for believers. Conceptual distinctions, however, cannot be avoided, and Weber makes a number of them, notably between asceticism and mysticism and between salvation and theodicy, which he was able to apply heuristically in his celebrated study, 'Die protestantische Ethik und der "Geist" des Kapitalismus' (1922), translated into English as *The Protestant Ethic and the Spirit of Capitalism* (1930), to show how Calvinist anxiety about predestination in the early modern age could be alleviated by the positive evidence of divine election provided by success in business.

A related 'scientific' way of looking at religion is as a cultural system. In an influential essay first published in 1966, the American anthropologist, Clifford Geertz (1926–2006), defines a culture as 'an historically transmitted pattern of meanings embodied in symbols, a system of inherited conceptions expressed in symbolic forms by means of which men communicate, perpetuate and develop their knowledge about and attitudes towards life' (1973: 89)[19] and a religion as 'a system of symbols

---

[18] The word 'Church' (*Église*) is used here in a generic sense.

[19] The thinking of Paul Ricoeur (1913–2005) seems to lie behind this. Compare his famous dictum, 'the symbol gives rise to thought' (Ricoeur, 1967: 247–57).

which acts to establish powerful, pervasive, and long-lasting moods and motivations in men by formulating conceptions of a general order of existence and clothing these conceptions with such an aura of factuality that the moods and motivations seem uniquely realistic' (90). Religion is thus fundamentally a set of interrelated symbols that communicates a particular world-view. Through its symbols, each religion provides its adherents with a 'model of reality' that makes the world intelligible to them and provides them with coordinates by which they can orientate their life.

In the course of the twentieth century, the sociology of religion, focusing on its comparative study, became an established academic discipline. This development has not been without its critics, who object to the construction of 'religion' as a cross-cultural analytical category supposedly free from ideological concerns. In the opinion of the British scholar Timothy Fitzgerald, who has spent his teaching career in university departments of religious studies, 'religion is really the basis of a modern form of theology, which I will call liberal ecumenical theology, but some attempt has been made to disguise this fact by claiming that religion is a natural and/or supernatural reality in the nature of things that all human individuals have a capacity for, regardless of their cultural context' (2000: 4–5). Fitzgerald argues that religion is generally approached in an ethnocentric fashion, on the assumption that the defining feature of religion is a common belief in the transcendent or the divine, without regard for the fact that Judaeo-Christian categories cannot be used cross-culturally. 'Religion', in his view, has no distinctive analytical validity. It is an ideological category that arose in the nineteenth century in connection with the growth of colonial empires and the need to impose Western values on them, including the distinction between religion and non-religion.

MODERN THEOLOGICAL CRITIQUES OF RELIGION

Most theologians nevertheless accept the analytical validity of the word 'religion'. They would agree with the British philosopher Richard Swinburne, who offers a definition of religion ('in the normal sense of the English word familiar to most of us') as 'an institutionalised system of belief and practice to which people belong, the practice of which is designed to secure their ultimate well-being and that of (at least) all the members of the religion' (2013: 54). The pluralism implied in a functional definition of this kind raises a problem. If Christianity is simply one religion among others, what does this make of its claim to be *the* religion? This was a question addressed by Karl Rahner, who presciently saw pluralism in a globalised world as presenting a greater threat to Christianity than religion's denial (1966: 116). Wishing to maintain, on the one hand, that there is no salvation apart from Christ ('according to Catholic teaching the supernatural divinisation of man can never be replaced merely by good will on the part of man but is necessary as something itself given in this earthly life' [123]), and, on the other, that salvation is intended by God for all human beings, Rahner concludes that all members of non-Christian religions must be regarded as 'anonymous Christians' and that the task of missionaries is to bring this to explicit consciousness (131).[20]

This is an approach to religion that despite its Christocentric concern accepts a sociological (some would say an imperialistic) construction of religion. At the opposite pole, though no less influenced by a secularising – in this case Freudian – construction of religion, is the approach of the Greek philosopher-theologian Christos Yannaras, who sees the category of religion in purely negative terms. In a book provocatively entitled *Against Religion*, he defines religion 'as humanity's natural (instinctive) need (1) to suppose that there are factors that generate existence and existent things, together with the evil that is intertwined with the fact of existence and (2) to extrapolate from this rational supposition methods and practices for the "management" of the supernatural factors, so that hopes of humanity's unending happiness are built up' (2013: 3). Religion is thus in essence the human creation of a psychological comfort zone.

By this definition, Yannaras appears to take up a position similar theologically to that of Karl Barth, who in Section 17 of his *Church Dogmatics* rejects the way the Christian faith has been treated as a species of the genus religion (2013: 3).[21] For Barth, religion is *Unglaube*, unbelief, or lack of faith, an attempt to replace the gift of God's self-communication with a human construct. As such, religion is idolatrous. Barth, however, does admit the existence of *true* religion, which is the creation of the Holy Spirit and within which the believer receives justification by the operation of divine grace. Yannaras is more radical than Barth in refusing to recognise any acceptable version of religion at all. For him religion (the word θρησκεία is still the current Greek term) is actually a

---

[20] This view has been very influential among Christian theologians of all denominations.
[21] For a good English translation of this section of *Church Dogmatics*, see Barth, 2013.

hindrance to authentic Christian faith-trust (πίστις), which is a mode of existence freed from egoism and natural determinism (2013: 37).

A different theoretical approach was proposed by the American Lutheran theologian George Lindbeck (1923–2018) in an influential book, *The Nature of Doctrine: Religion and Theology in a Postliberal Age*, first published in 1984. Drawing on Clifford Geertz and modern linguistic theory, Lindbeck proposes a 'cultural-linguistic' model of religion, which he claims combines the first two approaches (which I have illustrated with Swinburne and Yannaras, the former of which he would characterise as 'cognitive-propositional' and the latter as 'experiential-expressive') to propose a conceptualisation of religion as a 'comprehensive interpretative medium or categorical framework' that not only expresses but also shapes and moulds the believer's experiences (2009: 18, 65). This model treats a religion in postmodern fashion as a cultural construction analogous to a language with its own grammatical structure: 'religions resemble languages together with their correlative forms of life and are thus similar to cultures (insofar as these are understood semiotically as reality and value systems – that is as idioms for the construing of reality and the living of life)' (3). All religions cannot all be reduced to the same common core. Each religion is different because each has its own grammar, which enables its adherents to be religious in a particular way through ritual, prayer, and the giving of example, which are normally, in Lindbeck's view, much more important than doctrine (20). He summarises religion, according to his model, as 'idioms for dealing with whatever is most important – with ultimate questions of life and death, right and wrong, chaos and order, meaning and meaninglessness' (25).[22]

PERENNIALIST AND ESOTERICIST NOTIONS OF RELIGION

Even though 'religion' as the content of religious studies programmes may be a nineteenth-century ideological construct, the conviction that regardless of their being embedded in particular cultural contexts all religions have as their common core a universal sacred wisdom is deeply rooted. This is expressed most powerfully in the idea of the *philosophia perennis*, the perennial philosophy. The idea goes back to the Renaissance, when Marsilio Ficino and Giovanni Pico della Mirandola taught that the *Hermetic Corpus* together with the Neoplatonist philosophers and the

---

[22] For an application of this approach to the Early Church, see Theissen, 1999.

Greek Fathers expounded the same *prisca theologia*, the same ancient and eternally valid theological wisdom.[23] The popularisation of this wisdom, however, belongs to the late nineteenth and early twentieth centuries with the foundation of the Theosophical Society in 1875 and its offshoot, the Anthroposophical Society, in 1913. The leading figure of the former in its early days was Helena Petrovna Blavatsky, known as Madame Blavatsky (1831–1891), a Russian clairvoyant and esotericist with extensive connections among the nobility of her native country, where the writings of the German mystic Jakob Boehme (c. 1575–1624) made the Russian intelligentsia receptive to her ideas. The Anthroposophical Society was founded by Rudolf Steiner (1861–1925), originally a disciple of Blavatsky, who broke away on account of his dissatisfaction with the Theosophical Society's deepening rapport with Indian religion.[24] Steiner's ideas, like Blavatsky's, also resonated in Russia, where they influenced such Orthodox theologians as Pavel Florensky (1882–1937) and Sergius Bulgakov (1871–1944). The esoteric teaching of both Blavatsky and Steiner was based on their personal visionary experiences. For them, particularly for Steiner, religion was the quest of the inner 'I' to attain the highest level of spiritual development through withdrawal from everything transitory. Comparable ideas about realising the divine, or quasi-divine, kernel of the individual were further popularised in the West by such writers as Réné Guénon (1886–1951), Aldous Huxley (1894–1963), and Frithjof Schuon (1907–1998).

THE TURN FROM RELIGION TO SPIRITUALITY

A phenomenon of the late twentieth and early twenty-first centuries noted by many authors is a turning away, like the perennialists, from 'organised religion' to a personal quest for meaning through individual religious experience. In many bookshops today, titles that used to be found on shelves marked 'Religion' or 'Theology' are now to be found in a section called 'Mind, Body, Spirit'. A shift has taken place in the cultural paradigm of religion: 'we see a new model in which the sacred is intimate and close, a felt resonance within the self, and a deep and radiant presence in the natural world' (Tacey, 2004: 79). This new model of religion has

---

[23] The term *philosophia perennis* was first used by the Italian humanist Agostino Steuco in 1540.

[24] In 1878, the headquarters of the Theosophical Society were moved to Madras (now called Chennai) in India.

abandoned the traditional divide (traditional at least in the West) between sacred and profane, holy and unholy. It regards spiritual identity as quite distinct from religious affiliation. One's spiritual identity is not inherited from the tradition in which one was brought up but is constructed personally, partly by going beyond the traditional forms of Western religion to their origins and partly by searching eclectically among Eastern (Eastern Christian as well as Asian) spiritual teachings.

The new category of 'spirituality' has appealed to people searching for answers to the eternal questions about the meaning of life. Atheistic secularism, once assumed to be the normal fall-back human condition once religious faith begins to recede in the face of scientific progress, is now itself understood to be a nineteenth-century ideological construction. Religion is back as 'spirituality'. Inevitably, this spirituality has been exploited commercially in today's market-oriented world, both by its teachers and by its consumers, who are often large corporations seeking to improve the commitment and productivity of their employees. What has been called 'the commodification of religion as spirituality' (Carrette and King, 2005: 15) is a development that has latched easily on to the individualised search for meaning and self-transcendence in our consumerist society.

This search for meaning is often highly eclectic, drawing not only on Western religious teaching but also choosing elements from the Hindu, Buddhist, Sufic, or Eastern Orthodox traditions. Together with the subjectivisation and commodification of religion this has resulted in specific traditions no longer being 'owned' by the communities that created them but being available for selective appropriation in accordance with personal choice. Hesychast practices and the use of the Jesus Prayer are a case in point. These elements of Orthodox tradition have been adopted by a broad range of communities and movements, not only Roman Catholic but also Evangelical and esotericist.[25] Theosis, as we shall see, has followed a similar trajectory of reception.

THE MEANING OF THEOSIS IN EARLY CHRISTIANITY AND THE CHURCH FATHERS

Turning now to the second term of our binary, theosis, we may define it in a broad sense as a theological motif with roots in very early Christian

---

[25] For a review of the literature, see C. D. L. Johnson, 2010: 46–87.

tradition that seeks to express the content of salvation and its place in the divine economy as an interpenetration of God's life with ours. The term itself, as already mentioned, originated in the fourth century AD but its core meaning, 'becoming divine', goes back to the very origins of Christianity in first-century Judaism. The catastrophic Jewish revolt against Roman rule in the first and second centuries, which resulted in the suppression of much that was characteristic of Jewish life, including the Temple, sacrifices, pilgrimages, zealot movements, and contemplative communities such as the one at Qumran that produced the Dead Sea Scrolls, changed the character of Judaism. Only the Rabbinic form survived, its quietist emphasis on the study of Torah, prayer, and good works posing no political threat to the imperial government. Yet Rabbinic Judaism in this period was spiritually very fruitful, with the rise of Merkavah mysticism (ascent in the spirit to the throne-chariot of God) and the development of new speculations about the inner meaning of texts such Psalm 82:6 that fed straight into nascent Christian thinking on the divine destiny of the baptised.[26]

Recent studies in the New Testament (Blackwell, 2016; Byers, 2017) have demonstrated that an appreciation of the role of the deification motif is important if we are to gain a proper understanding of such fundamental constituents of Christianity as Pauline soteriology and Johannine ecclesiology. Paul's discussions of glory, immortality, adoption, and conforming to Christ's image (primarily in Romans 8 and 2 Corinthians 3–5, but also in Colossians 2, Galatians 3–4, 1 Corinthians 15, and Philippians 2–3) have been shown by Ben Blackwell to be themes, drawn from both the Jewish and Hellenistic worlds, that enable believers to participate through Christ in the divine attributes and so enter into a divine sphere of existence. Andrew Byers has argued convincingly for an equally participatory ecclesiology in the Fourth Gospel. The Johannine community is called to participate in the divine interrelation of Father and Son, the correlation of the Shema, 'YHWH is one' (Deut 6.4), with Jesus's prayer 'that they may all be one' (John 17.21), characterising the children of God as participants in the dyadic relationship of Father and Son through the operation of the Spirit.

Towards the end of the second century, deification becomes an important theme in Irenaeus of Lyon. Focusing on the realisation in humanity of the image and likeness of God, he is the first to enunciate the so-called

---

[26] For a fuller discussion of this, see Russell, 2004: 53–78.

exchange formula: because of his infinite love for us, Christ 'became what we are in order to make us what he is himself'.[27] That is not to say that we attain identity with Christ. What we attain is a community of life with him. Through his incarnation, Christ assumed our human nature; through our incorporation into Christ by baptism, we receive a share in his divine nature, which means principally a share in the properties of immortality and incorruption. This entry into the deified life through baptism is consolidated and deepened through participation in the Eucharist. Early Latin and Greek liturgical texts contain many allusions to the exchange formula.[28]

The second century also saw the entry of a new element into the Church's understanding of deification, that of spiritual ascent through moral development, intellectual application, and ascetic effort. This begins with Clement of Alexandria, who was the first to use the term 'deification', *theopoēsis* (θεοποίησις). Following the example of the Jewish philosopher Philo of Alexandria, Clement combined the Platonic injunction to flee from this world to the other by 'becoming like the divine so far as possible' (*Theaetetus* 176b) with the biblical statement that God created humankind in the divine image and likeness (Gen 1.26) to teach a doctrine of salvation as deifying assimilation to God through participation (another Platonic concept) in Christ's incorruption and moral excellence. Through the contemplation of intelligibles and the attainment of dispassion, in tandem with participation in the Church's sacrifice of worship and praise, the Christian 'studies to be a god'.

The philosophical foundations laid by Clement were built on (without acknowledgement) by Origen, the greatest Christian thinker before the golden age of the Church Fathers of the fourth and fifth centuries. Origen was not a convert from pagan philosophy, like Clement, but a biblical exegete, who developed his teaching through his meditation on Scripture. He nevertheless reveals an impressive philosophical competence in his more speculative writings, his discussions of the nature of participation

---

[27] Irenaeus of Lyon, *Against Heresies* V, Praef. For the Pauline thinking on which Irenaeus draws, see 2 Cor 8.9 and Phil 2.6–8. On Irenaeus's teaching on deification, see Blackwell, 2016: 35–70; Edwards, 2017a.

[28] On the Latin liturgical tradition, see Ortiz, 2019a. There is nothing as concise on the Byzantine liturgical tradition in this field, but useful discussions may be found in Gregorios, 2009. For comparable material in one of the branches of the Oriental Orthodox tradition, see Dagmawi, 2009.

in his *On First Principles*, providing him with a sound basis on which to elaborate the theme of deification in his works of exegesis. Deification for Origen is not principally a matter of philosophical ascent.[29] It is a dynamic participation in the divinity of the Father through sharing ecclesially in the spiritualising operation of the Spirit and the filialising work of the Son. The Spirit makes us holy so that the Son can make us sons and gods. The relationship of participation means that there is no danger of ontological confusion between Creator and creature, because participation entails two distinct terms, the participant and the participated in.

The fourth-century Greek Fathers, in turn, build on Origen. Their main concern is Christological, specifically the challenge to catholic Christianity presented by those who would make the Son ontologically inferior to the Father for the sake of preserving the transcendence of the divine. Origen had seen the Son as deified in relation to the Father but as deifying in relation to us. In view of the widening chasm, however, in the generation after Origen between the uncreated godhead and the created natural order, Christ could no longer be seen as himself deified, otherwise he would fall on the created side of the uncreated/created divide. At the same time, Christ's deification of the believer was found by Athanasius and others to be a compelling argument for the uncreatedness of Christ himself. That Christ can make created human beings sons and gods was not disputed. Athanasius argues that he can only do so if he is of the same uncreated nature as the Father. Believers are able to participate in the deified human nature assumed by the Logos through their assimilation to him by baptism and participation in the sacramental life.[30]

Athanasius's Christological arguments, which were so decisive in establishing the Nicene faith, were taken over by the Cappadocian Fathers, Basil of Caesarea, Gregory of Nazianzus, and Gregory of Nyssa, who attempt to combine them with the Platonic doctrine of the soul's ascent to God. Each does so, however, in a different way. Basil holds that the primary aim of the Christian life is to give glory to God but after that is to become like God so far as possible. Becoming like God through a moral and ascetic life gradually spiritualises the believer leading to the attainment of deification as an eschatological state. Like Basil, Gregory of Nazianzus emphasises the importance of the imitation of

---

[29] Origen's differences from Platonism are brilliantly discussed by Edwards, 2002.

[30] For an excellent discussion of the Alexandrian tradition on deification, see Edwards, 2017b.

God through the practice of virtue. This imitation renders believers akin to God, which results ultimately in their transcending the limitations of human life and coming to 'mingle' with the purest light. There is also a parallel process of ascent to the divine that is achieved liturgically. Christ deified the humanity that he assumed; this deified humanity is appropriated by the believer through baptism and nourished by the Eucharist. Deification, through following the contemplative life in tandem with the liturgical life, is thus the goal of every serious Christian. Gregory of Nyssa's emphasis is different again because he prefers to speak of *participating* in the divine attributes rather than of *mingling* with them. Deification for him is primarily a Christological term. He seems to have been wary of compromising the transcendence of God by attributing deification unequivocally to human beings, although, like Gregory of Nazianzus, he does extend deification to believers through their reception of the sacraments.

The ecclesial context of deification is thus sketched in only lightly and in a somewhat exploratory way by the Cappadocians. It was Cyril of Alexandria who fully integrated the theme of spiritual ascent to union with God with that of the corporeal participation attainable through Christ in the new ecclesial life inaugurated by him. Deification is a dynamic movement encompassing the entire trajectory of human life beginning with its emergence from non-existence into created existence and ending with its transformation in Christ through which it comes to share in the divine attributes of holiness, righteousness, and freedom from corruption and decay. A key concept for Cyril is that of participation. In his mature work he drops the technical terms of deification, preferring to rely on the Petrine expression, 'partakers of the divine nature' (2 Pet 1.4), which he sees as correlative to the Pauline emphasis on Christ's coming to share in our human nature (Heb 2.14), 'for the divine nature is God the Word together with the flesh' (*Com. on John* 6.1.653d). Salvation is in essence participation through the Spirit in Christ, who unites in himself the 'two vastly discrete things of the divine and the human (*Com. on John* 6.1.653e) and is thus participation in Christ's relationship with the Father. At the centre of this dynamic participation is the Eucharist. Cyril moves away from divinising contemplation to focus on the role of the practice of the virtues and the reception of the Eucharist as the path to theosis.[31]

---

[31] For an outstanding study of deification in Cyril, see Keating, 2004.

Deification in the Latin Fathers

Long regarded as a peculiarly Eastern perspective on salvation, deification has come to be seen in recent years as also embedded firmly within the Western tradition. The earliest studies were on Augustine, who uses the verb *deificare* (but not the noun *deificatio*) more frequently than any of his Latin predecessors, albeit still quite rarely in relation to the bulk of his writings.[32] Since then, work has also been published on Hilary of Poitiers and Ambrose of Milan, and, in a recent collective volume, on a representative range of Latin patristic writers.[33] What they all have in common is a commitment to the ontological transformation of human nature (not just its juridical justification) made possible for us by the incarnation, death, and resurrection of the Word of God. Christ became human that we might become divine. The Latin Fathers are more prone than their Greek counterparts to use mercantile imagery to express this exchange, but on the thematic level they convey the same message.

This fundamental unanimity follows naturally from the dependence of the Latins on the Greek tradition, the language of Christianity even in the West being Greek, of course, until well into the third century. Yet there is a difference in emphasis in the Latin Fathers compared with the Greek. The Latins did not have the same access as the Greeks to the Greek philosophical traditions, nor, apart from Hilary and Ambrose, who were good Hellenists, were they able to immerse themselves in Origen, whose importance for the Greek tradition on deification has already been noted. Some Latins also seem to have been wary of the technical language of deification. Even Rufinus, an eager champion of Origen, tones down the language on occasion.[34]

The Emergence of Theosis as a Doctrine

So how did theosis advance from being a pervasive theological theme (from being widely deployed, we might say, as a *theologoumenon*) to being a defined ecclesiastical doctrine (a *didaskalia* or *dogma*)? The line of

---

[32] The pioneer study of deification in Augustine is Capánaga, 1954. Later studies include Bonner, 1986 and 1990; Chadwick, 2002; Russell, 2004: 329–32; Meconi, 2013; and Haflidson, 2019.

[33] The earliest study on Hilary is Wild, 1950, now superseded by Sidaway, 2016 and 2019. On Ambrose, see Dunkle, 2019. For overviews of the Latin patristic tradition, see Bardy, 1957; Fokin, 2014; Ortiz, 2016; and, for a more extended treatment, Ortiz, 2019b.

[34] For more details on this, see Russell, 2019a.

development, as we shall see in Chapter 2, runs from Dionysius the Areopagite, through Maximus the Confessor and John Damascene, to Gregory Palamas. In these writers, theosis becomes integral to the theological structure of their thought. Defined dogma, however, arises only from the resolution of controverted teachings. It was only in Palamas's time, in the fourteenth century, that theosis became a matter of doctrinal controversy requiring an official pronouncement on its meaning and significance. At the Constantinopolitan Council of 1351, the patristic tradition on theosis was examined and those who claimed that the deity arising out of the gift of the Spirit was a created deity were condemned.[35] The saints who have been deified by union with God were defined as truly participating in the uncreated Godhead, not in the divine essence (because that would abolish their distinction from God) but in the divine energy.[36]

Modern Orthodox have naturally taken their cue from the synod of 1351, which although not an ecumenical council – ecumenical councils require the participation of Rome, which last occurred at the Nicene council of 787 – was nevertheless a council of the utmost solemnity whose findings were incorporated into the *Synodikon of Orthodoxy*, a list of proscribed errors read each year on the first Sunday of Lent. It is thus that deification comes to be defined by modern Orthodox as 'the religious ideal of Orthodoxy' (Kern, 1950: 394, cited by Mantzaridis, 1984: 12), as the realisation of humanity's true existence (Nellas, 1987: 15), as a doctrine that 'by the place it occupies in Orthodox theology, determines the shape of that theology' (Louth, 2007: 43).

MODERN RETRIEVALS OF THEOSIS

Is there a continuous history? It depends on how broadly theosis is defined. Although studies such as those of Blackwell and Byers have demonstrated that the theme of deification is not confined to writers who use the technical terms, it does make a difference, as Andrew Louth has said, whether or not you have a word for it (2020: 837). In Orthodoxy, even if the modern retrieval of theosis has accompanied the retrieval of Palamite theology, the word itself is present in texts such as Gregory of Nazianzus's *Orations* and Maximus the Confessor's *Ambigua* that have been read and studied in every generation. In 1782,

---

[35] Synodal Tome of 1351, paragraph 36 (Karmiris, 1968: 394; trans. Russell, 2020: 357).
[36] Synodal Tome of 1351, paragraph 40 (Karmiris, 1968: 396–98; trans. Russell, 2020: 361–63).

when Nikodemos the Hagiorite published these and other patristic spiritual texts in the *Philokalia*, his intention, as he reveals in the Preface, was to encourage the ascetic orientation of his readers towards the attainment of theosis. Yet in the early twentieth century, knowledge of deification in Greek and Russian academic circles was rare. It needed the retrieval of deification by different routes – by Florensky and Bulgakov developing the ideas of Soloviev, by Popov recovering the teachings of the Greek Fathers, by the Russian émigrés in Paris writing in French for a broad audience, by Stăniloae working on his Romanian translation of the *Philokalia* – for the Orthodox to reappropriate a central feature of their theology. These activities have also benefitted Western Christians, whose current broad awareness of theosis has been influenced by contact with Orthodox scholars and by acquaintance with Orthodox theological texts. Also important in the Western context since the Second World War is the revival of patristic studies and the renewal of philosophical interest in such ideas as Kant's making of the transcendent immanent or Bergson's *élan vital*.

HOW ARE RELIGION AND THEOSIS RELATED?

Theosis is not tied to any specific version of religion but it has different contours according to which version is under consideration. A taxonomy of religion might help us see this more clearly. Setting aside dismissive views of religion from Lucretius to Freud that have regarded religion as at worst harmful to humanity's interests and as at best an emotional prop with no basis in reality, we may group the different ways of understanding religion under four headings: phenomenal-theological (marked by a tension between θεοσέβεια and θρησκεία), experiential-philosophical (focusing on making of the transcendent immanent in actual experience), ethical (treating *religio* as a moral virtue), and semiotic (understanding religion in symbolic terms as a system of signs).

Under the first heading, the phenomenal-theological, *theosebeia* (θεοσέβεια), 'piety', 'reverence towards God') is pitted against *thrēskeia* (θρησκεία), the doctrines, rites, and structures that constitute a 'faith community'. Theosis in this context relates to *theosebeia* alone. It is not an external mark of religion but teaches a particular mode of appropriating salvation through faith. The thematic approach to deification belongs here. It may be noted, incidentally, that in the modern Greek context *theosebeia* is no longer available as a suitable term, having been used in the nineteenth century by Theophilos Kairis (1784–1853) as the basis for the name of his new theosophical religion, Theosebism, and has been replaced by *eusebeia* (εὐσέβεια).

The second way of understanding religion, in experiential-philosophical terms, relates to the actual experience of transcendence even in this life. It is the experience of transcendence that leads to theosis, the bond with the divine realised through the transcendent-immanent. But personal experience is needed *plus* 'the phenomenology of religion', cult and tradition, which are more than philosophising. The Palamite mode of theosis fits this understanding of religion, as does the Eckhartian.

The third way, which treats religion as a moral virtue, focuses on the final end. As Augustine puts it, to reconsider (*relegere*), to make a new choice is to direct ourselves towards God because our happiness and fulfilment lie only in him. In this case, theosis is to find the true fulfilment of our being in God.

The fourth way, the semiotic, which considers religion as a system of external signs, treats theosis as an element in a 'language' of participation in God. This is a way of discussing theosis favoured by many modern scholars, as it does not entail taking any position in advance on its experiential value.

The following chapters will focus on the first and second ways of relating theosis to religion, the phenomenal-theological and the experiential-philosophical. It is these ways that have proved most fruitful historically and that account today for the draw of theosis far beyond the walls of the academy.

2

Byzantium

The Flowering of the Eastern Tradition of Theosis

THEOSIS AND THE DEFENCE OF ORTHODOXY

The Role of Theosis in the Promotion of Chalcedonian Christology

The Late Roman Empire as a distinctive Christian polity began to take shape under the emperor Constantine I (324–337) – who founded New Rome, Constantinople, as a new capital free from the pagan traditions of Old Rome – and was consolidated by Theodosius I (379–395), who in 392 closed the pagan temples throughout the empire. It is called Byzantine (by modern scholars) from the time of Justinian I (527–565), who closed the Neoplatonist academy of Athens in 529, inaugurated the rebuilding on a colossal scale of the Great Church of Hagia Sophia in Constantinople in 537, and from 551, with the issuing of his *Edict on the True Faith*, made it a central policy of his reign to reconcile all his subjects to the orthodox Christian faith as defined by the Council of Chalcedon (451).[1]

The role of the emperor in Byzantium had from the beginning a strongly religious dimension (Dagron, 1996). Pope Gelasius I (492–496), writing to Justinian's imperial predecessor-but-one,

---

[1] Up to the fall of Constantinople in 1453 and beyond, the Byzantines called themselves *Romaioi*, Romans. With the revival of classical learning in the Palaiologan era (fourteenth century), the educated élite took to referring to Constantinople in archaic fashion as 'Byzantium' and its inhabitants as 'Byzantines'. The expression 'Byzantine Empire' was first used (somewhat pejoratively) by French scholars in the seventeenth century, partly in order to deny the Orthodox Greeks the title of 'Roman'. It has become established, however, as the normal modern term for the East Roman Empire from about AD 500, even among most (though not all) Greeks, and is used thus here.

Anastasius I (491–518), had laid down the theory of the two powers – the pope's *auctoritas* versus the emperor's (inferior) *regia potestas* – that was to have such fateful consequences for the history of Western Europe.[2] This was not how things were seen in Constantinople. The emperor's office did not derive its authority from any ecclesiastical sanction. Not only was it much older than the Church but it looked for its sacral dimension to the Old Testament model of kingship. In a brief treatise on the topic addressed to Justinian by a deacon, probably of Hagia Sophia, called Agapetos, the emperor is recognised as having received his dignity and authority directly from God but without thereby being absolved from the need to win the consent of his subjects or from the duty to master his passions, show temperance and mercy, and do everything to assist the salvation of those over whom he rules (*Ekthesis*, PG 86.1, 1163–85: partial trans. Barker, 1957: 54–61). The earthly kingdom is a preparation for the heavenly kingdom. Justinian is to see his office as his allotted path to salvation: 'Guide your kingdom aright here below, that it may become for you a ladder to the glory above' (59; trans. Barker, 1957: 60). Nor is this merely a personal and private ladder. The emperor's responsibility is to make the kingdom here below a ladder for all to mount to the glory above. Church and emperor are to work together (the famous *symphonia* of later Byzantine theory) for the salvation – indeed the deification – of all, which begins with knowing oneself, and thus knowing God, and leads ultimately to the attainment of the divine likeness, for 'he who knows God will become like God' (3; trans. Barker, 1957: 55).

The fundamental thesis of the Chalcedonian orthodoxy that Justinian was committed to upholding was that the divine Word of God entered the human state through the Incarnation, assuming a complete human nature without confusion, change, division, or separation. Christ (for soteriological reasons) became everything that we are, 'for that which is not assumed is not healed',[3] yet at the same time (for theological reasons) the

---

[2] Gelasius, *Ep.* 8 (text in PL 59, 41–47; trans. Barker, 1957: 108–9). The Rubicon was crossed on Christmas Day 800, when Pope Leo III crowned Charlemagne emperor, thinking that he was thereby demonstrating the superiority of papal over regal authority. Sir Richard Southern has described this action as 'the greatest mistake the medieval popes ever made in their efforts to translate theory into practice' (Southern, 1970: 99).

[3] Gregory of Nazianzus, *Ep.* 101, to Cledonius. Also: *Carmina Dogmatica*, PG 37, 468: Ὁ μὴ προσείληπται, οὐδὲ σώζεται. This was confirmed by the Sixth Ecumenical Council (Constantinople III) of 680, the Council in Trullo, which declared: τὸ γὰρ παρ' αὐτοῦ μὴ προσληφθὲν οὐδὲ σώζεται ('that which was not assumed by him is not saved'), ACO II, 2, 1–2, doc. 4, p. 76).

divine nature of the Word underwent no change or alteration, for that which is mutable is not divine. The hypostatic union (the union of the two natures, human and divine, in a single state of being) was effected by the deification of the human nature by the divine nature, the latter endowing the former (by the 'communication of idioms') with all the attributes of divinity, without, however, the humanness of the human nature being compromised in any way.[4] A correct understanding of the deification of Christ's human nature thus supported Chalcedon's dyophysite ('two-natures') Christology and was therefore an integral part of *eusebeia/theosebeia* – 'piety' or true religion.

In pursuit of his policy of reconciling the miaphysite opponents of Chalcedon to the Chalcedonian imperial Church,[5] Justinian held a colloquy in 532 in Constantinople between invited representatives from both sides. One of the participants on the Chalcedonian side was Leontius of Byzantium, *apocrisiarius* (representative in Constantinople) of the monks of Palestine, who appears to have already made a reputation for himself for his careful analysis of Christological language.[6] A little later, 'probably at some time in the 540s' (Daley, 2018: 203), in his *Three Books against the Nestorians and the Eutychians*, he discusses at length the importance of 'the communication of idioms' for avoiding the opposite extremes of either failing to unite the divine and the human in Christ (like the Nestorians) or of fusing them together to produce a third substance (like the Eutychians). In Christ, the human and the divine are not two different beings (ἄλλος δὲ καὶ ἄλλος), but, quoting Gregory of Nazianzus (*Ep.* 101.21), 'both are one by comingling, the divine, on the one hand, having been inhominated and the human, on the other, having been deified (θεωθέντος), or however you wish to put it' (Daley, 2017: 186).

---

[4] The 'communication of idioms', or exchange of properties (in Latin *communicatio idiomatum*; in Greek ἀντίδοσις τῶν ἰδιωμάτων), is an expression dating from the time of Cyril of Alexandria to signify that the properties of the divine nature may be predicated of the human, and vice versa, without altering the nature of either nature.

[5] 'Miaphysite' is the modern term given to the moderate opponents of Chalcedon (on account of their adherence to the Alexandrian *mia physis* slogan, 'one incarnate nature of God the Word') in preference to the pejorative label 'monophysite' that was attached to them in the aftermath of Chalcedon and is now properly applied only to the heretical Eutychian doctrine condemned at the council. The miaphysites (who understood *physis* in terms of *hypostasis*) denied that one could speak of two natures after the Incarnation. Their modern descendants are the 'Oriental' Orthodox – members of the Syrian, Coptic, Ethiopian, and Armenian Orthodox Churches – who are still not in communion with the 'Eastern' Orthodox Church.

[6] On Leontius of Byzantium, see Grillmeier with Hainthaler, 1995: 181–229; Daley, 2017: Introduction; Daley, 2018: 203–11.

Theosis is thus a convenient shorthand expression for how Christ's human nature is united with his divine nature without either nature annulling the other.

About a century after Leontius, Maximus the Confessor also draws on the Cappadocian tradition to explain how Christ can be a single hypostasis even though formed of two utterly different natures. The two natures completely interpenetrate each other with the result that the divine is humanised and the human divinised. In the fifth of his *Ambigua to Thomas* he says that Christ

does human things in a way transcending the human, showing, in accordance with the closest union, the human energy united without change to the divine power, since the [human] nature, united without confusion to [the divine] nature, is completely interpenetrated (περικεχώρηκε), and in no way annulled, nor separated from the Godhead hypostatically united to it. (PG 91, 1053B; trans. Louth, 1996: 175)

To explain how this can be, Maximus distinguishes between the *logos* of something (its essential nature) and its *tropos* (its mode of existence). By the Incarnation, human nature enhypostasised in Christ – human *nature*, it should be noted, not a human hypostasis or individual – is 'innovated', or made into something new, in its *tropos* while preserving its *logos* unchanged.[7] That is why Christ's humanity is real yet has powers that exceed the normally human (as, for example, the ability to walk on water). Such powers do not mean that any element naturally constituting the human has been suppressed or replaced by the divine. Maximus is convinced that the removal of the natural operation (energy) or the will from either of the natures for the sake of binding the natures together into a single hypostatic unit (as proposed by the imperial monothelete and monenergist initiatives designed to reconcile the miaphysites to the Byzantine Church) results in 'a mythical creation, wholly strange and foreign to any fellowship with the Father or ourselves' (*Opusc.* 7, PG 91, 76A; trans. Daley, 2018: 219). The incarnate Word is fully human and fully divine yet at the same time wholly one, the human operating divinely through its change of *tropos*, the divine operating humanly though its interpenetration of the human.[8]

In the following century, another Leontius, Leontius of Jerusalem, draws on the vocabulary of Dionysius the Areopagite to explain the

---

[7] For a full discussion, see Larchet, 1996: 249–73; 2015: 341–59.
[8] See Maximus's discussion of this in *Ambiguum* 42, PG 91, 1341D–44D (trans. Larchet, 2015: 343–44).

'synthesis' of Christ's divine and human natures as the product of the taking of the human into the divine by an act of 'ektheosis'.[9] It is not enough for Christ to be called a God-bearing man, for we too are called gods through having been deified by the grace of adoption.[10] The issue of monenergism and monotheletism had recently been settled definitively by the Sixth Ecumenical Council (Constantinople III) of 680, so it was no longer potentially confusing (even if it may have been previously) to speak about the union of the divine and the human in Christ in terms of the latter's deification. Indeed, Leontius of Jerusalem finds the language of theosis and ektheosis particularly well adapted to expressing the reciprocal exchange of attributes in accordance with the 'communication of idioms'.

Leontius's contemporary, John Damascene, brings the debate to a close, so far as the Byzantine tradition is concerned. The two natures of Christ, divine and human, may be distinguished numerically but are ontologically indivisible. Thus 'the manner in which the flesh was deified (τεθέωται) and yet did not suffer any change in its proper nature is the same manner in which the will and the activity were deified yet did not go beyond their proper boundaries' (*De fid. orth.*, 59; Kotter 2, 146.50–52; trans. Russell 2022: 200). In a comment on Gregory of Nazianzus's statement that by the Incarnation God made one entity out of two opposites, flesh and spirit, 'of which one deified and the other was deified' (*Orat.* 38, 13 and 45, 9; Moreschini 2000: 892 and 1144), John says that just as burning manifests not a change in what is burned but union with the fire, 'so too divinization (θέωσις) manifests union with divinity and enfleshment (σάρκωσις) union with flesh' (*De nat. comp. sive Contra aceph.*, 3; Kotter 4, 412.1–2). The miaphysites had made Cyril of Alexandria's expression, 'one enfleshed nature of God the Word', their favourite slogan.[11] John deploys the term 'theosis' as a counterpart to 'sarkosis' to indicate neatly how the Cyrillian expression may be interpreted in a manner perfectly compatible with Chalcedonian orthodoxy. The two natures of the incarnate Word form a single hypostasis that is not

---

[9] Leontius of Jerusalem, *Adversus Nestorianos* 1, 18 (PG 86, 1468C). On the dates of Leontius of Jerusalem (once considered to be a contemporary of his namesake of Byzantium), see Krausmüller, 2001; Dell'Osso, 2006. 'Ektheosis' is a Neoplatonic term (first used by Proclus), which was Christianised by Dionysius the Areopagite. For a discussion of the term, see Russell, 2004: 340.

[10] Leontius of Jerusalem, *Adversus Nestorianos* 3, 6 (PG 86, 1621C); 3, 8 (PG 86, 1625D and 1632B).

[11] On the history of this slogan, μία φύσις τοῦ θεοῦ λόγου σεσαρκωμένη, see Russell, 2016.

a new nature but the result of a two-way process of exchange between divinity and humanity.

By the late seventh century, theosis had thus become a useful Christological term that clarified the theological position of the imperial Church vis-à-vis the miaphysites of the empire's eastern provinces. The rapid Arab conquest of Syria, Mesopotamia, and Egypt in the 630s and 640s, however, made the reconciliation of miaphysites to the imperial Church no longer politically feasible.[12] The expansion of Islam also had another consequence, one that affected the religious life of the imperial heartland more directly. This was the controversy that arose over the legitimacy of images depicting Christ and the saints.

The Role of Theosis in the Iconoclast Controversy

Whether the veneration of images of Christ and the saints was legitimate or not was the main issue of the controversy named after the opponents of such veneration (the iconoclasts, or 'icon breakers') that was settled definitively in favour of images in 787 by the Second Council of Nicaea, later recognised in both East and West as the Seventh Ecumenical Council, even if the controversy still lingered on into the ninth century. The Empire's series of disastrous defeats in the seventh century at the hands of the Muslim Arab armies prompted many to think that God had withdrawn the divine protection that had ensured the victories of Roman arms in the past. One did not have to look far, it was thought, for the reason. In the Old Testament when God had allowed the enemies of Israel to triumph it was to punish his people for relapsing into idolatry. It was argued that by permitting the veneration of religious images, or icons, the Roman Empire, too, had relapsed into idolatry. From 726, with the publication of Leo III's edict ordering the destruction of religious images as idols, iconoclasm became the official imperial policy.

The high point of iconoclasm came in 754 when Leo's son, Constantine V (741–775) summoned a great council of 338 bishops, which met at the Hiereia palace in Chalcedon and condemned the veneration and manufacture of icons as idolatrous. The *Horos*, or Definition, of this council (which claimed the title of the Seventh Ecumenical)

---

[12] Syria was lost to the Empire in 636 (only four years after the death of Muhammad) as a result of the battle of Yarmuk. The reconciliation of miaphysite Syrians was not of course in the political interest of the Umayyad caliphate that was established in 661 with its capital at Damascus.

survives in the acts of the sixth session of the Second Council of Nicaea, where it is refuted paragraph by paragraph.[13] The principal argument of the *Horos* is Christological. The painted image of Christ falsifies the teaching of Chalcedon because either it accepts the hypostatic union of the two natures but by claiming to represent the totality of Christ reduces the divinity to something visible and finite or else it separates the two natures by claiming to represent the humanity alone. The divine and human natures of Christ are inseparable by virtue of the deification of the flesh assumed by the Word, but the act of depiction in images violates this inseparability (ACO series 2, III, 1–3, *Conc. univers. Nicaenum Secund.*, ed. Lamberz, 2008–16: 664; trans. Price, 2020: 472–73).

The patriarch Tarasios (who composed the refutation of the *Horos*) does not dispute the deification of the Lord's ensouled flesh through its union with the divine Word. That was perfectly orthodox. But he strongly denies that depicting the Lord either confuses the natures or separates them. The *Horos*, he insists, makes no distinction between image and archetype. It is not necessary for an image to represent all the properties of its archetype, any more than the portrait of a human being needs to represent the invisible aspects of the person depicted. The *Horos* goes on to say that it is utterly irrational to 'separate the flesh that was deified and moulded with the Godhead' because this implies that the flesh of Christ has a separate hypostasis; Tarasios indignantly denies that to depict Christ separates the natures or that it introduces a fourth person into the Trinity and repeats his assertion that the iconoclast error arises from a refusal to distinguish between the image and its archetype (Lamberz, 2008–16: 666; trans. Price, 2020: 473–74). 'We accept the sacred images,' he says, 'knowing them to be images and nothing else, since they bear only the name of the archetype and not the essence' (Lamberz, 2008–16: 670; trans. Price, 2020: 476).

The *Horos* then deploys another argument, based on the theology of the Eucharist, which again relies on the idea of deification. Just as Christ's body is holy because it has been deified by union with his divine nature, so the eucharistic bread is holy since it has been 'deified by the grace of consecration'. The bread and the cup of the Eucharist are therefore the true image of Christ's natural flesh, sanctified by the visitation of the Holy Spirit, 'through the mediation of the priest who by transformation changes the offering from being common to being holy' (Lamberz,

---

[13] For an analysis of the *Horos*, see Price, 2020: 427–32.

2008–16: 672; trans. Price, 2020: 476–77). Tarasios has no problem with the deification of the eucharistic species, but he objects to their being considered merely an image. There is no patristic support at all for calling 'the bloodless sacrifice' an image, he says. It is truly the body and blood of Christ.

A further point the *Horos* makes is that some people accept the argument that Christ cannot be depicted because of the inseparable character of the two natures but argue that this does not apply to the Theotokos and the other saints. The depiction of the saints, however, is also forbidden by the *Horos* for the sake of consistency: 'once the first has been rejected, there is no need for the latter' (Lamberz, 2008–16: 680–82; trans. Price, 2020: 482–83). Tarasios rejects this as a non-theological and therefore irrelevant justification. Against it he repeats the main argument of the supporters of icons, namely, that 'the honour paid to the image ascends to the archetype' (Basil, *On the Holy Spirit*, 18, 45) and adds that the same principle applies to the image of an emperor. The image is only a material object, but if it is dishonoured it is the emperor himself who is insulted.

Tarasios does not make use of John Damascene's argument that images of the saints may be venerated because the saints have been deified by divine grace, partly because this argument had been put forward by John to counter a different iconoclast move, and partly, perhaps, because arguments from deification had already been used by the *Horos*. The iconoclast move that John counters is the suggestion that it is sufficient to make images of Christ and his mother, the Theotokos, without multiplying images any further (*On the divine images* I, 19).[14] If images of Christ and the Theotokos are permissible, John declares, it is absurd to prohibit images of the saints. The saints are those who have become 'like God'. In fact, they have themselves become god, not by nature but by participation, 'just as iron plunged in fire does not become fire by nature, but by union and burning and participation' (*On the divine images* I, 19; trans. Louth, 2003: 33). Indeed, through their deification, the saints become the gods of whom the psalmist says: 'God stands in the midst of the gods' (Psalm 81[2]:6).

The theme of deification is thus employed by both sides of the iconoclast controversy, the deification of the flesh assumed by the Word as a result of the hypostatic union being taken by the *Horos* as a compelling

[14] Although John Damascene was anathematised by the council of 754, along with the patriarch Germanos and George of Cyprus, he is not cited by the council of 787.

reason for forbidding Christ's representation in images because his true character would thereby be falsified, whereas the deification of the saints by participation is taken by John Damascene as an equally strong reason for permitting the representation of the saints because they, like the Theotokos, share in the divine. It is telling that the iconophiles at the Second Council of Nicaea avoid using any argument from deification, very likely because such an argument had been used to good effect by the iconoclasts.

Deification, or theosis, thus played a significant role in the controversies between Chalcedon (451) and Nicaea II (787), which were all focused on Christological issues. Besides its Christological role, however, or rather in dependence upon it, for 'the flesh [of Christ] was both mortal in itself and life-giving through its hypostatic union with the Word' (*De fid. orth.*, 61; Kotter 2, 156.24–25; trans. Russell, 2022: 211), theosis had a further religious dimension as a term applicable to Christ's salvific work.[15] In order to explore this dimension we need to return to Dionysius the Areopagite.

THEOSIS AND THE CHRISTIAN'S ASCENT TO GOD

Dionysius the Areopagite

The theologian who retrieved the term 'theosis' is a mysterious figure who circulated his works under the name of the Dionysius mentioned in the Acts of the Apostles as an Athenian intellectual converted by St Paul.[16] His true name is not known.[17] Even his physical and cultural environment is contested, though it seems most likely to have been Syria/Palestine.

---

[15] For a succinct analysis of the difference between the Christological sense of deification (in which Christ's hypostatic principle, the Logos, is the sole principle of agency) and the anthropological sense (in which uncreated being enters into an already hypostasised human nature as divine activity or energy), see Tollefsen, 2012: 179.

[16] Acts 17.34. Dionysius has been the focus of much interest in recent years, as witnessed by Coakley and Stang, 2009. Studies of his approach to deification may be found in de Andia, 1986; Golitzin, 2013. Cf. Russell, 2004: 248–62.

[17] Golitzin, following E. Honigmann and M. van Esbroek, has suggested tentatively that the author of the *Corpus Dionysiacum* could be Peter the Iberian, a Georgian who spent his adolescence at the court of Theodosius II, travelled to Palestine to embrace the monastic life, and in 452 became bishop of Maiuma near Gaza (Golitzin, 2013, 399–406). Another suggestion, taking into account differences in style within the *Corpus*, is that it is a collective work, the product of several authors working as a team (Mainoldi, 2018: 483–89).

There is no doubt, however, that he belongs to the latter part of the fifth century, perhaps dying a little before the beginning of Justinian's reign. His works are first mentioned at the colloquy between Chalcedonians and their miaphysite opponents convoked by Justinian in 532. It was the miaphysites who cited Dionysius, even though he has nothing to say specifically on the issue of Christ's one or two natures.[18] The admissibility of citing him was challenged by one of the Chalcedonian bishops participating in the colloquy, who pointed out that Dionysius was unknown to the great Fathers of the fourth and fifth centuries.[19] Such scruples, however, were soon set aside, especially after John of Scythopolis (d. 550) produced an extensively annotated edition of the Dionysian corpus that was to become the source of all subsequent copies (Louth, 2009).

Although the work of Christ is evident on every page of the corpus, Dionysius does not speak explicitly of the deification of Christ's human nature. What he says is that 'the supremely infinite loving-kindness of the thearchic goodness ... transformed (μετασκευάσασα) the whole of what belongs to us beneficently into its opposite' (*Eccl. Hier.* III, Theoria, 11, 441AB; Heil, 1991b: 91). With regard to Christ's human nature, 'transformation' (μετασκευή) expresses best what Dionysius wishes to say about the ontological change brought about in the humanity which the divine Word assumed. The language of theosis is reserved by Dionysius for his discussions of the Christian's ascent to union with God.[20] This is because theosis is not an ontological state but a dynamic process, a participation of the believer in the divine attributes or energies, or rather, in one of them in particular, that of divinity. But as God is not apportioned among his energies but is wholly present in each of them, to participate in his deifying power (τὸ θεοποιόν) is to participate in the whole of God. One way of expressing this is by the image of descent and ascent. There is a descending movement on the part of God, which 'by the deification that comes from him' (τῇ ἐξ ἑαυτοῦ θεώσει) multiplies his oneness in creatures that have become deiform without diminishing or dividing his own supreme simplicity, for God infinitely transcends divinity (*Divine Names* II, 2, 649C; Suchla, 1990: 136). And there is a

---

[18] Dionysius does, however, speak of 'a new theandric activity' (καινήν τινα τὴν θεανδρικὴν ἐνέργειαν) in *Ep.* 4 (ed. Ritter, 161), which the miaphysites, by the change of one letter, appear to have read as 'a common theandric activity' (κοινήν τινα τὴν θεανδρικὴν ἐνέργειαν).

[19] This was Hypatius of Ephesus, who, it should be noted, did not query the authenticy of the attribution to Paul's Athenian convert but simply the admissibility of citing him.

[20] The discussion that follows draws on Russell, 2004: 248–62; and Golitzin, 2013: 183–86.

corresponding ascending movement on the part of creatures, 'so far as is attainable by them' (κατὰ τὸ ἐφικτόν), that raises them to the simplicity and unity of God, for those who have become deiform or deisimilar (θεοειδεῖς) have replicated God's unity. The divine initiative meets with a human response that renders creatures 'capable of being called by the same divine title as God' (*Cel. Hier.* XII, 3, 293B; Heil, 1991a: 43).

How, then, do creatures become deiform or deisimilar? Surprisingly, not by engaging in a process of philosophical abstraction that strips away the multiplicity of the phenomenal world in order to arrive at a more unified level of being but by meditating on the symbolism of the divine Liturgy. In the *Ecclesiastical Hierarchy*, Dionysius defines theosis (the first Christian writer to do so) as 'assimilation to God and union with him so far as is attainable' (ἡ δὲ θέωσίς ἐστιν ἡ πρὸς θεὸν ὡς ἐφικτὸν ἀφομοίωσίς τε καὶ ἕνωσις, *Eccl. Hier.* I, 3, 376A; Heil, 1991a: 91). He had already used the same phrase in the *Celestial Hierarchy* as a definition of the goal of 'hierarchy', a word of his own coinage (III, 2, 165A; Heil, 1991a: 17). 'Theosis' and 'the goal of hierarchy' are therefore to be seen as two different terms for the same reality. The proper context of theosis is thus liturgical, for in the Eucharist the earthly hierarchy imitates the angelic hierarchy, the bishop being a 'hierarch' who reveals to those in his charge the mysteries that have been entrusted to him. The ascent to the goal of hierarchy is through meditation on the symbolic meaning of the eucharistic rite.[21]

The eucharistic community, gathered round its bishop, is thus an analogue of the celestial hierarchy 'around God'. Embodied beings that we are, we need material means of rising up to the contemplation of the heavenly hierarchy. These material means are 'veils' that need to be lifted. Behind them, says Dionysius, is a spiritual reality that may be grasped intellectually if the material symbols of liturgical worship are read correctly:

[We need to reckon] the visible beauties as copies of the invisible beauty, the sensible perfumes as figures of the intelligible diffusion, the material lights as an image of the immaterial giving of light, and the expositions of the sacred teachings as images of the contemplative fullness according to the intellect, the orders of the clerical ranks here below as representative of the harmonious *habitus* [of the mind] ordered towards things divine, and the partaking of the divine Eucharist

---

[21] Hence the symbolic accounts of the Eucharist in the Byzantine tradition by, for example, Maximus the Confessor and Nicholas Kabasilas. For an analysis of the way Dionysius treats the symbolism, see Golitzin, 2013: 191–223.

as an image of participation in Jesus, and whatever else that is transmitted transcendentally to the heavenly essences but symbolically to us. (*Cel. Hier.* I, 3, 121D–24A; Heil, 1991a: 8–9; trans. Golitzin, 2013: 202, lightly adapted)

Alexander Golitzin describes this passage as a summary of the entire Dionysian project. As Dionysius himself immediately goes on to say, these images have been given to us 'for the sake of our own analogous deification' (ἕνεκα τῆς ἡμῶν ἀναλόγου θεώσεως: *Cel. Hier.* I, 3, 124A; Heil, 1991a: 9). Theosis is thus fundamentally a contemplative/liturgical participation through symbols in the supreme cause of all things conceived of as *theos*. Yet although it transcends matter, theosis is more than the product of an intellectual process, more than an ascent simply through negation. This 'more' is expressed by the terms 'ecstasy' (ἔκστασις) and 'union' (ἕνωσις), which are terms that characterise erotic love.

We tend to think of 'ecstasy' and 'union' as applying to the human yearning for self-transcendence. With Dionysius, these terms apply principally to God. Union refers to God as he is in himself, a triad of hypostases perfectly united in a manner beyond our comprehension. Ecstasy refers to God as he relates to what is not God, to the created order, by an act of separation or distinction (διάκρισις). It is God's going out of himself in active love for humankind (φιλανθρωπία) in order to unite himself with his creatures in accordance with their capacity to receive him (Golitzin, 2013: 155–57). There is a symmetry in the human application of these terms, with human beings moving in the opposite direction from separation to union under the impulse of their love for God (φιλοθεΐα).[22] The divine and the human meet and mingle in their respective ecstasies: 'Just as [God] departs from himself in order to enter into relation, so the creature is constrained, in obedience to the very thrust of its being, to transcend itself in union with the "rays of the unapproachable light"' (Golitzin, 2013: 156, with ref. to *Divine Names* IV, 11, 708D; Suchla, 1990: 156).

Maximus the Confessor

The person of Maximus the Confessor (c. 580–662) emerges much more clearly from his writings and from his role in the monothelete controversy

---

[22] The word φιλοθεΐα ('love of God') is not actually used by Dionysius – he speaks, rather, of the *eros* of all things for the beautiful and the good – but the φιλανθρωπία /φιλοθεΐα pairing conveniently summarises the symmetrical relationship he intends.

than does that of Dionysius the Areopagite, but in his case too there are uncertainties. For a long time a Greek hagiographical *Life*, composed perhaps in the tenth century, gave us all that we knew about his provenance and early life.[23] According to this *Life*, Maximus was born in Constantinople of noble parents and pursued a career in the imperial administration before embracing the monastic life. Then in 1973 a near-contemporary Syriac *Life* was discovered that gives a completely different account of Maximus's origins.[24] According to the Syriac *Life*, which comes from a monothelete source and is very hostile to Maximus, his origins were Palestinian and thoroughly ignoble. He is said to have been the child of a Samaritan linen-maker and his Jewish slave-girl. The couple and their children were baptised by a priest called Martyrios, who later arranged for Maximus and a younger brother to enter the Old Lavra of St Chariton, in the Pharan valley to the west of the Dead Sea. Today, although both versions have their partisans, scholarly opinion tends to favour the Syriac version. The Greek version accounts for the high level of Maximus's Hellenic culture and for his contacts (as witnessed by his letters) in government circles. The Syriac version, however, despite its tendentiousness, contains many persuasive elements. It accounts, for example, for Maximus's mastery of the Origenian method of biblical exegesis, in which every detail has a symbolic significance, and also for his taking Sophronius (later patriarch of Jerusalem) as his spiritual father. Nor does it leave his acquisition of an excellent education unexplained, for Palestine at the time was noted for the quality of its Hellenic culture, with Gaza an important centre of learning and the seat of a famous school of rhetoric. I am inclined, like the majority of scholars today, to accept the Syriac version of Maximus's origins.[25]

The inexorable advance of the Arab armies in the Eastern Mediterranean forced many monastics to seek refuge in Italy and North Africa, much of which at that time was still part of the Eastern Roman Empire. Maximus settled for a while in North Africa (in the area of modern Tunisia). It was here that in the 630s he wrote his most influential spiritual works, mainly in response to queries from fellow ascetics in North Africa and from Bishop John of Kyzikos. In these works (the

---

[23] The Greek Life exists in three recensions. For a discussion of their relationship and the text of the third recension, see Neil and Allen, 2003.

[24] The discovery was made by S. Brock, who published the text with a translation, notes, and commentary in Brock, 1973.

[25] Blowers, 2016: 25–42. For a judicious summary of the present state of research on the topic, see Allen, 2015.

Exposition on the Lord's Prayer, the *Mystagogy*, the *Questions to Thalassius*, and the *Ambigua to John*), Maximus sets out a comprehensive vision of the spiritual life as the appropriation by finite human beings of a new mode of divine life grounded in the theology of the incarnation.[26]

Maximus is not an easy writer. He does not, as a rule, write treatises analysing his theme according to a rational plan in the scholastic manner. His preferred literary genres are questions and answers (ἐρωταποκρίσεις), textual commentary (ἑρμηνεῖαι), or responses to difficulties (ἀπορίαι) encountered by his correspondents in their study of biblical and patristic texts. Often, he arranges his material in chapters (κεφάλαια), a literary form consisting of chains of short paragraphs, often a hundred of them (hence also the term 'centuries'), which was developed in a monastic context to facilitate slow meditative reading. These genres enable him to develop his thought by association, rather than by logical sequence, engaging in what Andrew Louth describes as a process of 'lateral thinking' enabling apparently diverse concerns to converge (Louth, 1996: 94) or what Paul Blowers calls 'an upward interpretative "spiral" into which Maximus desires to catch up his readers' (Blowers, 2016: 75). The reason for this preference is that Maximus is acutely aware of the polyvalency of language and thus of the different layers of meaning contained in the texts that he discusses. Christ is incarnated in different ways: pre-eminently in the flesh but also in the natural world, in Scripture, in the Eucharist, and in the theological writings of the Fathers. Each of these 'multiple incarnations', as Blowers calls them, in which the Word transfigures materiality and corporeality, can have several different meanings: all of them need to be brought into play in order for Maximus's writing to act as 'a conduit for the pedagogy of the Word' (Blowers, 2016: 73).

The incarnation of the Word in the flesh is the fundamental point of reference for theosis. The Word did not become flesh only to rescue a created world that had not gone according to plan. Far from being simply a response to human sin, the incarnation was intended from the beginning to bring creaturely being to fulfilment. Maximus's perspective is teleological, always looking back from the end-point (which alone gives meaning) to the beginning and to the various stages in between.

---

[26] The classic study of deification in Maximus is Larchet, 1996; see also Russell, 2004: 262–95. Outstanding recent books include Tollefsen, 2012, and Blowers, 2016.

Humanity was created to be the mediating link in creation, to recapitulate in the human microcosm the macrocosm of the universe. The instability of humanity's material existence, however, made this impossible to achieve without the coming of the Second Adam, to remedy sin certainly but more than that to introduce a 'wholly new way of being human'.[27] This 'wholly new way' – or 'newer mode' (καινότερος τρόπος) – of being human is by the transfiguration (not the *essential* change) of human nature through its participation in the divine. 'Participation', as Torstein Tollefsen has put it, is 'the presence of divine activity in the creature'. It takes place when the uncreated interpenetrates the created (without confusion, change, division, or separation, on analogy with the hypostatic union but with the created human being as the subject of the hypostasis, not the uncreated Word) so that 'the divine activity carries the human activity' (Tollefsen, 2012: 178, 180–83).

The distinction between 'natural principle' (λόγος) and 'mode' (τρόπος) is the key to understanding how human beings can remain unchanged *qua* human and yet be transformed – divinised – by the divine activity (ἐνέργεια) that interpenetrates them and 'carries' the human activity that is proper to them. This is how Maximus himself describes it:

> Generally speaking, all innovation (καινοτομία) is manifested in relation to the mode (τρόπος) of the thing innovated, not its natural principle (λόγος). The principle, if it undergoes innovation, corrupts the nature, as the nature in that case does not maintain inviolate the principle according to which it exists. The mode is thus innovated, while the natural principle is preserved, displays a miraculous power, insofar as the nature appears to be acted upon and to act, clearly beyond its normal scope. The principle of human nature is to exist in soul and body as one nature constituted of rational soul and a body; but its mode is the scheme in which it naturally acts and is acted upon, which can frequently change and undergo alteration without changing at all the nature along with it.[28]

Maximus goes on to exemplify this modal transformation in a series of Old Testament figures (Enoch, Elisha, Noah) and images (the burning bush, the dividing of the sea, the raining down of manna), in each case

[27] Maximus the Confessor, *Ambigua ad Ioannem* 7, PG 91, 1097C; trans. Blowers and Wilken, 2003: 70.
[28] Maximus the Confessor, *Ambigua ad Ioannem* 42, PG 91, 1341D; trans. Blowers and Wilken, 2003: 89–90. The language of innovation comes from Gregory of Nazianzus, who says in *Oration* 39, 13: 'Natures are innovated (καινοτομοῦνται φύσεις), and God becomes man, and "he who rides on the heaven of heaven in the sunrise" (Psalm 67. 33) of his own glory and splendour is glorified in the sunset of our baseness and humility.' On the relationship between *logos* and *tropos*, see also Larchet, 2015.

demonstrating innovation by God 'with respect to the mode of operation, not the principle of existence'.[29]

Here the 'upward interpretative "spiral"' by which Blowers character-ises Maximus's expository method is brought about by the use of sorites, or the heaping up of examples. Similar rhetorical techniques may be found elsewhere. In the *Exposition on the Lord's Prayer*, for example, there are the seven linked mysteries as the believer ascends from theology (knowledge of God), through filial adoption by grace (baptism), to equal-ity with the angels (through Christ's union of heaven and earth), to participation in the divine life (through the eucharist), to the unification of human nature (through Christ's healing of fallen humanity's divided will), to the abolition of the law of sin (through sharing in the salvation brought by Christ), and finally to the destruction of the tyranny of the evil one (through the flesh defeated in Adam proving victorious in Christ), the sequence as a whole comprising the mystery of deification.[30] In the *Mystagogy*, there is a similar ascent, this time through the various stages of the Liturgy to the climax of communion, when those who share in it worthily, 'can both be and be called gods by adoption through grace because all of God entirely fills them and leaves no part of them empty of his presence'.[31] And in *Questions to Thalassius* 59, the rhetorical figure of anadiplosis (in which the last word of a clause is repeated as the first word of the next clause) is employed to produce an interlocking chain of sixteen definitions, beginning with salvation as the end of faith and concluding with the infinite and more than infinite divine energy as 'the ineffable and more than ineffable pleasure and joy of those in whom the divine energy is active', all of this linked to theosis, which is defined in the twelfth definition as 'the boundary and limit of all times and ages, and of the things within those times and ages'.[32] Maximus occasionally offers simi-lar lapidary definitions of theosis, but they are always embedded within complex structures as he 'spirals' round his subject nudging the reader upwards to an ever richer understanding of the new deified mode of being made possible by Christ.

[29] Maximus the Confessor, *Ambigua ad Ioannem* 42, PG 91, 1344D; trans. Blowers and Wilken, 2003: 91.

[30] Maximus the Confessor, *Orationis dominicae expositio* 2, PG 90, 876C–80B.

[31] Maximus the Confessor, *Mystagogia* 21, PG 91, 697A; trans. Berthold, 1985: 203 (lightly modified).

[32] *Quaestiones ad Thalassium* 59, CCSG 22, pp. 53–59. The passage is translated in full in Blowers, 2016: 95–96.

Maximus's complex discussions are intended to allow for the expression of the Word's 'multiple incarnations' on many different levels. A text that illustrates this magnificently is *Ambigua to John* 10, an extended commentary on one of Gregory of Nazianzus's key statements on the nature of theosis:

If therefore it happens to anyone that, passing by means of reason and contemplation through matter and the fleshly, whether called cloud or veil, to become assimilated to God and united to the most pure light, so far as is permitted to human nature, this person is blessed by his ascent from here and his deification there, which is granted to those who genuinely live the philosophical life and transcend the material dyad through the unity the mind perceives in the Trinity.[33]

In the gospels, the penetration of the veil of matter that allows the human to become assimilated to God so far as is permitted to human nature is presented in a richly symbolic fashion in the transfiguration of Christ on the mountain (Matt 17.1–8; Mark 9.2–8; Luke 9.28–35). Maximus perhaps first comments on the Transfiguration in *Questions and Doubts*, where he resolves the apparent contradiction between Matthew, who says that the event occurred 'six days' after Jesus told his disciples that the Son of Man will come in glory within the lifetime of some of his hearers, and Luke, who specifies the interval between the same saying of Jesus and the transfiguration as 'about eight days'.[34] Maximus's solution is on two levels, the first that of rational analysis, the second that of *theoria*, or meditation on the symbolism of the text. On the first level, he maintains that Matthew is referring to the six days of actually climbing the mountain, whereas Luke is counting both ends of the series, from the day of departure to the vision of Christ transfigured on the summit. On the second level, Matthew's 'six days' represent the six days of creation, which in turn symbolise the acquisition of virtue and knowledge as the disciples ascend the mountain of theology together. Luke's 'eight days' point to the new creation of the eighth day. The first day is needed to overcome what contravenes nature in us, and then six days are needed to work through what is consistent with nature in order to arrive at the eighth day, which is that which transcends nature – a moral and spiritual progression from our fallen state, which is against nature (παρὰ φύσιν), to

---

[33] Gregory of Nazianzus, *Oration* 21, 2, in praise of Athanasius (PG 35, 1084C), quoted by Maximus the Confessor, *Ambigua ad Ioannem* 10, PG 91, 1105CD; trans. Louth, 1996: 96–97.

[34] Maximus the Confessor, *Quaestiones et dubia*, CCSG 10, p. 119. The text is an early one, dating to before c. 633/4 (Jankowiak and Booth, 2015: 29).

the long ascetic and moral struggle, which is in accordance with nature (κατὰ φύσιν), and finally to the deified mode of existence, which is beyond nature (ὑπὲρ φύσιν).

In *Ambigua to John* 10, Maximus takes this *theoria* a good deal further.[35] In the first place, when the apostles beheld Christ transfigured, the change that occurred was not in Christ but in their own sense faculties, which were enhanced by the operation of the Spirit 'lifting the veils of the passions from the intellectual activity that was in them'. They could then learn that the radiance that shone from Christ's face was a symbol – Christ, in this case, symbolising himself – of his divinity that transcends the mind. The white garments are a symbol of the words of Scripture, which are now grasped by the mind in all their clarity. Alternatively, the white garments symbolise creation, for the words of Scripture and creation – the written law and the natural law – are two paths to the same truth. After an examination of the two laws, exemplified by the Old Testament figures of Melchisedec, Abraham, and Moses, the discussion is brought round again to the Transfiguration. Now the luminous brightness of Christ's face leads the apostles 'in an ineffable and unknowable manner' to a direct encounter with the power and glory of God, while the white garments are the revelation of the magnificence of God in both Scripture and nature. Maximus then turns to the figures of Moses and Elijah, who were seen with Christ when he was transfigured. Here the polyvalency of the symbolism is rich indeed. Together, Moses and Elijah stand for the legal word and the prophetic word, for the wisdom of legislation and the divine gift of prophecy, for the ascetic struggle and spiritual contemplation, for marriage and celibacy, for life and death (each of them symbolising both the teaching that leads to life and the turning towards the passions that embraces death), for time and nature (for Moses was the first to count time through his narrative of the six days of creation and also instituted temporal worship, whereas Elijah guarded the *logoi* of creation inviolate within himself), and for the intelligible and the sensible creation. At this point, Maximus becomes aware that the richness of the layers of symbolism he is uncovering may be demanding too much of his readers, so he swiftly concludes by summing up concisely the significance of Moses and Elijah as representatives,

---

[35] Maximus the Confessor, *Ambigua ad Ioannem* 10, PG 91, 1105C–69B; trans. Louth, 1996: 96–134. This work belongs to the same period as *Quaestiones et Dubia* (Jankowiak and Booth, 2015: 28–29). Sherwood's classic date-list places the *Ambigua* a little after the *Quaestiones et Dubia*; Jankowiak and Booth reverse the order.

respectively, of apophatic and kataphatic theology. In this respect, they mirror the appearance of Christ, the light of whose face is theologically apophatic, revealing the divine glory that is beyond ineffability and unknowability, while the splendour of whose garments is theologically kataphatic, pointing to how God is manifested in created things.

The whole of this sustained passage is a remarkable tour de force. Blowers has aptly called it 'a resplendent icon of the dynamics of revelation' (Blowers, 2016: 79). Every detail is symbolic of how the Word is disclosed in both Scripture and creation. But there is no mechanical correspondence of symbol to signification. The narrative of the Transfiguration contains multiple levels of meaning, all validated by their mutual coinherence. The narrative's supreme symbol, however, which is different from all the others because it points not to something external but to itself, is the face of Christ. The vision of divine glory in Christ's face, a vision made possible by the moral and ascetical struggle of the beholders (symbolised by the six days of ascending the mountain) – but appropriated by them as the *theologia*, both apophatic and kataphatic (represented by Moses and Elijah) – is an iconic depiction of 'participation in the divine realities that transcend nature', 'assimilation of believers to that in which they are participating', and 'the identity of the participants with the participated that is permitted on the level of energy through the assimilation', which are the three interlocking definitions of *Questions to Thalassius* 59 immediately preceding the definition of theosis. It is thus that human beings – at least in the monastic context, for Maximus is writing primarily for monks – can come to participate in the 'newer mode' of being human.

The Maximian Heritage

The circumstances of Maximus the Confessor's death in 662, shortly after he was condemned for his opposition to the imperial government's official monothelete policy, mutilated, and sent into exile in Georgia, created difficulties for the reception of his thought in Byzantium.[36] He had greater influence in Palestine, where his work was known to John Damascene (c. 655–c. 750). In Constantinople, Photius (c. 810–c. 895) studied him but was not greatly impressed by him. Symeon the New Theologian (c. 949–1022), despite the centrality of theosis in his own thinking and

---

[36] On the reception of Maximus in the Byzantine tradition, see Louth, 2015a.

his sharing of a number of themes with Maximus, never alludes to him. It is only in the fourteenth century, in the context of the hesychast controversy, which came to revolve around the interpretation of Christ's transfiguration, that Maximus comes into his own.

John Damascene

John Damascene's argument from the deification of the saints for the legitimacy of venerating their icons along with those of Christ and the *Theotokos* has already been noted, as has his use of the concept of theosis on the Christological level to explain how the two natures of Christ are united without confusion through their unmixed interpenetration. On the anthropological level, the concept of theosis has a further role. Adam was created with the intention that 'in due time' (ἐν καιρῷ), when it pleased God, he should be united to God as a result of his unquestioning obedience and through this union he should be enriched by theosis (*De fid. orth.* 25b, lines 9–10; Kotter, 1973: 74). The serpent's promise, 'You shall be as gods', was not a temptation to Satanic pride, as some have thought, but a temptation to seize prematurely the gift that God always intended to give. The fall was therefore not a deliberate turning away from God but a misguided attempt to appropriate a supreme good before its proper time, its *kairos*. In true Maximian fashion, John Damascene uncovers a deeper layer of meaning that had eluded his predecessors, even Maximus himself. Maximus saw the invitation to become 'as gods' as a temptation to polytheism;[37] John sees it as the mistaken choice of evil under the guise of good.[38]

Symeon the New Theologian

The Damascene has nothing to say about the role of theosis in the Christian's spiritual life. This was to be a major theme of Symeon the New Theologian, who spent most of his monastic life in Constantinople, first at the monastery of Stoudios and then at that of St Mamas, where he

---

[37] Maximus the Confessor, *Quaestiones ad Thalassium* 44 (ed. C. Laga and C. Steel, CCSG 7, p. 299).

[38] Cf. Procopius of Gaza (c. 475–c. 538), a Palestinian like John (though a teacher of rhetoric rather than a monk), who in his commentary on Genesis puts into the serpent's mouth the argument that if Adam and Eve became like gods, they would always be able to enjoy God's company: νῦν γὰρ, φησίν, ὡς ἄνθρωποι οὐ δύνασθε πάντοτε εἶναι μετὰ τοῦ θεοῦ, ἀλλ' ἐὰν γενηθῆτε θεοί (*Com. in Gen.* 3, 1 (ed. K. Metzler, GCS, Neue Folge 22).

became *hegoumenos* (abbot) in 981.[39] Symeon, as Metropolitan Kallistos of Diokleia has put it, was 'a radical and a maximalist' (Ware 2003: 10). Indeed, in an address to his community of St Mamas, Symeon referred to himself as a 'most frenzied zealot' (ζηλωτὴς μανικώτατος) in his concern for the spiritual well-being of the brethren (*Cat. Disc.* 21, lines 139–40; Krivochéine, 1964: 362). This zealotry was to encounter strong opposition, not only in his own monastery (from which he was forced to resign in 1005) but also influential circles in the government and the patriarchate.[40] Its characteristic features were an emphasis on the central-ity of the relationship between a spiritual father and his disciple, an exaltation of personal spiritual experience, and a maximalist interpret-ation of deification.

We are well informed of the life of Symeon as a result of the autobio-graphical nature of much of his work and also of a *Life* by his disciple, Niketas Stethatos, written thirty years after his death.[41] Symeon's family belonged to the provincial aristocracy of Paphlagonia, a region of central Anatolia. At the age of twenty-seven, after studies in Constantinople and a brief career in the imperial service, he entered the monastery of Stoudios. He had already placed himself under the spiritual guidance of a Stoudite monk called Symeon Eulabes ('Symeon the Pious'). The elder Symeon, whose life showed something of the characteristics of a 'holy fool', was a controversial figure. The younger Symeon's putting his obedi-ence to him above that which he owed to his *hegoumenos* was probably the reason why he was obliged to leave and transfer to St Mamas. There he became *hegoumenos* himself after three years, but his hegoumenate was not a success. The demands he made on the community to lead a spiritual life of the utmost intensity led to a revolt that resulted in his resignation. Four years later, in 1009, at the instigation of Stephen of Nikomedeia, the patriarch's *synkellos* (confidant and successor desig-nate), he was tried for heresy (on the basis of his promotion of the cult

---

[39] The classic work on Symeon (originally published in French in 1980) is Krivocheine, 1986. Also important are H. J. M. Turner, 1990 and Alfeyev, 2000. Valuable studies on a more popular level include Golitzin, 1996–7 and Ware, 2003.

[40] On the historical context of Symeon's early life (and how his political career as a layman may have been cut short by the accession of Basil II), see McGuckin, 1996. McGuckin's reconstruction has been regarded by many scholars (e.g., Alfeyev, 2000: 32) as too speculative, but I find it entirely plausible.

[41] Niketas's *Life*, written on the occasion of the transfer of Symeon's relics to Constantinople by the patriarch Michael Keroularios, has been published by Hausherr and Horn, 1928. Much of Symeon's autobiographical writing is in his *Hymns*, which are not liturgical hymns but poems powerfully expressive of his inner life.

of his deceased spiritual father, Symeon Eulabes, with icons and an annual feast) and was exiled to a village on the Asiatic side of the Bosphorus near Chrysoupolis (now Üsküdar), where he died in 1022.

There is hardly a page in Symeon's writings where he does not mention the word 'light' (φῶς). One of his earliest spiritual experiences, even before he had embraced the monastic life, was of a divine radiance filling the room where he was and overwhelming him. In a discourse delivered to his monastic community of St Mamas, he speaks of a young man (no doubt himself) who lost all sense of where he was, and 'entering wholly into a state of immaterial light and seeming himself to have become light and forgetful of the whole world, became filled with tears and inexpressible joy and exultation' (*Cat. Disc.* 21, lines 88–100; Krivochéine, 1964: 372). In one of his 'chapters', he universalises this experience as the mark of someone who has internalised the light of the Holy Spirit. Such a person, he says, 'wholly consumed by fire, becomes like light', exemplifying the phrase, 'God united to gods and known by them'.[42] Indeed, it is a goal not only for monks but for all serious Christians.

The attainment of this goal is not achieved by the study of texts or by abstractive contemplation. It begins with baptism, is nurtured by the reception of the Eucharist, and is fulfilled eschatologically: 'O wonder! Like angels and sons of God, after death they will be gods united with God, those who are gods by adoption having been made like him who is God by nature' (*Hymn* 27, lines 93–95). Yet the fruits of it are already apparent in this life. Symeon's maximising of the implications of this scandalised many of his contemporaries:

I am called a heretic because I teach too that those who share in [the Spirit] are not only free from all lusts and passions and unseemly *logismoi*, but are also themselves gods abiding in God, and have come to exist outside the reach of the flesh and the world, and are not just holy themselves and live while in the body as if they had no body, but also look on all the rest of the faithful as holy, and not merely as holy but as people who have 'put on Christ' and have become christs; and I teach that he who has not acquired eyes of this kind for his heart is plainly a man who has not yet come to exist in Christ's light, and has not shared in it, for this is how Christ's light freely gives itself to be seen by all who are counted worthy to enter it through repentance. (*Ep.* 4, lines 468–78; H. J. M. Turner, 2009: 176–79)

---

[42] Symeon the New Theologian, *Theological, Gnostic and Practical Chapters* 3.28 (Darrouzès, 1957: 86), citing Gregory of Nazianzus, *Orat.* 38.7 (ed. Moreschini, 2000: 884), repeated in *Orat.* 45.3 (ed. Moreschini, 2000: 1136).

For Symeon, authority in the Church came from the Holy Spirit and was based on spiritual stature not on clerical ordination (Symeon Eulabes was not a hieromonk). Simply to be a genuine Christian required putting on Christ in baptism, living in Christ's divine light, and actually becoming Christ (or rather, *a* christ) through the operation of the Holy Spirit. Some have regarded Symeon's account of deification as too individualistic. Certainly, he is awestruck by the effect on his own person of the divine indwelling: 'I participate in the light. I share also in the glory, and my face shines like the face the face of my beloved, and all my limbs become light-bearing' (*Hymn* 16. 31–33). The body is not left out of such participation. We become Christ's members and Christ becomes each of our members, even our private parts (*Hymn* 15. 141–57). But there is also a strong sense in Symeon of the solidarity of all the faithful. It is not only oneself that has 'become Christ' but all the other Christians, too, in virtue of the sacramental context of deification. Even in this life, every aspect of the human person will become suffused with divine glory.

In the gospels, the divine glory is revealed most strikingly in the account of the Transfiguration. Symeon, however, only touches on the Transfiguration once, in the last of his *Theological and Ethical Discourses*. The hesychast, he says, should become like those who climbed Mount Tabor with Jesus and saw the change in his garments and the light of his face. But 'how many climbed Mount Tabor – and climb it even now – but did not see the transfigured Lord, not certainly because Jesus the Christ was not present there (for he is present) but because they were not worthy to see his divinity?' (*Eth. Disc.* 15, lines 41–52 and 121–26; Darrouzès, 1967: 446–48, 452; trans. Golitzin, 1996: 175, 178, adapted). It was not until the fourteenth-century, with the rise of the hesychast controversy, that attention became focused on the Transfiguration, thus stimulating a renewed study of Maximus the Confessor.[43]

Gregory Palamas

Symeon the New Theologian was steeped in the monastic tradition, that is to say, in the *experiential* tradition of theology, but he was not a learned theologian. He did not attempt to resolve difficult problems of biblical exegesis or doctrinal interpretation in the style of Maximus the Confessor,

---

[43] For a more detailed study of deification in Symeon the New Theologian, see Russell (forthcoming).

nor was he entirely consistent in his theological formulations.[44] Maximus's true successor in this respect was Gregory Palamas (1296/ 7–1357),[45] the author of the first monograph on deification, *On Divine and Deifying Participation*.[46]

Gregory was born in Constantinople, the eldest son of Konstantinos Palamas, a senator and trusted counsellor of the emperor Andronikos II.[47] At the age of twenty-four, he withdrew to Mount Athos to devote himself to a life of prayer in the hesychast tradition. It was there in 1336 that he first entered into correspondence with Barlaam of Calabria (c. 1290–1348), a Greek monk from Southern Italy who had established a reputation for himself in Constantinople as a philosopher and controversialist. At the emperor's invitation,[48] Barlaam had engaged in a disputation with a Latin delegation on the doctrine of the *Filioque*,[49] in which he had argued successfully against the Latins that no certain knowledge of the interior relations of the Trinity was possible, on the grounds that in logic apodictic proof requires premises that are self-evident, whereas the premises of Trinitarian doctrine are based on revelation. Palamas was alarmed by this argument because it implied that the Trinitarian doctrine of the Greeks was no more securely based than that of the Latins. He took issue with Barlaam on how we attain to knowledge of God. This led to a

---

[44] For example, on the one hand, he says (as Palamas was later to insist), 'I become totally god by communion with God ... not by essence but by participation' (*Hymn* 50, 200–201) and, on the other, 'we become participants of his divinity and his essence' (*Eth. Disc.* 1, 3, lines 83–84).

[45] The classic study of Palamas's life and thought (now somewhat dated) is Meyendorff, 1959. See also Russell, 2019b.

[46] This treatise (Περὶ θείας καὶ θεοποιοῦ μεθέξεως) (Sinkewicz, 2002: 141, no. 7) was written in the winter of 1341/2 while Palamas was staying at the monastery of Sosthenion on the Bosphorus (Rigo, 2021: 686) after the council of June 1341 that acquitted him of the charge of heresy. It builds on *Triads* 3.1 (summer 1340), which is also on deification, and indeed is subtitled 'On Theosis' (Περὶ θεώσεως) but is a more narrowly focused on refuting Barlaam's interpretation of a number of key texts from the *Corpus Dionysiacum*. On Palamas's use of Dionysius in the *Triads* see Titus, 2022.

[47] The *Life* of Gregory Palamas was written by his friend, the patriarch Philotheos Kokkinos, between 1357 and 1368. The text has been edited by D. Tsames, as no. 4 in the Thessalonian Byzantine Writers series (Thessaloniki: Centre for Byzantine Studies, 1985); trans. Russell, 2020: 52–210.

[48] By this time, Andronikos III (1328–1341), Andronikos II's grandson and successor.

[49] The *Filioque* is the Western Trinitarian teaching that the Holy Spirit proceeds 'from the Father *and the Son*', in contrast to the Eastern 'from the Father', as in the original version of the Nicene Creed. The Orthodox objected to the addition 'and the Son' (*Filioque*), even if qualified by the phrase 'as if from one principle', on doctrinal grounds because it seems to posit two sources for the Holy Spirit, and on ecclesiological grounds because Rome had made the addition to the Creed unilaterally at the beginning of the eleventh century.

consideration of the nature of participation. Both agreed that it was through participation in God that we arrive at knowledge of him; but for Palamas, participation implied sharing in the light of grace by which the divine interpenetrates the whole human person, whereas for Barlaam such divine illumination was rather an intellectual infusion of knowledge by God. From there, Barlaam went on to investigate the hesychastic teaching on the direct experience of God that lay behind Palamas's argument and came to the conclusion that Palamas's version of it was Messalian and implied a heretical fusion of the hesychast with God.[50] In 1340, he laid a charge of heresy against him at the patriarchate. In the following year, Palamas was acquitted by a Church council and his teaching was upheld as orthodox. Barlaam withdrew to Italy, but that was not the end of the matter. A common friend of Barlaam and Palamas, the monk Gregory Akindynos (c. 1300–1348), came forward with new complaints against Palamas centred on the nature of grace and the attainment of theosis.

Barlaam was a philosopher in the Neoplatonist tradition. Akindynos was a conservative monk who strongly objected to what seemed to him the new distinction that Palamas was seeking to make in the Godhead. This was the distinction between the divine essence (οὐσία) and the divine energies or operations (ἐνέργειαι), a distinction that for Palamas indicates two modes of divinity, essence being 'what God is' and energy 'what God does'. The distinction seeks to preserve, on the one hand, the supreme transcendence of God and, on the other hand, his accessibility to human beings. 'What God is' is beyond human knowledge or understanding. 'What God does', which we experience as his power, will, providence, grace, and so on, is accessible to us and yet is not less than God. Moreover, the goal of human life is to participate in God, to attain theosis, as St Maximus had said, and for this to imply neither being absorbed into God nor rendering God finite, like ourselves, the essence/ energies distinction is vital.

To Akindynos, the essence/energies distinction seemed to introduce two different levels of divinity, a higher imparticipable divinity and a lower participable one, or even a fourth hypostasis alongside the three Persons of the Trinity. He suggested that if we wanted to talk about the

---

[50] The Messalians (or Euchites) were a fourth-century rigorist monastic movement that taught the practice of perpetual prayer in order to drive out the demon that had entered the human soul as a result of the Fall and could not be expelled simply by Baptism. By the time of the hesychast controversy (on the Byzantine principle of identifying new heresies with old ones), they had been identified with the Bogomils, followers of a dualist heresy that had originated in Bulgaria in the tenth century.

divine energies yet avoid polytheism, these energies should be identified with the Son and the Holy Spirit. Palamas objected strongly to this because 'what God does' cannot be distributed in different ways among the Persons of the Trinity. It nevertheless seemed to Akindynos that Palamas was reifying the divine attributes, making them objective realities alongside God. This impression was strengthened by the fact that Palamas never says that the distinction is conceptual rather than real.[51] But although he avoids the expression 'conceptual' (κατ' ἐπίνοιαν), he never claims that the distinction is ontological. The thrust of his arguments is that the distinction is indeed conceptual but with a firm basis in reality. Akindynos and his followers, however, remained unpersuaded.

The essence/energies distinction had implications for the doctrine of grace. Palamas distinguished between uncreated and created grace, whereas Akindynos held that all grace, as experienced by human beings, was created. In Palamas's view, this made it impossible for divine–human communion to exist because human participation in God was thereby rendered purely passive without any bridging of the created/uncreated divide. Palamas distinguished between the divine giving of the gift (uncreated grace) and the human appropriation of the gift (created grace).[52] The biblical text on which he bases this is Joel 3.1 (also quoted in Acts 2.17), which reads: 'I shall pour out from my Spirit'. Note the 'from', says Palamas.[53] What is given derives from the Spirit but is not inferior to the Spirit himself – it is not created. The same is implied by John 1.16: 'From his fullness we have all received.' Through grace, the saints share in God but not in his transcendent essence. As St Maximus says, 'he who is deified by grace will become everything that God is short of identity of essence with him'.[54]

All through the controversy, the gospel accounts of the Transfiguration remained a fundamental point of reference.[55] They were discussed at

---

[51] In Russell, 2015, I suggest that this was because he was influenced by Eunomius's understanding of 'conceptual' (κατ' ἐπίνοιαν) as meaning 'fictional'.

[52] Palamas's expression for the giving of the gift is τὸ δωρεὰν δίδοσθαι, and for the gift as given τὸ δωρεὰν διδόμενον.

[53] Palamas, of course, is referring to the text of LXX, the Old Testament for the authors of the New Testament and the Church Fathers. The LXX reads 'I shall pour out from my spirit' (ἀπὸ τοῦ πνεύματός μου). In the English versions of Joel and Acts, the 'from' is omitted.

[54] Quoted by Palamas from *Questions to Thalassius* 22, lines 40–43 (CCSG 7, p. 139), in *Homily* 8, 13.

[55] For an interesting comparison between Palamas and Bonaventure with regard to the Transfiguration, see Dales, 2019b. On the topic of deification, the Franciscan Bonaventure is closer to Palamas than the Dominican Thomas Aquinas with whom Palamas is usually compared.

length in the Council of 1341, which pronounced judgement on Barlaam's accusation of heresy against Palamas and were appealed to in the following three hesychast councils. When the apostles beheld the transfigured Christ, what was it that they saw? Was the light that radiated from Christ's face and clothing a glimpse of uncreated divine glory, or was it a created light (in virtue of emanating from his flesh), or was it simply a construction in the mind of the beholder? Barlaam regarded the light as a symbol not possessing any genuine existence because of the transience of the apostles' vision (Russell, 2019b: 154). Akindynos was convinced that the light belonged to Christ's humanity and was therefore created, not uncreated. Others, in the later stages of the controversy, argued that it was both created and uncreated in view of Christ's twofold nature or that the apostles' experience of light was purely subjective, an image stimulated by perceptions received through the senses but created in the mind. Palamas himself, following Maximus the Confessor and John Damascene, had no doubt that the experience of the Transfiguration was the result of a change in the beholders, not in Christ, being a temporary enhancement of their natural faculties by grace that enabled them to see Christ as he really was.

The Transfiguration was a pledge of 'the future more perfect communion with God and deification, according to which "the righteous will shine like the sun in the kingdom of their father" and will be equal to the angels and sons of God according to the word of the same sun of glory' (Russell, 2020: 125–26). To claim that the light of the Transfiguration was created (and therefore subject to decay) or a mental image (and therefore insubstantial) was to attack the deification that is the goal of salvation and hence the Christian faith itself. The fourteenth-century Constantinopolitan councils upheld Palamas's teaching that the Transfiguration was a pledge of our own future deification, assembling a large number of patristic testimonies in support of it. After the council of 1347, Palamas was elected metropolitan of Thessalonike. In one of his sermons on the feast of the Transfiguration, he exhorts his people: 'Let us contemplate, then, with our inner eyes this great vision: our own nature, now co-existing forever with the immaterial fire of the Godhead. Taking of our "garments of skin", which we put on after the fall – our earthly and fleshly thoughts – let us stand on holy ground, each of us demonstrating through our virtue and our eagerness for God that our own ground in holy. So we will gain in confidence, dwelling in the light of God; and we shall be filled with light even as we press forward. And we shall share in his eternity, as we are filled with light' (Daley, 2013: 378). For what Christ is by nature we shall become by grace.

Theosis and Religion

In Byzantium, theosis summarised in a single word the whole of the Christian faith. Although the term was not formally defined by any council, it played a significant role in the Christological debates of the Fifth, Sixth, and Seventh Ecumenical Councils and became a focus of attention in the Constantinopolitan councils of the fourteenth century in the course of their seeking to clarify the meaning of the Transfiguration. It was thus an integral part of the religion – in the sense of *eusebeia* or *theosebeia*, not *thrēskeia* – that the emperors had a duty to uphold.

The essential character of theosis was both Christological and ecclesial. On the Christological level, the deification of the flesh assumed by the divine Word safeguarded the unity of Christ's hypostasis without detracting either from his humanity or from his divinity. On the ecclesial level, the deification of the believer is accomplished not primarily by philosophical contemplation but by participation in Christ, by 'putting on' Christ in baptism and by deepening the Christification thus attained through participation in the Eucharist. Both the Christological and the ecclesial senses of theosis had been fully developed by the fourth and fifth centuries, the great age of the Fathers. What happened subsequently was the working out of the implication of these senses in new contexts, notably (1) on the Christological level, in the struggle after Chalcedon, to explain the unity of the person of Christ without abandoning the Chalcedonian Definition or compromising either the divinity or the humanity of Christ and (2) on the ecclesial level, in the controversy after Barlaam's portrayal of the hesychasts as 'Messalians' (i.e., Bogomils), to explain the analogous deification of the human being without this entailing different levels of divinity.

After the council of 1351, the uncreated nature of theosis, in virtue of its being an operation (energy) and gift of the Holy Spirit, became the official teaching of the Orthodox Church. The *Synodal Tome* issued shortly after the council declared:

Moreover, since indeed those who oppose the archbishop of Thessalonike say that this gift of the Spirit and energy, that is to say, deification (θέωσις), by which the saints are deified, and is called deity (θεότης) by the saints, is a created divinity, supposedly proving this from the fact that God is said by the great Dionysius to be the cause of its subsistence, and it is called by him an imitation and a relation of those who participate, the sacred synod declared that they were speaking impiously. (36, Karmiris, 1968: 357; trans. Russell, 2020: 357)

This was the first time that a council (not an ecumenical council but nevertheless a Constantinopolitan council of the first importance) had ever pronounced a judgement on the nature of theosis. Shortly afterwards, the council's anathematisation of the opinions of Palamas's opponents was inserted into the *Synodikon of Orthodoxy*, the list of heresies read out liturgically each year on the first Sunday of Lent. Henceforth, belief in the uncreated nature of theosis as the divine energy that is communicated to the saints by the Holy Spirit and interpenetrates their humanity even in this life was a required element of *eusebeia/theosebeia*.

POST-BYZANTINE POSTSCRIPT

After the fall of Constantinople to the Ottoman Turks in May 1453, the ecumenical patriarchate was reconstituted by the sultan, Mehmet the Conqueror, as the governing body of the Orthodox entrusted with collecting the Christian poll tax and ensuring the civil obedience of the *Rum millet*, the 'Roman nation', that is, of all the Orthodox Christians of the Ottoman Empire, not only Greeks but also Bulgarians and Arabs. In the sixteenth century, the Orthodox were fully occupied guarding, on the one hand, against defections to Islam and, on the other, against losses to Latin Catholicism through the proselytising activities of Jesuit and Dominican missionaries. In the seventeenth century, Greek schools began to be founded, which started to raise the educational level of the Christian population. Preachers, however, still concentrated on much-needed basic moral teaching. The kind of spiritual formation that permitted the study of works explaining the role of theosis in the Christian life was only available to monks at the great monastic centres of Patmos and Mount Athos. A new initiative to spread this spiritual teaching beyond the walls of the monastery came in the eighteenth century. A movement of reforming monks called the *Kollyvades*, led principally by Athanasios Parios (1722–1813), Makarios of Corinth (1731–1805), and Nikodemos the Hagiorite (1749–1809), using 'the great and resplendent light of printing', as Nikodemos calls it (Cavarnos, 2008: 37),[56] sought to offer the Orthodox a middle way between the submissiveness to the political status quo counselled by the hierarchy and the revolutionary fervour preached by secularisers such as Adamantios Korais (1748–1833)

---

[56] Printing presses were not permitted in any of the realms of the Ottoman Empire directly controlled by the imperial government in Constantinople. Most Greek works were printed in Venice.

and Rigas Feraios (1757–98). This middle way was a turning inwards, an interiorisation of the Orthodox faith (along quite modernist lines),[57] in pursuit of which Nikodemos, with the help of Makarios, who had the appropriate contacts to ensure financial sponsorship, published such works as the *Philokalia* (Venice, 1782), the *Evergetinon* (Venice, 1783), and, in a vernacular version, the works of St Symeon the New Theologian (Venice, 1790). These had very little influence, however, on contemporary Greeks, especially after the establishment of the modern Greek state on Western lines in 1833, with a state church based on the Lutheran model and a German-inspired university. As we shall see in Chapter 6, it was the Russians, within the context of the intense religious ferment of the last decades of the nineteenth century, who were to appropriate the Byzantine teaching on deification more fully and transmit it, via the post-Revolution Russian exiles in Paris, not only to Western Christians but also to the Greeks themselves.

---

[57] For discussions of this movement towards the interiorisation of Orthodoxy at a time when many Greeks saw their religion simply as a badge of communal identity, see Russell, 2017b and 2018.

3

The Latin Heirs of Dionysius

Theosis in the Mediaeval West

The first readable Latin translation of Dionysius was completed by the
Irish scholar John Scotus Eriugena (c. 810–c. 877) in 862. Nearly forty
years earlier, in 824, a luxury copy of the works of the Areopagite had
been sent to Louis the Pious (778–840), Charlemagne's son and successor,
by the iconoclast emperor Michael II (820–929) as part of a diplomatic
initiative to persuade Louis to use his influence with the pope in the
iconoclast cause. The Areopagite's works were considered a suitable gift
because the Franks identified him with the martyr Dionysius, or Denis,
who was the first bishop of Paris. Hilduin, abbot of Saint-Denis, was
asked by Louis to make a translation, but Hilduin's text was so difficult to
follow that Eriugena, Alcuin's successor as head of the Palace School at
Aachen, was asked by Louis's son, Charles II the Bald (823–877), to
undertake a fresh translation. In 875, Eriugena's translation was provided
with notes in the form of an interlinear gloss by Anastasius
Bibliothecarius (c. 810–c. 878), the learned chief archivist of the Roman
Church. It was thus that Dionysius became accessible to Western
scholars.

Through his translation of Dionysius, Eriugena was the first to introduce the noun *deificatio* (his translation of 'theosis') to readers of Latin.
The verb *deificare* had already been used by Augustine but, buried as it is
in the vast corpus of his work, had not attracted much attention. In his
Periphyseon, Eriugena remarks on the oddity of the avoidance of the
term, suggesting that it must have seemed incomprehensible and

incredible to people incapable of ascending beyond carnal thoughts and for this reason was not preached publicly but was something only to be discussed among scholars (*Periphyseon* 5, CCCM 165, 217). Eriugena has a point. In Ambrose, for example, the term is very rarely used in catechetical material addressed to neophytes. It tends to be reserved for the more advanced (Dunkle, 2019). Eriugena's translation of Dionysius, perhaps partly for the same reason, did not have much impact in the earlier Middle Ages until it was taken up in the twelfth century by Hugh (d. 1141) of the abbey of St Victor in Paris, who wrote a commentary on *The Celestial Hierarchy* (Rorem, 2009). In around 1167, a new translation was produced by the otherwise unknown John Sarracenus, which removed many of the obscurities of Eriugena's version. In the next century, between 1240 and 1246, yet another translation was made, this time by Robert Grosseteste (c. 1170–1253), bishop of Lincoln and a notable Greek scholar. This translation stimulated the renewed study of Dionysius by a friend of his, the Victorine Thomas Gallus, abbot of Vercelli (d. 1246), but its influence was more limited than that of the earlier translations (Coolman, 2009). The Dominicans Albert the Great (c. 1200–1280) and Thomas Aquinas (c. 1225–1274) based their own work on the translations of Eriugena and Sarracenus, as did the Dominican mystical theologian, Meister Eckhart (c. 1260–c. 1328). Subsequently, whether through the translations of Eriugena-Sarracenus or Grosseteste-Gallus, Dionysius exercised an important influence on such figures as the author of that masterpiece of English mystical writing, *The Cloud of Unknowing* (around 1370), the Flemish mystical theologian Jan van Ruusbroec (1293–1381), the French schoolman Jean Gerson (1363–1429), and the German cardinal Nicholas of Cusa (1401–1464), the last of whom also benefitted from the fifteenth-century translation of Ambrogio Traversari (c. 1368–1439). The renewed study of Dionysius initiated by Hugh of St Victor thus had far-reaching consequences, one of which was the popularisation in certain religious circles of the notion of deification as the goal of the spiritual life.

THE AFFECTIVE MYSTICAL TRADITION: BERNARD AND BONAVENTURE

The Dionysian version of deification, however, was not the only one in the field. In the form in which it was appropriated in the West, especially by the Dominicans, it embraced an intellectual mystical theology based the acquisition of experiential knowledge. Its rival belonged to the affective tradition, which taught the attainment of deification not so much through knowledge as through love. This tradition was the older of the two. Drawing principally on Augustine and Gregory the Great, it found its greatest exponent in the Cistercian Bernard of Clairvaux (1090–1153).[1] Subsequently, as Dionysius's writings became more widely available, the affective was combined with the intellective approach, as we find in the Franciscan tradition, especially in Bonaventure (c. 1217–1274), and in the fourteenth-century flowering of mystical writing in northern Europe.

Bernard was born to a noble family at Fontaine, near Dijon, the capital of Burgundy. In 1112, at the age of twenty-two, he embraced the monastic life at the newly reformed Benedictine foundation of Cîteaux (from which the name Cistercian derives), bringing with him thirty additional postulants, including his five brothers.[2] Within three years, he was sent by the abbot, Stephen Harding, to found another house at Clairvaux, near Bar-sur-Aube in northern Burgundy, where he rose to be abbot and one of the most influential ecclesiastics of his day. His greatest spiritual work is the course of eighty-six sermons on the Song of Songs, which he gave to his community at Clairvaux in chapter after Prime. These sermons are an astonishing tour de force, which – despite sending some of his audience to sleep on their first delivery[3] – are still gripping today. In his exegesis of the Song of Songs, Bernard interprets the three kisses bestowed on the beloved's (i.e., Christ's) feet, hand, and mouth as indicating the three stages on the way to union with God – the purgative, the illuminative, and the unitative – that go back to Dionysius the Areopagite.[4] The ascent culminates in the transformatory vision of divine glory, when, 'gazing confidently on the glory of the Lord with unveiled face, you will be transformed into that same image with ever-increasing brightness, by the work of the Lord's Spirit' (*Sermon* 36, 6, with ref. to 2 Cor 3.18). This transformation is not reserved exclusively to the life to come. It may

---

[1] For an important earlier figure, John of Fécamp (c. 990–1078), author of a popular devotional treatise, the *Confessio theologica*, which presents the hypostatic union as the model for our own glorification in the resurrected and glorified Christ, see Faesen, 2019.

[2] On Bernard's life and thought, see Evans, 2000.

[3] Bernard reprimands them in *Sermon* 7, 2, but without naming them. The long hours spent in church (Matins began at 3 a.m., Prime at about 6 a.m.) were understandably demanding for the hard-working Cistercians.

[4] *Sermons* 3 and 4 are on the first two kisses, *Sermons* 7 and 8 on the third kiss. Cf. Dionysius , *Celestial Hierarchy* III, 2 165B; VII, 3, 209CD; *Ecclesisatical Hierarchy* V, 3, 504ABC; VI, Contemplation, 537BC. Bernard presents the three stages as ascending steps of love, Dionysius depicts the same three stages as ascending steps of knowledge.

be experienced fleetingly even in this life, as Bernard explains near the end of his course of sermons, hesitatingly recounting a personal experience of the presence of Christ in the soul for the encouragement of his community (*Sermon 74*, 5).

It is love that unites humanity with God, and divine love, when it is experienced, transforms the human person. In his sermons to his community, Bernard does not call this 'deification', but he does do so in another work, *De diligendo Deo* (*On the Love of God*), addressed to Cardinal Aimeric, a fellow Burgundian, who from 1123 to 1141 was chancellor of the Roman Church. Here the passage on deification (like Augustine, he only uses the verbal form) comes at the climax of a discussion of four grades of love, the first being love of oneself for oneself; the second, love of God for oneself; the third, love of God for the sake of God; and the fourth, love of oneself entirely for God's sake in ecstatic self-forgetfulness. In this fourth grade, 'nothing remains mixed in it which is properly our own'. 'To be touched in this way,' says Bernard, 'is to be deified' (*Sic affici, deificari est*).[5] It is like a drop of water that falls into a large quantity of wine and loses its own nature, taking on the taste and colour of wine, or like red-hot iron that takes on the characteristics of fire, or like air pervaded by the light of the sun that seems itself to become light (*De diligendo Deo*, 28; SC 393, pp. 130–32). These examples had been developed by Greek writers to suggest how Christ's divine and human natures were united without confusion, the divine transforming the human but without obliterating its nature. Transferred by Bernard, however, to the soul of the human believer, they were to alarm a reader such as Jean Gerson, who saw the image of a drop of water in a butt of wine, in particular, as suggesting that the identity of the human individual might be totally lost through deification.[6]

---

[5] The word *deificare* is used only twice by Bernard in all his voluminous writings, here and in the first of his sermons on the Assumption, where he refers in much the same way to 'a deified attachment' (*affectio deificata*) (*Sancti Bernardi Opera*, eds. J. Leclercq, H.-M. Rochais, and C. H. Talbot, vol. 5, p. 262.16). Nevertheless, through Bernard the theme of deification enters into the Cistercian 'school' more widely, being taken up by his friend and disciple, William of Saint-Thierry (c. 1080–1148), on whom see Sergent, 2015.

[6] Jean Gerson, *Theologia mystica*, Consideratio XLI (Vannini, 1992: 194). Bernard's image is the reversal of Aristotle's drop of wine in a large quantity of water (*On generation and corruption* 328a23–28). It is also reminiscent of Gregory of Nyssa's drop of vinegar mingled in the sea (*Against Eunomius* III, 3, 68–69), an image that has continued to trouble theologians to the present day.

In the generation after Bernard, the affective mystical tradition begins to be combined with the Dionysian. The first notable exponent of this amalgamation is Bonaventure (c. 1217–1274).[7] Born Giovanni di Fidanza in Bagnoregio, a small hilltop town near Viterbo in central Italy, he was given the name Bonaventure when he joined the Franciscans. In 1257, he became minister general of his order and did much to establish the Franciscans alongside the Dominicans in higher education. His approach to deification may be studied most conveniently in his spiritual masterpiece, the *Itinerarium mentis in Deum* (*The Soul's Journey into God*).[8] The circumstances of its writing are described in the work itself. In early October 1259, Bonaventure was staying in La Verna, the retreat in the Apennines where in 1244 St Francis had had his vision of the Crucified as a six-winged seraph and had received the stigmata. While meditating on Francis's experience, it came to him that the six wings could be seen to represent the six stages of the spiritual journey to God, ascending steps from the contemplation of the Creator from the evidence of him afforded by the created world to the contemplation of the Trinity itself as the highest good. Beyond these steps lies the ecstatic stage, when 'all intellectual activities must be left behind and the height of our affection must be totally transferred and transformed into God' (*et apex affectus totus transferatur et transformetur in Deum*) (*Itinerarium* VII.4; trans. Cousins, 1978: 113). Bonaventure does not use the term *deificatio* or its cognates,[9] but he leaves us in no doubt that by the transformation of our affection, or attachment, 'into God' (with an emphasis on the exercise of the will) he means the Dionysian participation in divine unity, for immediately afterwards he quotes Dionysius's great hymn to the Trinity from the beginning of *The Mystical Theology* and the Areopagite's advice to his friend Timothy to leave behind all sensible and noetic things and ascend 'to the supraessential ray of the divine darkness' (*Itinerarium* VII.5; trans. Cousins, 1978: 14, quoting Dionysius, *Mystical Theology* 1.1).[10]

---

[7] On deification in Bonaventure, see T. Johnson, 2012, and the fine series of recent studies by Douglas Dales (Dales, 2017, 2019a, 2019b, 2021).

[8] The Latin text is in *S. Bonaventurae Opera omnia*, published by the Franciscans of Quaracchi, vol. 5, pp. 293–313; Eng. trans. in Cousins, 1978: 53–116.

[9] Douglas Dales has pointed out to me in a personal communication (dated 27 June 2023) that Bonaventure does, however, use the term 'deiform' (*deiformis*) quite frequently in his writings. He also gives great and unusual prominence to the Holy Spirit in his theology.

[10] On Bonaventure and Dionysius, see Dales, 2021.

THE INTELLECTIVE MYSTICAL TRADITION: ALBERT THE GREAT AND THOMAS AQUINAS

In 1273, Bonaventure was created a cardinal in order to help Pope Gregory X prepare for the Second Council of Lyon (1274), the main business of which was to be the reconciliation of the Greek Church to the Church of Rome.[11] Among the distinguished theologians invited by the pope to attend that council was also Albrecht of Lauingen, known to posterity as Albertus Magnus or Albert the Great.[12] Albert's long career (he was over eighty when he died) began with studies at Padua, where he entered the Dominican Order in 1229. After teaching in Germany, mainly in the Rhineland, he spent some time at the University of Paris (where Thomas Aquinas was one of his students) before returning to the Rhineland in 1248 to direct the new Dominican *studium generale* at Cologne. He subsequently became Dominican Provincial of Germany and in 1260 was appointed bishop of Ratisbon. In the following year, however, he resigned his see, having speedily put right the problems he encountered there, so as to be able to concentrate on his intellectual work.

This work exhibits an interesting evolution.[13] The crucial period was 1248 to 1254, when Albert had a free hand in Cologne to organise the course of studies to be followed by advanced students. It was at this time that he wrote his commentaries on the entire Dionysian Corpus, the *Celestial Hierarchy*, the *Ecclesiastical Hierarchy*, the *Divine Names*, the *Mystical Theology*, and the eleven *Epistles*.[14] In Paris, he had based his lectures, as was the practice there, on the Bible and Peter Lombard's

---

[11] Bonaventure's understanding of Trinitarian truth was deeply influenced by, and sympathetic to, the classic Greek approach with its roots in Cappadocian theology. This is probably the reason why he was so successful at the Second Council of Lyon in winning the confidence of the Orthodox delegation, who were so distraught at his death there (personal communication from Douglas Dales, 27 June 2023).

[12] Thomas Aquinas was also to have attended the council as an expert theologian but died on his way to it. Boniface, who died at Lyon before the council ended, was buried in the Franciscan church in Lyon (now the church of the Oratorians) but his tomb was destroyed during the seventeenth-century wars of religion.

[13] Albert is the subject of a brilliant study by Bernhard Blankenhorn, OP. See esp. Blankenhorn, 2015: 122–212, on which much of what follows depends.

[14] Blankenhorn describes this as 'a possible first in the history of Western theological education' (2015: 122). In the East, George Pachymeres (1242–c. 1310), a patriarchal official best known as a historian, produced a Greek paraphrase of the *Corpus Dionysiacum* about twenty years later.

Sentences, but in Cologne the emphasis moves to Dionysius.[15] The shift of focus is matched by a shift in Albert's anthropology. Whereas in his *Sentences* commentary the intellect is hampered in its knowledge of spiritual realities because it is tied to a fallen body; in the commentary on Dionysius, the intellect's spiritual knowledge is mediated by the body and material symbols. Thanks to Dionysius, Albert takes an altogether more positive view of the body.[16] Earlier he had relied on Augustine's distinction between the higher intellect, which alone knows immaterial realities, and the lower intellect, which knows material objects. Now the lower intellect (the agent intellect) plays a vital role in the way we know God but only through darkness, which is actually divine light from our own embodied perspective. Another shift in Albert's thinking as a result of his reading of Dionysius is his rejection of 'the notion that created grace and glory are secondary efficient causes of divine life. He insists that only a direct divine act divinises. This doctrinal evolution moves Albert closer to the Areopagite's understanding of divinisation' (Blankenhorn, 2015: 134).

Albert, however, has no role for the liturgical dimension that is so important for Dionysius. It is the intellect operating in the light of faith – not through syllogistic thought – that leads us to the knowledge of God. Faith is indispensable; cognition alone is insufficient, for our finite minds cannot comprehend God. And yet, 'because although through the obscurity that is left in us from the eminence of splendor we fall short of comprehending the divine eminence, still, because we somehow attain it by leaving all behind, the mind is deified and illuminated (*mens deificatur et illuminatur*)' (*Super Dion. myst. theol.* I, 457.26–30; trans. Blankenhorn, 2015: 167). Negation, in the sense of the cessation of all natural cognition, leads to union with God through an infusion of divine light that deifies the mind. When he comes to consider Moses's union with God, Albert refers to this again, speaking of it as a process 'by which the mind is elevated above itself' (*quo mens supra se elevator*), that is to say, beyond its own nature (*Super Dion. myst. theol.* I, 462.38; cf. Blankenhorn, 2015: 175–76). This noetic ecstasy, which is the product

---

[15] Albert did not know Greek: 'His lectures rely on the Eriugena and Sarracenus translations as well as the scholia and interlinear gloss' (Blankenhorn, 2015: 123).

[16] Blankenhorn considers that Aristotle, on whose work Albert was also writing commentaries at this time, also made a contribution through the principle (cited by Albert) that cognition begins with the senses (Blankenhorn, 2015: 126).

not of intellectual effort but of grace received in faith, gives the soul a mode of knowing God that transcends nature.

Yet it is in the negations themselves that the mind is united with God. This because the negations through what they negate imply eminent affirmations about the nature of God. They are 'the highest peak (*summum verticem*) of mystical sayings', says Albert, 'insofar as in negations of all things we come into him [God] as into something hidden' (*Super Dion. myst. theol.* I, 457.12–14; trans. Blankenhorn, 2015: 166).[17] All 'sensibles and intelligibles' must be left behind, he goes on to assert, because being comprehensible by the intellect they are finite and therefore less than God. What takes their place is the divine light, which is not a noetic object, because in that case it would be finite, but the supreme principle of cognition received in silent non-comprehension. This light, the *lumen gloriae*, elevates the soul, in virtue of its having been created in the divine image, to union with God but not to comprehension of him.

Albert brings Dionysius to the fore in the West as the supreme guide to ascent to union with God – through the intellect, certainly, but by negations, not by way of propositions and syllogisms. 'As in Dionysius', says Blankenhorn, 'Albert's negative knowledge is not the knowledge of nothing'. The infusion of divine light through faith enables the theologian to penetrate to the true meaning of the Scriptures. In Dionysius, it is the bishop who guides his flock to the goal of theosis through his expertise in hierarchic 'science'. 'Albert's hierarch', in Blankenhorn's words, 'is not a bishop who unveils the hidden meaning of liturgical symbols and liturgically proclaimed Scriptures, but the scholastic theologian who, in faith, has learned the proper distinctions. Albert himself is the hierarch for his Dominican students in Cologne …. We are witnessing the birth of the theologian's mysticism' (Blankenhorn, 2015: 199).

The greatest of these Dominican students was Thomas Aquinas. Born in about 1225 to an aristocratic family of Roccasecca, near Aquino in the kingdom of Naples, he received his earliest education at the nearby Benedictine abbey of Monte Cassino. From there he went on to the newly founded University of Naples, where he joined the Dominicans, who sent him to Paris for his higher studies. At Paris, he became a student of Albert the Great, following him in 1248 to Cologne, where he attended his courses of lectures until 1251. This was the time when Albert was writing his commentaries on the Dionysian Corpus. Thomas's exposure to

---

[17] According to the anonymous *Parisian Scholia* on the *Mystical Theology*, the 'mystical sayings' are 'the arcane words of sacred Scripture'.

Dionysius, however, did not make him as narrowly focused a follower of the Areopagite as his teacher. Other influences, Greek as well as Latin, fed into his understanding of union with God.

By 1256, Thomas was back in Paris, now as a teacher lecturing on the standard texts, the Bible and the *Sentences* of Peter Lombard. Three years later, we find him in Italy, first at Orvieto and then at the priory of Santa Sabina in Rome, where he was asked to set up a new Dominican house of studies. During this period (1261–1268), he embarked on an intense study of the Greek Fathers, one of the fruits of which was the *Catena Aurea*, a vast commentary on the Gospels compiled from passages from a broad range of Greek Fathers, including Dionysius.[18] In the same period, he wrote his only commentary on Dionysius, the *Expositio super Dionysium De divinis nominibus*.[19] In this work, he emphasises the utter unknowability of God on account of his transcending the ability of our mind to comprehend him. The best we can do is to arrive at an understanding of him by way of abstraction (for which Thomas uses the term 'remotion'):

> The most perfect [state] to which we can attain in this life in our knowledge of God is that he transcends all that can be conceived by us, and the naming of God through remotion (*per remotionem*) is most proper .... The primary mode of naming God is through the negation of all things, since he is beyond all, and whatever is signified by any name whatsoever is less than that which God is. (*De div. nom.* I, iii, 83–84; trans. O. Davies, 2002: 54)

Yet negation is limited in its function. Like Dionysius, Thomas balances negations with affirmations in the course of the mind's contemplative ascent to God. But although he draws on Dionysius's threefold way of knowing God 'in the negation of all things, by pre-eminence, and in the cause of all things' (ἐν τῇ πάντων ἀφαιρέσει καὶ ὑπεροχῇ καὶ ἐν τῇ πάντων αἰτίᾳ) (*Div. Names*, VII, 3, 872A; Suchla, 198.1–2) he is indifferent to Dionysius's ascending order. Sometimes he speaks of knowing God 'by negation, or causality, or pre-eminence' (*per negationem vel causalitatem*

---

[18] On Thomas's Greek researches, especially the translation he commissioned of parts of the commentaries of Theophylact of Ochrid (bringing Theophylact for the first time to the attention of Latin theologians), see Peters, 2019.

[19] *Commentary on Dionysius' On the Divine Names.* Thomas also refers frequently in his other writings to Dionysius's *Celestial Hierarchy* and *Ecclesiastical Hierarchy* (but rarely to his *Mystical Theology*, except in the commentary on the *Divine Names*). For detailed studies of different aspects of Thomas's use of Greek patristic teaching, see Dauphinais, Hofer, and Nutt, 2019, and for his use of Dionysius in particular, Blankenhorn, 2015: 215–441.

vel excellentiam) (*De malo*, q. 16, a. 8); at other times he says that God is known 'by the mode of pre-eminence and causation' (*per modum excellentiae et causationis*) (*Summa theol.* Ia, q. 13, a. 1, *resp.*). This is because in Thomas's case the ascent does not take us *beyond* the intellect.[20]

The end of all things, says Thomas, is to become like God, in view of the fact that all things are drawn to God as their final end in order to share in his goodness (*Summa contra Gent.* III, ch. 19). The end of intellectual beings, in particular, is to become like God in the manner appropriate to them, which means by knowing God, or apprehending him mentally (*Summa cont. Gent.* III, ch. 25). Dionysius had used a similar form of words for his definition of theosis: 'Theosis is likeness to God and union with him so far as is attainable' (*Eccl. Hier.* I, 3, 376A; Heil, 1991b: 66.12–13). Thomas prefers to stay with biblical expressions for his references to deification: 'But of all creatures', he says, the most excellent are those that are called gods by participation' (*Summa theol.* I, q. 4, a. 3, obj. 1). His allusion is to two texts, Psalm 82.6 ('I said, you are gods and all of you sons of the Most High') and 2 Peter 1.4 ('partakers of the divine nature'), but he does no more than merely allude to these.[21] His explicit reference is immediately to Dionysius, who says that likeness to God can never be perfect because all things fall short of their cause (*Summa theol.* I, q. 4, a. 3, resp. obj. 1 and 4, citing *Divine Names* X, 7, 916A and IX, 6, 913C). For Dionysius, it is self-evident that the cognition of God exceeds the human mind and therefore that the vision of the divine essence, seeing that the latter occupies an inaccessible realm transcending all caused being, is excluded. Thomas agrees that the cognition of God 'through his nature' exceeds the power of finite minds, but he believes that it is nevertheless accessible to us 'by the light of glory'.

Thomas does not follow Dionysius in distinguishing between God's nature and God's light (a distinction that was to be developed by Gregory Palamas, with the help of the Cappadocians, as the distinction between the divine essence and the divine energies) but he comes near to it with his

---

[20] Blankenhorn makes the important point that for Thomas 'the *Mystical Theology* remains a work of *sacra doctrina*, not a guide to transcend all active cogitations about revelation. Instead of signalling the need to pass beyond all human thought and discourse because of their inherent limits, the work is all about identifying the limits of our thought and discourse, but precisely through a rational reflection that remains bound to those limits' (2015: 324). With regard to apophaticism, Thomas thus draws attention to a fundamental principle of language and therefore of thought.

[21] On Thomas's understanding of participation and his use of 2 Peter 1.4, see Spezzano, 2015: 129–42.

teaching (drawn from Albert the Great) on the *lumen gloriae*, the light of glory.[22] The *lumen gloriae* is 'the mode by which God elevates the created intellect, uniting it to himself' (Boersma, 2019: 138). Thomas is clear (quoting Dionysius, *Divine Names* I, 1, 588A) that the divine essence cannot be seen through any created likeness, because the superior cannot be known by the inferior.

> Therefore it must be said that to see the essence of God there is required some likeness in the visual power, namely, the light of glory which is spoken of in the Psalm (35.10): In thy light we shall see light. The essence of God, however, cannot be seen by any created likeness representing the divine essence as it is in itself. (*Summa theol.* I, q. 12, a. 2, resp.; trans. Pegis)

The participation of the beholder is in the light, not in the divine essence, yet because the light is not less than God, the beholder sees God 'as he is' (1 John 3.2). The way Thomas puts it is that the divine essence becomes the intelligible form of the created intellect:

> The divine essence is being itself. Hence, as other intelligible forms which are not their own being are united to the intellect by means of some being whereby the intellect itself is informed and made in act, so the divine essence is united to the created intellect, as the object actually understood, making the intellect in act through itself. (*Summa theol.* I, q. 12, a. 2, resp. obj. 3; trans. Pegis)

As Blankenhorn remarks, 'Thomas can only save the intelligibility of the Areopagite's doctrine by making it more kataphatic.'[23] For Dionysius, union with God takes place beyond mind. Thomas brings the union into the realm of intelligible experience, but for Thomas it is not the way of negation that deifies. Noetic ascent may well perfect the intellect. Ultimately, however, deification takes place through union with God by faith as revealed by the Scriptures. It is within the context of faith that believers may be called gods by participation.[24]

THE BEGINNING OF THE NORTHERN EUROPEAN MYSTICAL TRADITION: MEISTER ECKHART

The importance of Albert the Great's *studium* at Cologne can scarcely be exaggerated. Not only did it introduce Thomas Aquinas to Dionysius, but

---

[22] On the *lumen gloriae* in Aquinas, see Spezzano, 2015: 36–39; and Boersma, 2019.

[23] Blankenhorn, 2015: 355. Palamas was to make a similar move, but by means of the essence–energies distinction.

[24] On this aspect see Spezzano, 2015: ch. 4, 'The Incarnation and Participation in the Divine Nature'.

it also contributed to the intellectual formation of one of the greatest mystical theologians of Northern Europe, Meister Eckhart.[25] Eckhart, it should be said, was not an isolated figure. The German provinces of the Dominican Order in that era contained a number of remarkable men who were at the forefront of *scientia divina*. These included Hugo Ripelin of Strasbourg (d. before 1268), Ulrich of Strasbourg (1220/5–1277), Dietrich of Freiberg (c. 1250–d. after 1310), and Berthold of Moosberg (d. after 1361), not names well known today outside specialist circles but significant for the high quality of their philosophical and theological work.[26] Hugo wrote an important theological *Compendium*, influenced by Albert's commentary on the *Divine Names*. Ulrich, who was one of Albert's best students, wrote a *Summa on the supreme good*, which also draws on his teacher's work on Dionysius. Dietrich, who knew Eckhart personally, wrote a treatise *On the beatific vision*, which seems to owe something to Proclus as well as Dionysius. Berthold certainly drew on Proclus, writing the only mediaeval commentary on *The Elements of Theology*. Eckhart belonged to the same intellectual milieu as these scholars. He was the only one to be indicted for heresy, however, for reasons, as we shall see, that were not entirely within his control.

Eckhart was born in the village of Hochheim,[27] in Thuringia, in around 1260. He joined the Dominicans when he was about fifteen and pursued his early studies at the Dominican *studium particulare* at Erfurt. From there he went for his higher studies to the *studium generale* at Cologne, arriving a year or two before Albert the Great died. After further studies in Paris, he rose swiftly in the Dominican Order. From 1290 to 1300 he was prior of the Dominican house in Erfurt, during which time he also served as vicar of Thuringia. After another spell at the University of Paris, where he received the title of Master (Meister) and acceded to the Dominican chair of theology, he became his order's provincial of Saxony (a huge area that contained forty-seven Dominican convents for men and nine for women). For several years, he fulfilled a number of demanding pastoral responsibilities both as an ecclesiastical administrator and as a popular preacher and spiritual director, until he returned to Cologne in

---

[25] For a very readable introduction to Eckhart's life and thought, see Harrington, 2018. Also useful are Haas, 1987; O. Davies, 2006: 30–72.

[26] On these figures and their work, see de Libera, 1984.

[27] There are two villages called Hochheim, one near Erfurt, the other near Gotha; it is not clear which one is intended in the sole reference in the manuscripts that mentions Hochheim.

1324 as director of the Dominican *studium generale*. It was there that he delivered many of his surviving sermons and wrote most of his works.

Cologne, however, also saw the rise of the serious difficulties that Eckhart began to experience with the ecclesiastical authorities over the doctrinal content of his works, particularly his sermons. The archbishop of Cologne, Heinrich of Virneburg, was engaged at that time in a struggle to extirpate the Brethren of the Free Spirit, groups (either real or imaginary) that believed that their perfect union with God absolved them from the constraints of moral and ecclesiastical rules.[28] Convinced that many of the numerous Beguines and Beghards of Cologne were infected by such ideas and that Eckhart's teaching was encouraging them, Heinrich became determined to convict Eckhart of heresy. On Eckhart's appeal to the Holy See, the case went to Avignon, where a commission was appointed by Pope John XXII to examine his works. Eckhart wrote in advance, declaring his intention to abide by the Holy See's decision and retract whatever did not conform to the Church's teaching.[29] He died, however, at Avignon before judgement was given condemning seventeen of the twenty-eight suspect propositions that had been culled from his Latin and German works.[30]

The judgement, which was promulgated in March 1329 by the bull *In agro dominico*,[31] put a stop to the copying of Eckhart's Latin works, but his sermons in the vernacular (Middle High German), which had been taken down by hearers in the form of *reportationes* (verbatim reports), continued to circulate. It was actually from these that many of the condemned propositions had been derived, and it is not difficult to see what it was that had disturbed the examining commission. The four propositions relating to deification that were declared erroneous were (1) that we are fully transformed and converted into God in the same way as in the sacrament the bread is converted into the body of Christ, so that there is no distinction; (2) all that God the Father gave His only-begotten Son in human nature He has given to me, without exception;

---

[28] The Brethren of the Free Spirit were not a sect but a tendency that existed (or was thought by heresy hunters to exist) within the Beguine/Beghard movement of lay communities outside the strict control of the ecclesiastical authorities. On the 'heresy of the free spirit', the most complete study is Leff, 1967: 308–407.

[29] As Eckhart rightly pointed out in a defence made in Cologne in 1327, shortly before his appeal to the Holy See, heresy resides not in the expression of wrong opinions but in the determination to maintain them, that is to say, not in the intellect but in the will.

[30] The trial documents have been published by Théry, 1926.

[31] Text in Denzinger, 501–29; trans. Walshe, 2009: 26–28.

(3) everything that Holy Scripture says of Christ is entirely true of every good and holy man; (4) all that is proper to the divine nature is also proper to the just and godly man, with the result that such a man performs everything that God performs.[32] At his trial, Eckhart withdrew the analogy between the divinised bread of the Eucharist and the divinised Christian believer but reiterated his conviction that the goal of the Christian life was total assimilation to God. Deification was not an alien concept to Eckhart's judges, but the maximalist expression that the Dominican gave it (without, however, using the term *deificatio*, or its vernacular equivalent) seemed to them to go beyond the bounds of orthodoxy. How did Eckhart get himself into this position?

For his doctrine of God, Eckhart appeals to a wide variety of authorities, including Aristotle, Augustine, Avicenna, and especially Maimonides, but his fundamental frame of reference is Dionysian. As Vladimir Lossky has shown, his notion of God as unnameable name (*nomen innominabile*) and hidden existence (*esse absconditum*) – that is to say, his conviction that God is best expressed by oxymorons that unite apophasis with kataphasis – derives from the Areopagite.[33] Maimonides, to whom Eckhart always refers with great respect as Rabbi Moses, and who is his leading authority in his consideration of the divine names in the *Commentary on Exodus*, is strictly apophatic.[34] Eckhart agrees with him that 'nothing affirmative is properly and aptly said about God' (*Commentary on Exodus* 47; trans. McGinn, 1986: 58), but for Eckhart God is not simply the negation of all names: one must go beyond negation to 'the negation of negation' (*negatio negationis*) in order to arrive at the purity of affirmed Being.[35]

The kataphatic turn in Eckhart's thinking aligns him with Albert and Thomas, but from that point he parts company from his Dominican confrères. First, he makes a distinction in the divine being between God as he is in himself (*gotheit*) and God as he relates to the created order (*got*):

---

[32] Denzinger, 510–13, propositions 10 to 13; trans. Walshe, 2009: 26–27.

[33] Lossky, 1998: 13–26. Lossky has also provided compelling evidence for Eckhart's having read Dionysius in the light of Thomas Aquinas's commentary on the *Divine Names* (18, 26–28).

[34] Rabbi Moses ben Maimon (1138–1204), known as Maimonides, was the author of an influential work, *The Guide for the Perplexed*, which was translated into Latin from Arabic in about 1240.

[35] 'Negatio autem negationis medulla, puritas et geminatio est affirmati esse' (Eckhart, *Commentary on John*, f. 121ᵛ, cited, with other examples, by Lossky, 1998: 68 n. 103).

So all creatures speak of 'God' (*got*). And why do they not speak of the Godhead (*gotheit*)? All that is in the Godhead is one, and we cannot speak of it. God is active and does things, while the Godhead does nothing, for there is no activity in it, nor has it ever sought any activity. (Quint, 1977: 273; trans. O. Davies 2006: 46)

These two modes of divine being are closely related. Eckhart speaks of God's 'melting outwards' through the superabundance of his goodness and love. In a sermon in which he comments on 'the gate of the Lord's house' (Jeremiah 7.2), he says:

God's house is the unity of his being. What is one is best all alone. Therefore unity stands by God and keeps God together, adding nothing. There he sits in his best part, his *esse*, all within himself, nowhere outside. But where he melts, he melts outside. His melting-out is his goodness, just as I have now said of knowledge and love. (*Sermon* 35; Quint, 1977, *Sermon* 19; trans. Walshe, 2009: 207)

In a sermon delivered a few days later, he went over the same ground in connection with the gate of the town of Nain, where Jesus raised the widow's son (Luke 7.11 ff.), this time relating the 'melting outwards' to the Persons of the Trinity:

I spoke recently of the gate through which God melts outward, which is goodness. But essence is that which keeps to itself and does not melt outward – rather it melts inward. But that is unity, which remains on in itself, apart from all things, and does not communicate itself, which goodness is where God melts outward and communicates himself to all creatures. Essence is the Father, unity is the Son, goodness is the Holy Spirit. Now the Holy Spirit takes the soul (the sanctified city) in her purest and highest and bears her to her source which is the Son, and the Son bears her further into his source, which is the Father, into the ground, into the beginning, where the Son has his being, where the eternal wisdom is in like repose 'in the holy and sanctified city', in the innermost. (*Sermon* 36; Quint, 1977, *Sermon* 18; trans. Walshe, 2009: 212)

The 'ground' (*grunt*) is an important term in Eckhart. Along with the divine 'spark of the soul' (*seelenvünkelîn*), it expresses an element common to both God and the human person on account of the soul's having received its being directly from God. 'He who is nameless, who is the negation of all names', is the '"hidden God" (Isa 45.15) in the ground of the soul where God's ground and the soul's ground are one' (*Sermon* 51; Quint, 1977, *Sermon* 15; trans. Walshe, 2009: 273). Eckhart is equivocal on whether this ground or spark is uncreated or created. On one occasion he declares:

I said recently in one place that when God created all creatures, if God had not previously begotten something that was uncreated that bore within itself the image of all creatures – that is, the spark, as I said at St Maccabees if you were listening – this spark is so akin to God that it is a single impartible one, and contains in itself the images of all creatures, imageless images and images above images. (*Sermon* 53; Quint, 1977, *Sermon* 22; trans. Walshe, 2009: 280)

The 'spark' (*fünkelîn*) here is only akin to God; it is not identical with God. But there are other passages in the sermons that seem to blur the distinction between God and the soul. For example:

The humble man and God are one, the humble man has as much power over God as he has over himself, and whatever is in the angels, that the humble man has for his own. What God performs the humble man performs, and what God is, he is: one life and one being. (*Sermon* 50; Quint, 1977, *Sermon* 14; trans. Walshe, 2009: 267–68)

And driving home the point in the same sermon, Eckart insists:

So if you want God to be your own thus, you must make yourself his own and bear in mind nothing but him: then he will be the beginning and the end of all your activity, just as his Godhead depends on his being God. To that man who thus in all his actions means and loves nothing but God, God gives his Godhead. Whatever that man performs God performs. (*Sermon* 50; Quint, 1977, *Sermon* 14; trans. Walshe, 2009: 269)

Yet the spark of the soul, even if apparently uncreated, is still only 'akin to God'. Created and uncreated are in fact distinguished in Eckhart, though perhaps not as absolutely as in most orthodox theologians. The reason for this is that creation did not take place in time. When questioned at Avignon on this point, Eckhart maintained that since time only began with creation, creation must have existed eternally in the mind of God outside time, otherwise the decision to create would have entailed change in the Godhead. Moreover, the creation of humankind in the image of God – and therefore, in principle, from all eternity – implied for Eckhart a very high conception of the human soul. Each human being is an only-begotten son, to be distinguished from the second Person of the Trinity only by virtue of having been 'eternally at rest and asleep in the hidden understanding of the eternal Father, immanent and unspoken', unlike the divine Word who has issued from God and has been uttered:

And so, if you ask me, since I am an only son whom the heavenly Father has eternally begotten, whether I have eternally been that son in God, my answer is: Yes and no. Yes, a son in that the Father has eternally begotten me, not a son by way of being unborn. (*Sermon* 53; Quint, 1977, *Sermon* 22; trans. Walshe, 2009: 280–81)

The origin of the soul, begotten as it is directly by the Father, sets the terms for its incarnate existence. The soul's constant struggle after its infusion into the body is to return to its source. The *exitus–reditus* theme permeates Eckhart's thinking. The soul has come from God and will return to God, transfigured by divine light. The context for this thinking is not, as often maintained, (pagan) 'Neoplatonic' but Dionysian. As Eckhart himself states, 'St Dionysius says the angelic nature is like the revelation of the divine light. With the angels and through the angels and by the divine light – that is how the soul must strive to return to God, till she returns to her first source.'[36] The return requires a rigorous ascetical programme that detaches the soul from the corporeal and assimilates it to its highest part, the intellect:

Accordingly it is necessary for a man to have trodden under foot all things that are of the earth, and whatever may becloud the understanding, so that nothing remains but what is akin to the understanding. If she works still with the understanding, she is akin to it. This soul that has thus transcended all things, is lifted and supported by the Holy Spirit and borne with him into the ground whence it emanated. Indeed he bears her into her eternal image whence she has emanated, into that image after which the Father has shaped all things, into that image in which all things are but one, into the vastness and profundity wherein all things again shall find their end. (*Sermon* 54; Quint, 1977, *Sermon* 23; trans. Walshe, 2009: 285–86)

The full recovery of the *imago Dei* is the teleological goal for which humanity was created: 'the beginning exists for the sake of the end' (*Sermon* 51; Quint, 1977, *Sermon* 15; trans. Walshe, 2009: 273). Curiously, Eckhart does not call this end 'deification', but he does say that when the light that streams forth from God 'breaks through into the soul', 'it makes her like God and divine, as far as may be, and illumines her within' (*Sermon* 48; Quint, 1977, *Sermon* 31; trans. Walshe, 2009: 260). The phrase 'like God and divine, as far as may be' recalls Dionysius's definition of theosis: 'the attaining of likeness to God and

---

[36] Eckhart, *Sermon* 44 (Quint, 1977, *Sermon* 58; trans. Walshe, 2009: 243). In distinguishing between Neoplatonic and Dionysian, I am not denying that Dionysius develops insights drawn from pagan Neoplatonists. But like Alexander Golitzin, I hold that in relation to the Neoplatonists Dionysius was a Christian thinker who 'was free to abandon their elaborate machinery of emanation while exploiting the opportunity that . . . was present in their doctrine of transcendence' (Golitzin, 2013: 67). Eckhart does draw occasionally on Neoplatonic texts, such as Macrobius's *Commentary on the Dream of Scipio*, the *Liber de Causis* (a compilation thought at the time to be by Aristotle), and Proclus's *Elements of Theology* (translated into Latin in 1268 by the Dominican, William of Moerbeke), but his fundamental orientation is decidedly Dionysian.

union with him so far as possible.'[37] But although Eckhart may perhaps be consciously echoing Dionysius's definition, and indeed speaks of the soul as being made divine, he does not actually use the term 'theosis'. In these German sermons, he is speaking to ordinary people where Greek technical terms would be totally inappropriate. In struggling to express the overcoming of division, even the division between subject and object, he comes out with a statement that even by Eckhart's standards is startling: 'The eye with which I see God is the same eye with which God sees me; my eye and God's eye are one eye, one seeing, one knowing and one love' (*Sermon* 57; Quint, 1977, *Sermon* 12; trans. Walshe, 2009: 298). Yet despite his claim that God and the soul share the same ground, transcending all division, Eckhart is careful in the final analysis to exclude any *ontological* identity between the two. He offers the following analogy to clarify his position:

I take a bowl of water and put a mirror in it and set it under the disc of the sun. Then the sun sends forth its light-rays both from the disc and from the sun's depth, and yet suffers no diminution, The reflection of the mirror in the sun is a sun, and yet it is what it is. So it is with God. God is in the soul with his nature, with his being and with his Godhead, and yet he is not the soul. The reflection of the soul in God is God, and yet she is what she is. (*Sermon* 56; Quint, 1977, *Sermon* 109; trans. Walshe, 2009: 293)

The soul remains what she is. Her divinity is a reflected divinity, not an ontological transformation of her nature. Yet it is a reflected divinity that brings the *Imago Dei* in which the human being was created to perfection, the divine form becoming a *habitus* that renders the human soul by grace that which the unique Son is by nature.[38]

The key to understanding how Eckhart came to be condemned for heresy is his 'yes and no', his method of saying and unsaying, particularly in his preaching.[39] The perfected human soul is both God and not-God. The statements proclaiming the identity of God's ground and our ground through our having been created from eternity need to be balanced by

---

[37] Dionysius, *Eccl. Hier.* I, 3, 376A; Heil 1991b: 66.12–13. Eckhart could be drawing directly on Dionysius's source in Plato, *Theaetetus* 176b, since his allusion to the phrase omits the characteristically Dionysian word 'union', but the tone and context of his discussion of divine illumination is Dionysian (cf. *Cel. Hier.* XIII, 3, 301D–4B; *Divine Names* I, 3, 589BC).

[38] On this point, Lossky's discussion, 'La théologie de l'Image et la transformation déificatrice' (1998: 358–69) is illuminating.

[39] As in the passage quoted above from *Sermon* 53 (Quint, 1977, *Sermon* 22; trans. Walshe, 2009: 280–81).

other statements insisting that the divinity of the soul that has returned to its source is a participated divinity attained by grace, not a merging with the uncreated Godhead. This has aptly been called a '"dialectics" of identity and difference' (D. Turner, 2009: 124). It was not difficult for trained theologians to convict Eckhart of heresy simply by focusing on one side of the dialectic. His German audiences, however, were deeply moved by the grandeur of the spiritual vision he set before them. It is not surprising that despite the condemnation of 1329 he continued to be widely read.

DIONYSIUS IN A POPULAR KEY: FROM TAULER TO THE AUTHOR OF *THE CLOUD*

Although Eckhart still attracted a broad readership after 1329, his condemnation did have an inhibiting effect on theologians. Two of his Dominican disciples, however, Johannes Tauler (c. 1300–1361) and Heinrich Seuse (c. 1295–1366) (Anglicised as Henry Suso), developed his thinking in a less risky direction. Neither of them was a student of Dionysius himself, but their occasional use of language reflecting Eckhartian apophaticism brings them into the circle of authors who may be considered as influenced in some degree by Dionysius.

Tauler, who was born in Strasbourg, entered the Dominicans at a very young age. He does not appear to have pursued his theological studies at university level or sought an academic career. Instead, he became a popular preacher and spiritual director, especially of women religious. As with Eckhart, his sermons were taken down as *reportationes*, but unlike Eckhart, he seems to have edited them personally, for they show signs of literary polishing. In Tauler we have Eckhart without the dialectics. Although Tauler refers to the 'spark of the soul' (*seelenvünkelîn*) and the ground (*grunt*) of one's being, he is always careful to distinguish between what God is by nature and what we become by grace. For example:

The soul takes on the form and nature of God. Through grace it becomes all those things which God is in his own nature because, by becoming united with God, by sinking into him, it is raised above itself into God. And then it is wholly coloured by God so that if the soul could see itself, it would think that it was itself God. Whoever could see it would see it clothed in God, coloured by him, contained in his nature and manner of Being, all by grace, and such a person would be blessed by this sight, for in this union, which happens not by nature but by grace, man and God are one. (*Predigten*, Hoffman, 1979: 277; trans. O. Davies, 2006: 78–79)

There are clear echoes here of Eckhart. The soul becomes 'wholly coloured by God' – the expression *got var* (God-coloured) is Eckhartian – but there is no impression of a blurring of the edges between the human and the divine, such as we find in Eckhart when he is focusing on only one side of his dialectic. The divine ground and the ground of the soul merely 'correspond' to each other; they do not form, as in Eckhart, 'one life and one being'.[40] Tauler, in fact, is more ecclesiastical, more conventionally devout, than Eckhart. He speaks of the believer being 'transformed into God' (a phrase already made familiar by Bonaventure), but such transformation is principally through self-abnegation and participation in the Eucharist.[41] At his trial in Avignon, Eckhart had retracted his analogy between the deification of the human soul and the transubstantiation of the elements of bread and wine in the Eucharist. Tauler recasts the analogy in an unobjectionable fashion, pushing it back to the stage of the transformation of the grape by the action of the sun:

What noble and precious fruit God grows from the person who cultivates their vine in such a way that the divine sun can work upon it and penetrate it! Then the sun shines and works upon the grape and brings it to glorious fruit . ... Then the sun shines more brilliantly still and casts its heat upon this fruit and makes it more and more transparent, the sweetness in it grows and the skin of the fruit becomes ever thinner so that God is close to it constantly. However often we look at it, we always find that it is illumined by the divine sun from within, more clearly than any sun ever shone in the sky, and thus all our ways are transformed into God so that we neither perceive nor delight in any thing nor know any thing more truly than God, though in a manner which transcends the powers of reason and rational knowledge. (*Predigten*, Hoffman, 1979: 50–51; trans. O. Davies, 2006: 97)

The appeal to the transformative effect of the rays of the divine sun, to the divinisation that these bring about, and to the transcending of the mind's cognitive powers evoke Dionysius, but the context is very different. Instead of metaphysics, we are given moral exhortation and devotional encouragement – certainly of a very high quality but it is the affective not the intellective approach that predominates.

Suso, who came from the area of Lake Constance near Switzerland and joined the Dominicans in around 1308, takes the affective approach a

---

[40] Eckhart, *Sermon* 50 (Quint, 1977, *Sermon* 14; trans. Walshe, 2009: 268); cf. Hoffman, 1979: 336, trans. O. Davies, 2006: 81.
[41] *Predigten*, Hoffman, 1979: 211, trans. O. Davies, 2006: 93. Cf. Bonaventure's *Itinerarium mentis in Deum*, VII.4, cited above, p. 68.

good deal further. His is the world of popular mediaeval piety. Although he held Eckhart in the highest regard – defending his distinction between *gotheit* and *got* by insisting on its conceptual nature[42] and commending the transformation of the experienced contemplative into the divine image so that he becomes one with it by restricting such transformation to a few rare souls whose virtue, in any case, only 'appears divine' (trans. O. Davies, 2006: 106, from Bihlmeyer, 1907: 338) – his more characteristic work is his hundred meditations on Christ's passion. He appears to have had some knowledge of Dionysius (he refers to the *Divine Names*: O. Davies, 2006: 48, citing Bihlmeyer, 1907, 328–29), but beyond an emphasis on the divine unity and on the 'still and unmoved darkness' that is the essence of the Godhead (O. Davies, 2006: 105, citing Bihlmeyer, 1907: 330), Dionysius has left very little mark on him.

The Low Countries produced a number of writers on spiritual themes in the fourteenth century, none more important than Jan van Ruusbroec (1293–1381) – ordained a secular priest, not a religious – who left his native city of Brussels in 1343 in order to establish himself a few kilometres to the southeast in a forest hermitage at Groenendaal. Like Tauler, he did not have a university education. He wrote his many books in the vernacular (Middle Dutch), which ensured a wide circulation for them and brought many visitors to his hermitage in search of spiritual counselling, some of whom stayed eventually to form a community around him. Such knowledge of Dionysius as Ruusbroec possessed came to him mediated by other writers, chiefly, it would seem, by Eckhart. He has a keen sense of the 'hidden brightness' and 'incomprehensible light' of the deity (*Die Gheestelike Brulocht* (The Spiritual Espousals) 77 and 80, trans. Van Nieuwenhove, 2003: 55), to which we ascend by a process of interior transformation 'beyond reason and distinction' (*Gheestelike Brulocht*, trans. Wiseman, 1985: 150), which he combines with a Bonaventurean emphasis on the primacy of divine love.[43]

One of the most important Dionysian elements in Ruusbroec is the *exitus–reditus* theme, which he is likely to have derived from Meister Eckhart. Like Eckhart, he applies this theme to the inner life of the Trinity – to the procession from, and return to, the Father – but in Ruusbroec's case, the emphasis is on the role of the Spirit rather than, as in Eckhart, on that of the Son. The Father is the eternal beginning of the

[42] Henry Suso, *The Book of Truth*, trans. O. Davies, 2006: 105, from Bihlmeyer, 1907: 330.
[43] On the priority of relational over ontological categories ('love', *mine*, rather than 'being', *wesen*) as the basis for union with God in Ruusbroec, see Cooper, 2019.

Persons, begetting his eternal Wisdom, the Son, 'as ceaselessly being born from him' and 'as outflowing in personal distinction from the Father's substance' and flowing back to him in the contemplation of his source. The Holy Spirit emerges (in the Western fashion) 'as an eternal pleasure' from the mutual contemplation of Father and Son, eternally flowing forth as the third Person out of the other two, and 'flowing back into the nature of the Godhead' (*Vanden XII Beghinen*, 2a 600–12; trans. Van Nieuwenhove, 2003: 83). The created world flows out from its origin in the Father through the Son, who is his Wisdom and Image, and because the world lives in the Image, 'all things live according to a divine mode'. The rational creature, which is specifically the image of the Image, seeks knowledge of its Creator in accordance with its created capacity, 'for it flows out as creature and therefore it knows and loves with limitation in the light of grace or glory' (*Dat Rijcke der Ghelieven* I, p. 77; trans. Van Nieuwenhove, 2003: 103). It is in virtue of this outflowing that the creature can return to unity in God, the rational creature thus participating in the 'complete return' of the Word to the Father.

There are two kinds of unity of the rational creature with God, one essential, the other active. The essential unity takes place when the spirit, 'according to its essential being, receives the coming of Christ in its bare nature, without intermediary and without cease'. In this mode, 'the spirit in the most intimate and highest part of its being, in its bare nature, ceaselessly receives the impress of its eternal Image and of the divine resplendence and becomes the eternal dwelling place of God' (*Gheestelike Brulocht*, b 1627–35, trans. Wiseman, as cited, lightly modified, by Van Nieuwenhove, 2003: 105). 'Essential' in this context refers not to a substance but to a relation, a relation that we have with the Father (as cause) through participation in Christ, the agent of our transformation:

> The essential unity of our spirit with God does not exist by itself, but abides in God, and it flows forth from God, and it hangs in God, and it returns back into God as into its eternal cause, and in this mode, it is never parted from God nor will it ever do so .... And this this unity is above time and place and always acts without cease after the mode of God, only it receives the impress of its eternal Image passively, insofar as it is God-like but creature in itself. This is the nobility which we have by nature in the essential unity of our spirit, where it is naturally united with God. (*Gheestelike Brulocht*, b 1655–65, trans. Wiseman, cited by Van Nieuwenhove, 2003: 106)

Our life in God's image is a given that is entailed by our creation as rational beings. The essential unity, however, is a passive one. For its relational nature to bear fruit we need to participate actively in the Person of Christ, whose humanity is already deified through the hypostatic union: 'Therefore, with God's grace, we have to renounce ourselves and our own personality and conform to our nature deified in Christ. Thus we are transformed by the eternal truth, which is Christ himself' (*Van den Gheesteliken Tabernakel*, II, p. 114, trans. Van Nieuwenhove, 2003: 131).

The active unity is the work of the Spirit, the one will and one love in both the Father and the Son, who flows out of them eternally and transforms us by the fire of divine love:

When we are lifted up above the disquiet of desires and the practices of virtues in purity of spirit, then we are empty, without activity. And there the Holy Spirit gives his eternal shining into our pure spirit; there we are wrought, and we undergo [God's work]. For the Holy Spirit is a consuming fire, which consumes and swallows up in its very self everything that it catches. Where it is hottest, there our spirit burns and undergoes the love of God; and [when it is] more than hot, it is burned up and undergoes transformation (*die overforminghe*) by God. But where it is [totally] burned up and one spirit with God, it is inactive, essential love. And that is the highest scale of love that I understand. (*Vanden XII Beghinen*, 2b 853–63; trans. Van Nieuwenhove, 2003: 165, lightly adapted)

The active unity results paradoxically in the cessation of activity – that is to say, in the cessation of merely human activity. Through the conflagration of everything that is egocentric, the soul becomes perfectly theocentric and in its state of pure deiformity (for which Ruusbroec has coined the term *overforminghe*, literally 'over-formation') participates in the bond of love between the Father and the Son, thus entering fully into the life of the Trinity. We should note, as Van Nieuwenhove has emphasised, that self-transcendence in Ruusbroec 'does not refer to a psychological experience but to a radical transformation of the human person, whose self-centeredness has been "burnt away"' (Van Nieuwenhove, 2003: 56). Psychological experiences come and go but the transformation that deifies is the result of the *habitus* of love that produces an ontological change: 'For if we possess God in immersion of loving, that is: lost to ourselves, God is our own and we are his own and we sink away from ourselves for ever, without return, in our possession that is God. This sinking away is essential, with habitual love' (*Vanden Blinkenden Steen*, 600–604; trans. Van Nieuwenhove, 2003: 56).

Ruusbroec's younger English contemporary, the anonymous author of *The Cloud of Unknowing*, is not usually thought to show signs of dependence on the Rhineland mystics and yet the passage from

Ruusbroec's *Sparkling Stone* quoted above could easily be thought to have come from his pen. There is in the *Cloud* author the same emphasis on the superiority of love over knowledge, the same stripping of self, the same loving lifting up of one's 'being – naked and blind as it is – to God's blessed being, beings which are one through grace, though different, of course, in nature'.[44] The *Cloud* author, however, moves on a different theological plane, one that is much closer to Dionysius the Areopagite. Indeed, he is the author of the first rendering in a vernacular language (the East Midland dialect of Middle English) of Dionysius's *Mystical Theology*, which he translated and adapted from the Latin versions of Johannes Sarracenus and Thomas Gallus.[45] His Dionysius is thus already a Westernised Dionysius, in which the intellective dimension has been subsumed by the affective.

In Dionysius's *Mystical Theology*, the context of the ascent of Moses to the darkness at the summit of Sinai is liturgical.[46] Moses is the hierarch who within the darkness of the summit (the altar) encounters the transcendent deity in a mystical vision beyond the realm of sense, so as to be a type to his flock of 'an ordered ascent from ignorance and sin into the knowledge of, participation in, and union with, God' (Golitzin, 2013: 237). For the author of *The Cloud*, the darkness represents something that stands *between* us and God, namely, our cognitive powers themselves. There are in fact two clouds that contemplatives must negotiate. The first is the cloud of forgetting, which they must put between themselves and the world of sense. The second is the cloud of unknowing, which they must also put behind them if they are to encounter God. 'Why?' asks the *Cloud* author. 'Because [God] may well be loved, but not thought. By love he may be caught and held but by thinking never' (*Cloud*, 6; trans. Wolters, 1978: 68). It is by the will, not by the intellect, that contemplatives attain to God: 'A naked intention directed to God,

---

[44] *The Epistle of Privy Counsel*, ch. 5, trans. Wolters, 1978: 173. The consensus of opinion is against a Dominican influence (O. Davies, 2006: 163–64) but Dom David Knowles (Knowles, 1960: 76–77) has not implausibly seen in the *Cloud* author's 'insistence upon naked faith' a reflection of 'the characteristic features of the Dominican school of the Rhineland'.

[45] This is his *Translacioun of Dionise Hid Divinite*, available in modern English in Wolters, 1978: 205–18, under the title *Dionysius' Mystical Teaching*. The author says himself that in order to explain the difficulties of the text, 'I ... have made much use of the Abbot of St Victor [Thomas Gallus], a distinguished and worthy expositor of the same' (Wolters, 1978: 207).

[46] I follow Golitzin here, who argues this interpretation in detail in Golitzin, 2013: 227–38.

and himself alone, is wholly sufficient' (*Cloud*, 7; trans. Wolters, 1978: 69).

The union that is attained by this 'blind groping for the naked being of God' (*Cloud*, 8; trans. Wolters, 1978: 72) is transformative and deifying, for then 'you will be worshipping God in union with himself, for what you are you have through him and, indeed, it is himself'' (*Epistle of Privy Counsel*, 4; trans. Wolters, 1978: 170). Yet even though what the contemplative becomes is what God is, there is no blurring of the ontological distinction between the Creator and the creature:

> For he is God by nature and without beginning; and you once were nothing at all. And when afterwards you, by his power and love, were made something, you by your deliberate act of will made yourself less than nothing. And it is only by his wholly undeserved mercy that you were made a god by grace, inseparably united to him in spirit, here and hereafter in the bliss of heaven, world without end! (*Cloud*, 67; trans. Wolters, 1978: 141)

A 'god by grace':[47] this expression, common among the Greek Fathers from at least the fourth century, and familiar to Western theologians through Augustine's sermons and commentaries and also to some extent through Latin translations of the Greek Fathers, very likely came to the attention of the *Cloud* author through William of Saint-Thierry (an author popular among the Carthusians), who states at the end of his *Golden Epistle*: 'in an ineffable and unfathomable manner the man of God is found worthy not to become God, but to acquire by grace what God is by nature'.[48]

THE RETURN TO THE INTELLECTIVE TRADITION: FROM JEAN GERSON TO NICHOLAS OF CUSA

In 1399, Jean Gerson, chancellor of the University of Paris, was asked what he thought of Ruusbroec's *Spiritual Espousals*. The reason for this seems to have been a move on the part of the Groenendaal community,

---

[47] 'Only bi his mercy withouten thi desert arte maad a god in grace': *The Cloud of Unknowing*, ed. Gallacher, lines 2277–78.

[48] Trans. O. Davies, 2006: 165, from PL 184, 348: 'cum modo ineffabili inexcogitabileque fieri meretur homo Dei non Deus, sed tamen quod Deus est ex natura, homo ex gratia'. William, a Benedictine abbot who became a Cistercian in 1135 at Signy, knew the Carthusians well, having stayed for several months at the Charterhouse of Mont-Dieu to recover from nervous exhaustion after a hard campaign to convict Peter Abelard and William of Conches of unorthodoxy. His *Golden Epistle* is addressed to the Carthusians of Mont-Dieu.

eighteen years after the death of their revered founder, to test whether there was any support in university circles for Ruusbroec's canonisation. Gerson's response was a bitter disappointment to them.[49] In the chancellor's view, Ruusbroec's book was a work of pseudo-erudition that sought to raise private inspiration above the Church's tradition on humanity's final beatitude. Even worse, in one part the book, says Gerson, Ruusbroec goes so far as to confuse the distinction between the Creator and the creature. Gerson is prepared to concede that the author is not an obdurate heretic because he later disavows his erroneous opinions. Nevertheless, as a result of the absence of any sound theological framework, the *Spiritual Espousals* is a very bad book. Despite Groenendaal's protests, Gerson's magisterial put-down put a stop to any hopes for Ruusbroec's canonisation. He was not beatified until 1908 and has still not advanced beyond the title of 'Blessed'.

Throughout his busy public career, the issues raised by the controversy with Groenendaal were never far from Gerson's mind. Of the four treatises that constitute his most important spiritual work, *De Theologia Mystica*,[50] the first and longest, the 'Speculative', was based on six lectures that he gave in the University of Paris in 1402–1403. The second, the 'Practical', was written four years later in Genoa, where Gerson had several months to spare while he waited in vain for the rival popes, Benedict XIII of Avignon and Gregory XII of Rome, to turn up for a promised meeting. The third treatise, the short 'Bibliography' of the best authors on contemplation, headed by Dionysius the Areopagite, was added to the work at a later stage.[51] And the fourth treatise, the 'Scholastic elucidation of mystical theology', was written in Lyon and was completed, according to the colophon, on 1 June 1424.

On Mystical Theology was a work that Gerson himself appears to have especially prized, referring to it frequently in his other writings (Hobbins, 2009: 23). It contains his mature judgement on the nature of

[49] Warner, 2007: 1–2. The standard work on the Groenendaal–Gerson dispute is André Combes's exhaustive *Essai sur la critique de Ruysbroeck par Gerson* (Combes, 1945–59).
[50] The critical edition was published by André Combes (Combes, 1958). My references are to the convenient reprint with a facing-page Italian translation by M. Vannini (Vannini, 1992).
[51] The remaining authors are Richard of St Victor, John Cassian, Augustine, Gregory the Great, Bernard, Hugh of St Victor, Bonaventure, and the only Greek author apart from the Areopagite, John Climacus, who had been translated into Latin by Angelus Clarenus (1255–1337). Among several works by modern authors appended at the end of the list is Ruusbroec's *Spiritual Espousals*, the third part of which, says Gerson, is suspect.

contemplation and on the contemplative's goal of union with God. Each treatise, apart from the Bibliography, is divided into 'Considerations', each Consideration being a stated thesis followed by a discussion. This is a structure that allows Gerson to reflect in a less formal way on his topic than would have been possible in treatises based on strict dialectical arguments. In the prologue to the first treatise, he announces his intention to fulfil the promise made to his students at the end of his previous course of lectures, namely, to show whether knowledge of God is better attained in a spirit of penitence or by intellectual inquiry. Right from the start, he makes his Dionysian orientation clear. Appealing to the Areopagite as his authority (but in fact echoing Albert the Great on Dionysius), he says that the meaning of mystical theology is 'hidden theology' (*theologia occulta*). He will therefore discuss what the best doctors have written on contemplation, meditation, rapture, ecstasy, and the mind's going out of itself (*et de mentis excessu*), for mystical theology is not a matter of intellectual inquiry: it is founded on experience.[52]

It is only in the last part of the treatise, after demonstrating that although mystical theology is founded on experience, it is nevertheless the most reliable form of knowledge with an objective character susceptible of rational analysis, that Gerson comes to consider the true nature of union with God. In *Consideratio* XL, he sets out seven different types of spiritual union, culminating in the hypostatic union of the divine and the human in Christ and the essential union of the three Persons of the Trinity, but the only one relevant to his theme is the union of love: 'Love unites the lover with the beloved, and therefore sets him firmly and stably next to him' (Vannini, 1992: 188). Such affective union is achieved through the conformity of the will to God.

In *Consideratio* XLI, Gerson goes on to consider in what sense this loving union may be considered a transformation. He accepts that the term 'transformation' may be used legitimately because it has the support of 'the divine Dionysius and the holy fathers', but he finds it problematical on account of the ease with which unorthodox interpretations may be drawn from it (Vannini, 1992: 190). Among the works that interpret transformation wrongly, he singles out Ruusbroec's *Spiritual Espousals*,

---

[52] *Gerson, Theologia Mystica, Prologus*, pp. 54–56. At the beginning of *Consideratio* III (p. 68), Gerson sums up his argument thus far: 'Theologia mistica, sicut innitur experientiis perfectiori certitudine cognitis, ita perfectior atque certior debet iudicari' ('Mystical theology, in that it is founded on experience known with perfect certainty, must be judged more perfect and more certain').

adding, however, that the author had corrected his error in other works, 'by affirming that such a soul always remains in its own being, which it possesses in its own kind, but is said to be transformed merely figuratively (*sed dicitur tantummodo similitudinarie transformari*), as we say of close friends that they are "one heart and soul"' (Vannini, 1992: 192). It is only this metaphorical sense that Gerson is prepared to concede to the word 'transformation'.

Perfectly orthodox works, particularly St Bernard's, may also be misused in Gerson's view. Bernard's image in his *Homilies on the Song of Songs* of a drop of water falling into a butt of wine, for example, could be taken to mean that the soul is transformed into God without any distinction remaining. Or his statement in *De praecepto et dispensatione* that 'the soul is more truly where it loves than where it is the animating power' could be thought to imply that the soul passes entirely into God. Other examples are given of potentially misleading analogies, such as that of iron becoming incandescent in a fire (a popular patristic image), the iron remaining itself while taking on the properties of fire, or the transformation through transubstantiation of the bread and wine of the Eucharist (recalling Eckhart's condemned Proposition 10), or the union of matter and form (this time alluding to Aquinas), by which matter receives its perfection through its form. Gerson himself prefers to explain the soul's transformation differently:

> From the analogies adduced we would conclude that love, like heat, has by nature the capacity to bring together and unite things that are homogeneous and separate and divide things that are heterogeneous. There is no doubt that whereas spiritual realities have a certain homogeneity or similarity with each other, corporeal or earthly realities are unlike each other. Therefore everything spiritual or divine that is found in the human person is separated in some way by vivifying love from that which is earthly and corporeal. Thus there is in the human person a division between spirit and soul, that is to say, between what belongs to the spirit, what belongs to the soul, and what belongs to the senses, and so the precious element is separated from the paltry. And because 'God is spirit' (John 4.24) and likeness is the cause of union, it is clear why a rational spirit when cleansed and purified is united to the divine Spirit: because it has been made like him. (*Consideratio* XLI; Vannini, 1992: 196–98)

'Transformation' for Gerson means the assimilation of like to like, which brings about a moral, not an ontological, change, a union of intimate contact with the divine that does not blur the distinction between Creator and created.

In the brief fourth treatise of *On Mystical Theology*, which he completed only five years before his death, Gerson sums up his final thoughts on union with God. He begins with one of the Lord's sayings to his disciples, 'To you it has been given to know the mystery of the kingdom of heaven' (Matt 13.11), qualifying it with the statement: 'I thank you, Father, Lord of heaven and earth, because you have hidden these things from the wise and experienced and have revealed them to little ones' (Matt 11.25). Union with God is not the product of learned research; it is the product of divine love received in humility. Nevertheless, a basic reading list is indispensable. Gerson recommends just three authors: Dionysius the Areopagite (the *Mystical Theology* and the *Divine Names*, especially Chapter VII), Bonaventure (the *Itinerarium Mentis*, Chapter VII), and Hugh of Balma (the *De duplici via ad Deum*). The last of these is mentioned anonymously in the fuller bibliography of the third treatise as the modern author of a work with the incipit *Vie Syon lugent*. Here, in the fourth treatise, he is named correctly as Hugo de Balma and his work is given the title *De duplici via ad Deum*.[53]

Hugh of Balma, a Carthusian who was prior of the Charterhouse of Meyriat in the Bresse, north-east of Lyon, from 1289 to 1304, was a significant writer on the contemplative life in the Dionysian tradition of Thomas Gallus.[54] His *Mystical Theology* was written to recall his Carthusian brethren from the academic theology (*theologia speculativa*) that he felt was claiming too much of their attention to the mystical theology (*theologia mystica*) proper to their contemplative vocation. The work is divided into three parts reflecting Dionysius's 'three ways' of purgation, illumination, and union. But what is of particular interest to Gerson is Hugh's consideration of the 'difficult question' of the relationship between the 'two ways' of knowledge and love, for if love takes precedence, as Gerson believes it should, it is difficult to determine how love for God can exist without previous knowledge.[55] You cannot love what you do not know, yet the Western consensus gives priority to love. How is this paradox to be resolved?

Gerson takes a somewhat different line from Hugh, who develops a double idea of the intellect's contemplation in terms of *anagogia*, which consists, on the one hand, of an upward movement from below based on

---

[53] This is Gerson's title for Hugh of Balma's *Mystical Theology*, a long work published in two volumes in the Sources Chrétiennes series (Barbet and Ruello, 1995–96). Later in the fifteenth century, the *Mystical Theology* was wrongly attributed to Bonaventure and was only restored to Hugh of Balma in the early twentieth century.

[54] On Hugh of Balma's use of Dionysius, see de Andia, 2006.

[55] On Hugh's 'two ways', see de Andia, 2006: 242–23; on Gerson's appropriation of Hugh's teaching, see Vial, 2009.

theological reflection and the elevation of the mind and, on the other, of a downward movement from on high that elicits a burning desire to mount yet higher. Gerson has nothing so elaborate. He is attracted more by the notion of *synderesis*, which he derives from Bonaventure and defines as 'an appetitive power of the soul that receives directly from God a certain natural inclination towards the good, through which it is drawn to follow the motion of the good from the apprehension of the simple intellect presented to it'.[56] Mystical theology consists solely in love, and such love is infused supernaturally in those who desire wisdom, becoming in them an acquired *habitus*. Yet this love infused from on high is accompanied *simultaneously* by cognition, for Gerson acknowledges that there can be no mystical theology without some kind of knowledge of God. Refusing to accept that we can only know God by negation, for as Gregory the Great says, 'Love itself is knowledge' (*Homiliae LX in evangelia*, 27; PL 76, 1207), he offers a powerful analogy of our knowledge of God in the way that a baby relates to its mother, the baby pressing 'itself on the breasts giving it milk and this becomes a kind of soothing experiential operation that is not reflective, or declaratory, or propositional' (*Theologia Mystica* IV, *Consideratio* XI; Vannini, 1992: 330; cf. 2 Sam 6.21–22).

Many, says Gerson, have discussed the two types of contemplation, the affective and the intellective. Gerson would unite them in a loving knowledge, a *cognitio affectualis*, accessible to the simplest believer, by which 'the intellect is carried to God outside the here and now, that is to say, outside space and time, and without any admixture of mental representations (*fantasmata*)' (*Theologia Mystica* IV, *Consideratio* XII; Vannini, 1992: 334). Gerson does not call this rapture 'deification', a term that does not appear in any of the four texts that he regards as essential reading. Nor is he willing to call it 'transformation', which does appear in Bonaventure and Hugh but is a dangerous term, in his view, because of the use made of it by Ruusbroec and others. For the unreserved acceptance of 'deification', and indeed of the Greek term 'theosis', we need to turn to Gerson's younger contemporary, Nicholas of Cusa (1401–1464).

Like Gerson, Nicholas was to become one of the leading churchmen of his day. He was born in 1401 in Kues, a small town on the River Mosel not far from Trier in north-west Germany – hence his name Nikolaus of Kues, Latinised as Nicolaus Cusanus. Studies in canon law at Padua were

---

[56] *Gerson, Theologia Mystica* I, *Consideratio* XIV; Vannini, 1992: 98. Cf. Bonaventure, *In libros Sententiarum* II, d. 39, a. 2, q. 1, concl.

followed by philosophy and theology at the University of Cologne, where he was introduced by his teacher, Heymericus de Campo (1395–1460), to Albert the Great's commentaries on Dionysius and also to the works of Raymond Llull (c. 1233–c. 1315). His ecclesiastical career began in 1425 with his entry into the household of the archbishop of Trier, Otto of Ziegenhain, as his secretary. In 1433, he took part in the Council of Basel, where, after initially supporting the conciliar movement, he switched his allegiance (alarmed, no doubt, by the threat to church unity posed by the council's chaotic proceedings) to the papacy. All through the 1430s and 1440s, he worked for the papal cause in Germany and was also used by Pope Eugenius IV in negotiations for reunion with the Greeks. Created a cardinal in 1448, he was appointed bishop of Brixen in the Tyrol shortly afterwards and papal legate for Germany. Problems with Sigismund, duke of Austria and count of the Tyrol, however, eventually forced him to resign his see. The last four years of his life were spent as a curial cardinal in Rome.

Early in his career, Nicholas came to be employed in the collection of ancient manuscripts. Cardinal Giordano Orsini, one of the leaders of the Italian Renaissance, was in Germany as papal legate and enlisted Nicholas's aid in tracking down manuscripts of classical Latin authors.[57] Later Nicholas had the opportunity to acquire manuscripts on his own account, building up an impressive personal library, which he bequeathed to the hospice he founded in the town of his birth. This remarkable collection, which still remains intact in the institution in which it was originally deposited, contains only two Greek patristic texts, a fine tenth-century manuscript of some of the homilies of St John Chrysostom and an undated commentary on the *Carmina Arcana* of St Gregory of Nazianzus by Niketas David Paphlagon (Marx, 1905: 42–43). Unlike the Latin manuscripts, these are not annotated in Nicholas's own hand, which suggests that his Greek was too elementary for him to study them in the original.[58] Among the Greek texts he possessed in Latin, pride of place belongs to Dionysius the Areopagite, whose treatises and letters Nicholas possessed in the translation of Ambrogio Traversari.[59] The library also

[57] Nicholas discovered a manuscript containing the lost plays of Plautus.

[58] On Nicholas's knowledge of Greek, see Casarella, 1995.

[59] Marx, 1905: 39–40. Nicholas would have met Traversari at the Council of Basel, where the latter, who had become prior general of the Camaldolesi in 1431, was a papal legate. But it was not until later that he acquired Traversari's translations of Dionysius. The mathematician, Paolo del Pozzo Toscanelli, a friend from his university days at Padua, is known to have sent him a copy of Traversari's translation of the *Mystical Theology* in

contains the translations by Robert Grosseteste of the *Celestial Hierarchy* and the *Mystical Theology*, together with the commentary by Thomas Gallus on Grosseteste's version of the *Celestial Hierarchy* (Marx, 1905: 39, 41). There is also a copy of Hugh of St Victor's commentary on Eriugena's version of the *Mystical Theology*, with marginal notes in Nicholas's own hand (Marx, 1905: 40). No other patristic author, except Augustine, is so well represented as Dionysius in the cardinal's library.

Deification is a major theme in Nicholas's works.[60] Among the writers we have been considering in this chapter, he is the first since Eriugena to have used the Greek term 'theosis', which he would have encountered in Eriugena's *Periphyseon*, a work he is known to have studied carefully.[61] Deification, however, presents quite a different aspect in Nicholas compared with his late-mediaeval predecessors. As Nancy Hudson remarks, this is because for Nicholas 'theosis is a *metaphysical* rather than an epistemological category' (Hudson, 2007: 46). He is not concerned, as Gerson is, with the relationship between the affective and the intellective mystical traditions. Nor does he focus on the nature of mystical experience, as the Rhineland mystics do, although he does not ignore it. What absorbs him is the search for comprehension – 'to become a perfect master' (*perfectum magistrum*), as he puts it – of what is true and eternal.[62] In his fundamental work, *De docta ignorantia* (*On Learned Ignorance*), written in 1440, the idea for which, he says, came to him on the ship bringing him back from Constantinople, where he had been sent on a papal mission, he expresses an acute sense of the mystery of the universe.[63] This mystery is rooted in the world's affinity to its divine cause and its ultimate return to that cause, an *exitus–reditus* encompassing the whole of reality that Hudson aptly calls 'the theotic destiny of creation'

1443. In *Apologia doctae ignorantiae*, 10, Nicholas mentions that he received Traversari's translation of the *Divine Names* from 'our most holy Lord, Pope Nicholas' (Nicholas V, 1447–1455).

[60] The only monograph (a helpful one) dedicated specifically to Nicholas's understanding of deification is Hudson, 2007.

[61] Cf. Eriugena, *Periphyseon* 5, quoted above, at the beginning of the chapter. Nicholas refers frequently to the *Periphyseon* in his *De docta ignorantia*.

[62] Cusanus, *De filatione Dei* II, n. 60, line 3; trans. Jasper Hopkins, 1994: 345. English translations of all of Nicholas's works may be found on Hopkins's website: www.jasper-hopkins.info. The Latin originals are also accessible online at www.cusanus-portal.de.

[63] The work was therefore conceived in early December 1437. The title, as Nicholas makes clear in *Apologia doctae ignorantiae discipuli ad discipulum*, n. 50, is based on Dionysius's statement in *Letter I to Gaius* that 'the most complete ignorance is knowledge of him who transcends everything that is known' (Dionysius the Areopagite, *Letter* I, 1065B; Heil and Ritter, p. 157); cf. Hudson, 2007: 40–41.

(Hudson, 2007: 47). In his discussions of this mystery, Nicholas develops his own philosophical language in a struggle to do justice to the dynamic asymmetrical relationship existing between the uncreated One and the created many.[64] He speaks of God as the absolute maximum, as the coincidence of opposites, as not-other, in order to indicate God's absolute transcendence and yet at the same time his unifying immanence in everything that exists. In the words of Clyde Miller, 'Coincidence underlines the Oneness that comprehends all else in undifferentiated and unlimited unity. It is not that creatures coincide with God or God with creatures, but that in God all else coincides as nothing else than God' (Miller, 2017: 2.1). Theosis is fundamentally the intellectual apprehension of what is entailed by this truth.

In around 1450, Nicholas's *On Learned Ignorance* was attacked by John Wenck, a teacher of theology at the University of Heidelberg, on the grounds that it compromised the transcendence and unicity of God. According to Nicholas, Wenck's animosity towards him dated from the Council of Basel, since when, as an unrepentant conciliarist, he had not forgiven Nicholas for changing sides (Cusanus, *Apologia doctae ignorantiae*, 5; trans. Hopkins, 1988: 462). Wenck summarises the coincidence of opposites as entailing that 'God – an equality of being-all-things and without any change in himself – exists in oneness with the humanity of the maximum [man] Jesus' and is outraged that this 'abominable thesis asserts an equality-of-being between divinity and humanity' (Wenck, *De ignota litteratura*, 38; trans. Hopkins, 1988: 444). One of the corollaries that Wenck draws from this is 'that each blessed one is Christ and God', differing from God not ontologically but only in degree (*De ignota litteratura*, 41; trans. Hopkins, 1988: 448). He declares that in his entire life he has not come across a writer, even Meister Eckhart, as heinous in this respect as the author of *De docta ignorantia*.

In *De docta ignorantia*, Nicholas only alludes to deification in passing. The text that he devotes specifically to the topic is his short treatise *De filiatione Dei* (*On Becoming a Son of God*), written in the summer of 1445 at the request of Conrad of Wartberg, a canon of the monastery of Meinfelt (now Münstermaifeld, near Koblenz).[65] Conrad had asked Nicholas for an exposition of John 1.12: 'But to all who received him,

---

[64] For excellent overviews of Nicholas's philosophical thinking, see Hopkins, 2009; Miller, 2017.

[65] Codex Trevirensis 1918/1466 states that it was completed on 27 July 1445.

who believed in his name, he gave power to become children of God.'[66] Nicholas begins at once with a concise definition: 'To put my view summarily: I judge that being sons of God is to be regarded as nothing other than deification, which, in Greek, is called theosis'. And he adds immediately: 'But you know that theosis is ultimacy of perfection, which is called both knowledge of God the Word and intuitive vision [of him]' (*De filiatione Dei* I, 52.2–5; trans. Hopkins, 1994: 341, modified).

Theosis is thus an ascent to the vision of God, which is the vision of truth, yet it is not the result of a purely intellectual process. It is participation in a divine power (the power of filiation bestowed by the Word) that calls for intuitive apprehension rather than dialectical reasoning and, moreover, requires the presence of faith:

This [power of filiation] is a super-wonderful participation in divine power, so that our rational spirit has this power in its own intellectual strength. It is as if the intellect were a divine seed – the intellect whose power in the believer can reach such heights that it attains *theosis*. It attains, that is, the ultimate perfection of the intellect – in other words unto the apprehension of truth, not as truth is bedarkened in figurativeness and symbolisms (*obumbrata in figura et aenigmate*) and various degrees of otherness in this sensible world, but rather as truth is intellectually visible in itself. And this is that sufficiency which our intellectual power – which, in the case of believers, is actualized by the arousal of the Divine Word – has from God. For he who does not believe will not at all ascend; rather, he has condemned himself to be unable to ascend, by closing off for himself the pathway [of ascent]. For nothing is attained without faith, which first sets the pilgrim on his journey. (*De filiatione Dei* I, 53.1–12; trans. Hopkins, 1994: 341–42, slightly modified)

God cannot be attained by the intellect alone, because he utterly transcends it. But he can be attained by participation in the Word by faith, a participation that produces a modal, not an ontological, change in the believer. The sonship of the many is a participation in the sonship of the Word, so that the many become sons in a different mode (*De filiatione Dei* I, 54.1–12; trans. Hopkins, 1994: 342). 'This mode can perhaps be called "participation in adoption"' (*De filiatione Dei* I, 54.22–23; trans. Hopkins, 1994: 342). In the next world, there will be a further change but again in a modal, not an ontological, sense: 'I do not think that we become sons of God in such a way that we will then be something [essentially] other than we are now; instead, *then* we will be in another manner than that which *now* we are in our present manner' (*De filiatione*

---

[66] The Greek of John's Gospel has τέκνα, 'children' (which the Latin Vulgate, followed by Nicholas, renders as *filii*). Hence the 'son' and 'sonship' of Hopkins's English translation.

Dei II, 56.1–3; trans. Hopkins, 1994: 343). It is thus that deification not only transcends discursive reason but 'surpasses the limits of every mode of intuition' (*De filiatione Dei* I, 54.5; trans. Hopkins, 1994: 342).

This transcendence of the self through participation in the Word gives one access to truth, which 'alone is the intelligibility of everything intelligible'(*De filiatione Dei* III, 69.6–7; trans. Hopkins, 1994: 349). It implies the overcoming of otherness without the loss of personal identity. An illustration that Nicholas develops at some length in order to convey this idea is that of an image reflected in a straight mirror that is then reflected from the straight mirror to curved mirrors. The straight mirror is God's Word. The curved mirrors are ourselves, who reproduce a distorted reflection of the divine image. Our task is to straighten our curved mirrors so as to reproduce the divine accurately. 'And so, Brother', concludes Nicholas, addressing his confrère, Conrad of Wartberg, '[mentally] remove the quantitative contractions of the sensible mirrors, and free your conception from place and time and all things sensible, elevating yourself unto the rational reflected brightness, where in clear reason our mind beholds the truth' (*De filiatione Dei* III, 68.1–4; trans. Hopkins, 1994: 342).

Truth is thus attained through rising above all contradictions, alterities, disjunctions, negations, and affirmations, and ultimately even above multiplicity itself, to arrive at the oneness of pure intellectual life:

Therefore, sonship is the removal of all otherness and all difference and is the resolution of all things into one thing – a resolution that is also the imparting of one thing unto all other things. And this imparting is theosis. Now, God is one thing in which all things are present as one; He is also the imparting of oneness unto all things, so that all things are that which they are; and in the [aforementioned] intellectual intuition *being something one in which are all things* and *being all things in which there is something one* coincide. Accordingly, we are rightly deified when we are exalted to the point that in a oneness [of being] we are (1) a oneness in which are all things and (2) a oneness [which is] in all things. (*De filiatione Dei* III, 70.1–7; trans. Hopkins, 1994: 349)

Theosis is accordingly the attainment of unity, in the Dionysian manner, by a graced intellectual ascent. If Nicholas's treatises and dialogues were all we had, we would have to conclude that his concept of theosis is rigorously, even exclusively, intellectualist; but we also have his sermons.

Nicholas has left a large body of sermons (293 in the Heidelberg edition of his works), several of which relate theosis explicitly to the Church's sacramental life. Like Eckhart, Nicholas drafted in Latin even the sermons he intended to preach in German to lay congregations.

What we have are therefore not the sermons as preached (few of them are *reportationes*) but Nicholas's sermon notes. The style is naturally different from that of the learned writings, but interestingly even the vocabulary differs. As Hopkins points out, 'whereas in the treatises and the dialogues Nicholas sticks with the terms *"deiformis"* and *"Christiformis,"* he prefers in the sermons the expressions *"in Christum transformari"* and *"in Deum transformari"*' (Hopkins, 2003: xix). This is language reminiscent of Bonaventure, which suggests that in his preaching Nicholas deliberately sets aside his austerely philosophical frame of reference and draws instead on the popular affective tradition on deification. In a characteristic passage, he speaks of the transformation of the inner man into the exact likeness of Christ through putting on the form of the Lord in baptism (Sermo CCLXXII, Domine adjuva me (preached in Brixen on 13 March 1467), 13.1–17; trans. Hopkins, website: 142.). This is the patristic teaching (drawing on Phil 2.6–11) that the Word became what we are so that by putting on Christ in baptism we might become what he is. In the peroration of the same sermon, however, Nicholas echoes Ekhart's condemned analogy with the Eucharist – by participation in the Eucharist the Christian's soul is transformed 'into the life of the spirit of Christ', just as at the altar by faith and mystical prayers the material bread is transformed into the living body of Christ – though now with the authority of a bishop and member of the College of Cardinals.

THE PLACE OF THEOSIS IN LATE MEDIAEVAL RELIGION

In the ninth century, Eriugena suggested that the reason why the term 'theosis' was not found in Latin writers was that what it denoted was so exalted and so open to misinterpretation that it was 'something only to be discussed among scholars (*inter sapientes*)' (*Periphyseon*, 5). A review of how deification was treated up to the fifteenth century proves Eriugena right. Ecclesiastical authority (or more often, the self-appointed heresy-hunter) was always suspicious of a maximalist interpretation of how the human person becomes united with God – but usually when such an interpretation was expressed in popular sermons or didactic works, rather than in learned treatises. Thus Eckhart was attacked by Henry of Virneburg, Ruusbroec by Jean Gerson, and Nicholas of Cusa by John Wenck, all three because they seemed to their critics to be opening the door to pantheism. Deification in the Latin West, more so than in the Greek East, needed to be carefully nuanced in order not to incur official censure.

Yet those works, especially in the vernacular, in which the notion of deification was embedded enjoyed a wide readership. Religion, as the Middle Ages drew to a close, came to imply, even for the laity, a greater focus on the interior life. Meister Eckhart, Johannes Tauler, and Jan van Ruusbroec present this life as the perfection of the image of God in the soul through the transformative action of Christ and the Holy Spirit until, as Tauler puts it, through grace 'the soul takes on the form and nature of God'.[67] In the *Cloud of Unknowing*, written for a non-ordained monastic, the interior life is given a Dionysian colouring as the 'blind groping for the naked being of God', which is rewarded by the attainment of deifying union.[68] By the end of the fourteenth century, religion for many of the laity was no longer mainly a matter of liturgical feasts, confraternities, pilgrimages, and processions but had become primarily the interior search for God.

Among the classics of spiritual writing, Bonaventure's *Itinerarium mentis in Deum* stands out. It was highly regarded not only by Jean Gerson, who gave equal weight to the affective and intellective traditions, but also by Nicholas of Cusa, who strongly favoured the intellective tradition. For Bonaventure combined a fervent affective spirituality with a warm admiration of Dionysius's *Mystical Theology*. Behind all the later discussions of deification lie the writings of Dionysius the Areopagite. The authority of Dionysius was unquestioned, resting as it did on the assumption that that the author of the Dionysian corpus was the Athenian philosopher converted by St Paul. Even after Neoplatonic texts by Proclus and others began to be available, it was assumed that they were later than Dionysius and therefore dependent on him. Commentaries on one or other of Dionysius's treatises, or even on the whole corpus, were composed by Hugh of St Victor, Albert the Great, Thomas Aquinas, and Thomas Gallus. The Victorines Hugh and Thomas, together with Bonaventure himself and the author of *The Cloud of Unknowing*, interpreted Dionysius in accordance with the affective mystical tradition. By contrast, Albert, Eckhart, and Nicholas of Cusa assimilated Dionysius to the intellective mystical tradition but gave priority to negations and intuitive intellection rather than to syllogistic and discursive reasoning. Whether they privileged love or knowledge, however, these writers all held Dionysius to be the supreme guide to the interior life, the goal of which was union with God interpreted as a spiritual transformation, or theosis.

---

[67] Tauler, *Predigten*, p. 277; trans. O. Davies, 2006: 78.
[68] *The Cloud of Unknowing*, ch. 8; trans. Wolters, 1978: 72.

With Nicholas of Cusa, the first to retrieve the term 'theosis', we find an interesting distinction between, on the one hand, *transformation* into Christ or into God as set out in his popular preaching and, on the other, *deification* or *theosis* as discussed in his treatise on divine filiation addressed to a monastic audience. The reality signified by these different terms seems to be the same. Nevertheless, theosis was not a term that Nicholas appears to have considered suitable for a popular audience. It was an expression to be reserved to the *sapientes*.

Among the texts consulted by Nicholas were the teachings of 'Thrice-great Hermes', the so-called Hermetic Corpus. These texts first became available in the West during the Renaissance and enjoyed a great *succès d'estime*, partly because they did not require any great philosophical expertise on the part of the reader. It is to this low-level teaching on deification that we now turn.

4

'Light the Lamp within You'

A Recurring Esoteric Tradition

For the student of intellectual history, it is an exciting experience to enter the cathedral of Siena. On the floor at the entrance is a wonderful pavement of inlaid coloured marble by the artist Giovanni di Stefano showing the figure of Hermes Trismegistus, executed in 1488. Flanking Hermes, in the aisles, are the Sibyls. As one moves up through the basilica, one crosses a mosaic of a she-wolf suckling Romulus and Remus, an inlaid marble allegory of the Mount of Wisdom, and lastly, before arriving at the altar, an inlaid marble panel with scenes depicting Moses on Mount Sinai. The whole programme is a visual rendering of Lactantius's presentation in the *Divine Institutes* of the unity of all genuine wisdom, which ascends through the philosophers and prophets to Christ himself.[1]

Only a decade or so before Giovanni di Stefano was commissioned to make his image of Hermes, the Hermetic Corpus had been translated into Latin from a newly discovered Greek manuscript by Marsilio Ficino (1433–1499).[2] A few years after Ficino's translation, Giovanni Pico della Mirandola (1463–1494) had a large part of the main kabbalistic writings translated for him from the original Hebrew by a learned Jewish convert.[3]

---

[1] In *Divine Institutes* IV, 6, Lactantius specifically mentions Hermes Trismegistus and the Sibyls and quotes passages there and elswhere from the *Asclepius*. The point Lactantius is making is that pagan prophets and philosophers also testify to Christ.

[2] The manuscript was located in Macedonia by a monk who brought it to Florence in 1463 and presented it to Cosimo de' Medici. It is housed today in the Biblioteca Laurenziana (Laurentianus, LXXI 33 [A]).

[3] The translator was Samuel ben Nissim Abul Farag, a Jewish convert from Agrigento, Sicily, who took the name Raimondo da Moncada and was also known as Flavius

This was a period in which new sources of ancient wisdom were being explored eagerly by leading intellectuals of the Italian Renaissance. Study of this ancient wisdom (*prisca sapientia*), a perennial wisdom as it was thought, flourished throughout Europe in the sixteenth century but was later marginalised by the confident new orthodoxies of the Protestant Reformation and the Council of Trent. It came to be associated with magic and alchemy and heterodox opinions about the way God, humanity, and the world interacted. Yet the 'perennial philosophy' continued to be influential right up to modern times as an important component of Western culture and in the late-nineteenth and twentieth centuries played a significant role in the Christian retrieval of theosis. In this chapter, we shall review a range of spiritual movements that, from the second to the twentieth centuries, have predicated a divine destiny for the human soul so as to gain an understanding of how theosis relates to religion's esoteric aspect.

GNOSIS AND HERMETISM

Who were the gnostics? The evidence for the use of the term 'gnostic' as a self-designation is very slight. In the third century, Plotinus wrote a treatise 'Against the gnostics',[4] and Clement and Origen report that there were some who called themselves gnostics,[5] but none of the texts of the so-called gnostic scriptures discovered at Nag Hammadi in Egypt in 1945 actually describes itself as written by a gnostic or originating from a gnostic community.[6] As for the terms 'gnosticism' and 'the gnostic religion', these are simply modern constructs reflecting 'the hypothesis of social-historical continuity based primarily on supposed theological similarity' (M. A. Williams, 1996: 43). Yet there *were* those who claimed privileged access to hidden knowledge either through direct revelation or through a charismatic teacher. And they did produce texts in the first three centuries of the Christian era, which were lost after ecclesial Christianity had established its dominance until some of them were

---

Mithridates. Both Ficino and Pico were members of Cosimo de' Medici's Platonic Academy.

[4] Plotinus, *Enneads* II, 9. In § 9, he attacks the gnostic version of deification as purely individualistic and lacking in intellectual and moral effort.

[5] Clement of Alexandria, *Stromateis* III, 30, 1; Origen, *Contra Celsum* 5, 1.

[6] The expression 'the Gnostic scriptures' is the title of Layton, 1987, and appears on the cover of the paperback edition of Robinson, 1988, published by HarperCollins in 1990.

recovered in Coptic translation buried in a jar at Nag Hammadi.[7] Several
of these texts share a belief in the soul's divine origin and teach that
salvation consists in the soul's return to its source. Notable among them
are *The Gospel of Thomas*, *The Gospel of Truth*, and *The Teachings
of Silvanus*.

    The Gospel of Thomas is the earliest of the three, going back perhaps
to the beginnings of East Syrian Christianity in late first-century Edessa.[8]
It is therefore contemporary with the canonical gospels, the product of an
ancient rhetorical culture in which oral and scribal traditions (written
texts at the time being 'published' by being read aloud to an audience)
were not in sharp contrast with each other but coexisted easily. *The
Gospel of Thomas* did not make it into the scriptural canon, which began
to be defined in the late second century, no doubt because of its esoteric
emphasis. It is, in any case, not a gospel in the sense of a continuous
narrative but a collection of 'secret sayings' attributed to Jesus intended to
direct the hearers' attention inwards, for 'the kingdom of God' (in the
Greek version, 'of the father') 'is inside you' (cf. Luke 17.21) as well as
outside, and that is principally where it is to be sought. For the path to
knowledge is through self-knowledge – drawing on the 'know yourself'
(γνῶθι σαυτόν) of the Greek philosophical tradition – which results in the
understanding that 'it is you who are children' (in the Greek version, 'the
sons') 'of the living father' (3; trans. Layton, 1987: 380). Certainly, the
divine is transcendent, yet it also penetrates the whole of creation. Jesus
says: 'It is I who am the light (that presides) over all', but in the same
saying declares: 'Split a piece of wood: I am there. Lift a stone and you
will find me there' (77; trans. Layton, 1987: 394). For the believer, the
personal intimacy with the divine made possible by Jesus can lead to
complete assimilation to him: 'Whoever drinks from my mouth will
become like me; I, too, will become that person, and to that person the

---

[7] Who buried the jar and why is a question that has given rise to much speculation. The texts
were written on papyrus and assembled in thirteen leather-bound codices in the fourth
century (the approximate date being established from the cartonnage used in the binding).
The most satisfactory explanation is still that of James M. Robinson, who suggested that
they came from the library of a nearby Pachomian monastery and were carefully secreted
when Athanasius, archbishop of Alexandria, condemned the use of non-canonical scripture in his Festal Letter of 367.

[8] The full text of the *Gospel of Thomas* survives only in Coptic (English translation Layton,
1987: 376–99; Robinson 1988: 124–38; Meyer, 2007: 133–56). The Greek fragments are
conveniently edited in Bernhard, 2007: 20–47. For a useful discussion of its historical
context, see Uro, 2003: 106–38.

hidden things will be shown forth' (108; trans. Layton, 1987: 398). True knowledge is hidden from the profane but revealed to the Christified.

The Gospel of Truth is a little later, dating from the second century.[9] It, too, is not a gospel in the narrative sense but rather a spiritual homily of great beauty mapping out the journey of the soul, which emanates from the Father, becomes estranged from him through ignorance and error, and is brought back to him by the Word, Jesus Christ. Error is personified as the producer of forgetfulness and fears. The elect who have overcome this forgetfulness and surmounted these fears through eating the fruit of the knowledge of the Father, which is what Jesus Christ became through being nailed to a tree, are not only discovered by Christ within himself but also discover him within themselves. It is this knowledge that enables those who possess it to ascend through the Father's aeons and emanations to the Father himself. There they attain to truth, or rather, 'they themselves are the truth; and the Father is within them and they are in the Father, being perfect, being undivided in the truly good one, being in no way deficient in anything, but they are set at rest, refreshed in the Spirit' (42; trans. Attridge and MacRae in Robinson, 1988: 51). This perichoresis, or mutual interpenetration, of the perfect and the Father looks forward to Eckhart, although Eckhart, of course, had no knowledge of *The Gospel of Truth*.

The Teachings of Silvanus belongs to yet another genre, that of wisdom literature.[10] A sage instructs his disciple: 'From now on, then, my son, return to your divine nature. Cast from you these evil, deceiving friends .... Cast from you death, which has become a father to you ... return, my son, to your first Father, God' (90–91; trans. Peel and Zandee in Robinson, 1988: 383–84). Our inner nature is divine because 'the soul has come into being from the thought of the Divine' and in some fashion shares in God. Our task is to light the lamp within us (106; trans. Peel and Zandee in Robinson, 1988: 390), for we are temples of divinity, temples from which Christ has cast out the dealers and merchants. The Gospel says: 'Knock and it will be opened to you'; but the sage says: 'Knock on yourself that the Word may open for you' (117; trans. Peel and Zandee in Robinson, 1988: 395). Reconnecting through Christ with our inner

---

[9] The language of composition was Greek, but it survives only in a Coptic translation from Nag Hammadi (trans. Layton, 1987: 250–64; Robinson, 1988: 38–51; Meyer, 2007: 31–48).

[10] It, too, was composed originally in Greek but survives only in a Coptic translation discovered at Nag Hammadi (Eng. trans. Robinson, 1988: 379–95; Meyer, 2007: 499–522).

nature is to become conscious of our innate divinity and thus to find the means of returning to our origin, the Father.

These three texts are not 'gnostic' in the commonly received sense of presupposing a world created by an inferior, even hostile, deity from which the possessor of gnosis must escape in order to attain salvation. But they do presuppose the location of divine knowledge within the human person, rather than 'out there', an occult knowledge that needs an expert guide in order to become accessible. The same is true of the Hermetic Corpus, a portion of which was also discovered in Coptic translation at Nag Hammadi.[11] These writings, too, dating from the first to the late third centuries, are cast in the form of a master addressing a disciple, only in this case the master is not a Christian sage but Hermes Trismegistus, the Thrice-great Hermes.[12] In an atmosphere of awe and reverence, intended to evoke the sense of an Egyptian temple, Hermes imparts his teaching to his disciples, Asclepius and Tat. Even more emphatically than in the Christian gnostic writings, the core of the human person in the Hermetic Corpus is treated as divine, either simply in virtue of its divine origin or because through striving for knowledge under the guidance of Hermes it undergoes a number of transformations that render it fully divine. In a key discourse addressed to Asclepius (and in fact entitled *The Key*), Hermes says that to attain deification is to attain the vision of the beauty of the Good, an experience that is impossible in the body. This prompts Asclepius to ask a series of questions:

What do you mean by 'being deified' (ἀποθεωθῆναι), father?
The transformations (μεταβολαί), my child, of every divisible soul.

Divisible in what sense?
Did you not hear in the *General Discourses* that that all the souls circulating in the world, are from the single soul of the All, as if split off from it? The transformations, then, of these souls are many, some more fortunate, others the opposite ... human souls gain hold of the principle of immortality by being transformed into daemons and then they pass thus into the choir of the gods ... and this is the most complete glory of the soul. But if a soul enters into human beings yet remains evil, it will neither taste death nor partake of the Good, but will retrace its steps and return to the state of the reptiles. This is the condemnation of an evil soul. Evil for

---

[11] On gnosis in the Hermetic Corpus, see especially Fowden, 1993: 104–15.

[12] The critical edition by A. D. Nock, with a French translation by A. J. Festugière, was first published in four volumes in 1945–1954. I use here the convenient one-volume reprint with an Italian translation by V. Schiavoni (2018). There is an annotated English translation by B. P. Copenhaver (1992).

the soul is ignorance …. By contrast, virtue for the soul is knowledge. He who knows and is good and devout is already divine.

Who is such a man, father?
One who does not speak much or hear much …. For he who is God and Father and the Good is the subject neither of speech nor of hearing. (CH X, 7–8; Schiavoni, 2018: 172–74; my trans.)

A human who has acquired the divine intellect, *nous* (ὁ ἔννους ἄνθρωπος), is one who has come to know himself (CH I, 21; Schiavoni, 2018: 76).[13] And it is this knowledge of his true origin and his final end that raises him to a divine state of being and enables him to know and worship God, who transcends all human thought, in utter silence.

In other discourses, deification is defined further as determined first by the orientation of the will (the rejection of the corporeal and the choice of the divine, the vision of which draws one like a magnet draws iron) (CH IV, 7 and 11; Schiavoni, 2018: 118, 122), and then by divine action, which banishes ignorance and brings about spiritual rebirth (παλιγγενεσία): 'When the decad supervenes, my son, a spiritual birth occurs and drives out the dodecad and we have been deified (ἐθεώθημεν) by this birth.'[14] The emphasis on the need for ascetic effort and spiritual rebirth brings Hermetism close to Christian gnosis, but as Garth Fowden says, 'it would be a mistake … to imagine that Christian gnosticism either substantially influenced Hermetism, or can be used to illuminate it, except by way of general analogy' (Fowden, 1993: 114). In Fowden's view, it can nevertheless be asserted confidently that 'Hermetism represents the sort of pagan intellectual milieu with which Christian gnostics read the books of Hermes, both technical and philosophical' (1993: 114). It may be added that this is equally true of the Early Modern period once the Hermetic Corpus had become available in Latin translation.

---

[13] Although ἄνθρωπος is masculine only in grammatical gender, the disciple addressed is assumed to be male.

[14] CH XIII, 10; Schiavoni, 2018: 240. The 'decad' comprises the ten divine powers, which drive out the 'dodecad', or the twelve vices. On rebirth, Fowden comments that this 'is emphatically not a repetition of physical birth, but a bursting into a new plane of existence previously unattained, even unsuspected, albeit available potentially' (1993: 108).

KABBALAH

Before we turn to the Early Modern period, we need to look briefly at another esoteric tradition that fed into the Renaissance, that of the Kabbalah.[15] 'Kabbalah' is defined by Gershom Scholem as 'the traditional and most commonly used term for the esoteric teachings of Judaism and for Jewish mysticism, especially the forms which it assumed in the Middle Ages from the 12th century onward' (Scholem, 1988: 3). The relationship of Kabbalah to rabbinic Judaism in the twelfth century in some respects resembles that of the contemporary Franciscan Spirituals to the Catholic Church, neither movement breaking with the broader religious community but the former, with its Neoplatonic and gnostic orientation, and the latter, with its attraction to Joachimite ideas of a new age of the spirit, pushing against the authority of the rabbinate and the papacy, respectively. In point of fact, since its emergence in the second century AD, rabbinic Judaism has never been without its mystical side.[16] The rabbinic dialectical style of exposition, called out for a complementary emphasis on intense prayer and personal experience of God. The Merkavah mystic's ecstatic ascent to the throne-chariot of God of Rabbi Yohanan ben Zakkai's time did not dispense with the study of Torah, any more than the rabbi's status as an authoritative interpreter of the law precluded out-of-body experiences, as the story of Rabbi Ishmael's ascent to the seventh heaven in the *Third* or *Hebrew Book of Enoch* testifies. Jewish Neoplatonism (based on Plotinus and Proclus and influenced by the Islamic school of Neoplatonism) also contributed to the mystical tradition from its beginning in the ninth century. The ninth-century work known as *Ibn Chasdai's Neoplatonist* describes how the rational soul, if it is righteous, 'goes to the world of intellect and reaches the light which is created from the Power, its pure brilliance and unmixed splendour and perfect wisdom, from where it had been derived' (Rudavsky, 1997: 173). This Neoplatonic tradition supported the Kabbalah, Moses ben Simeon of Burgos representing this in a literal fashion at the end of the thirteenth century with his dictum: 'the mystic stands on the head of the philosopher' (Wolfson, 1997: 453). Kabbalah was not a phenomenon isolated

---

[15] My account of Kabbalah is based on Scholem, 1988, which although criticised for dichotomising 'the intellectual currents of mysticism and philosophy in too simplistic a fashion' (Wolfson, 1997: 452) is still the best detailed study.

[16] For an overview of the Jewish mystical tradition, see Wolfson, 1997.

from the rabbinate or from the philosophical tradition and quickly became integrated into Jewish spiritual life.

Kabbalah first emerged in Provence, principally under the influence of Isaac the Blind of Narbonne (d. c. 1235), 'the first kabbalist to devote his work entirely to mysticism' (Scholem, 1988: 45). By the mid-thirteenth century, Gerona, on the other side of the Pyrenees in Catalonia, had become an important centre of Kabbalah, largely through the work of Moses de Leon (d. 1305). It was at Gerona that the Zohar (the [Book of] Splendour) was produced, probably by Moses de Leon, with its teaching about the divine emanations known as the *sefirot*. Parts of this work were among the Hebrew sources that Pico della Mirandola had translated for him.

The Zohar, which was written between 1270 and 1300, contains a large number of independent sections. It is more like a collection of books than a single work, drawing as it does from a wide range of Hebrew writings, mainly the Babylonian Talmud and a variety of midrashim and targums, and interspersing this material with its own exegetical discussions.[17] Central to the Zohar is the theory of the *sefirot*. These are emanations from the hidden being of God that in the Neoplatonic manner relate divine unicity to created multiplicity. They are divine – 'He is They and They are He' (Zohar 3: 11b, 70a, cited by Scholem, 1988: 101) – identical with the essence of God and yet separate from him.[18] The *sefirot* emanate from *Ein-Sof* (the Emanator) 'as if one candle were lit from another without the Emanator being diminished in any way' (Scholem, 1988: 102). In the diagrams illustrating the first printed texts of the Kabbalah, the ten *sefirot* are grouped together in a 'tree', each *sefirah* connected vertically with the one directly above it and the one directly below it and also laterally with those to one side of it. In a later development, Moses Cordovero (1522–1570), whom Scholem calls 'the chief exponent of Kabbalah' and its 'main systematic theologian' (73) refined the structure of the *sefirot* still further, positing different elements, the *behinot*, within each *sefirah*, through which one *sefirah* is connected with the next. This seems to be inspired by the Neoplatonic doctrine of the henads that emanate from the One in linked series of causes and effects and revert again to the One through each henad participating in the one above it and being participated in turn by the one below. The Kabbalah

[17] The contents of the Zohar are listed by Scholem, 1988: 214–19.
[18] My summary makes the system sound tidier than it is. Scholem points out that, whereas the earlier kabbalists saw the *sefirot* as wholly identical with God's substance, later writers were more inclined to emphasise their separation from him (1988: 101–2).

uses the symbolism of reflected light to express such reversion: 'This reflected light can re-ascend from any *sefirah*, particularly the last one, back up to the first' (115). It can thus act as a ladder leading the contemplative soul back to its source, the Oneness from which it originated.

The soul in the Kabbalah, as in Greek thought, is tripartite. But whereas in Greek thought every soul has three 'parts', the appetitive, the incensive, and the rational, which mediate between the flesh and the mind, the three 'parts' in the Kabbalah are incremental, the second two being acquired additionally only by those souls that have grown in spiritual understanding. The fundamental 'part' is the *nefesh*, which is the vital principle in every human being. To this is added the *ru'ah* when a person has begun to apprehend spiritual realities. Finally, the *neshamah*, a divine spark that emanates from God, is also acquired by those who apply themselves devoutly to the study of the Torah and are thus rendered capable of entering into communion with God. The Kabbalah rarely speaks about *union* with God. Its preferred term is *devekut*, 'communion'. Scholem reports that 'Moses de Leon mentions a supreme but temporary condition in which the soul finds itself standing before God in a state of contemplation and ultimate bliss' (160) – a fleeting *ekstasis* – but only a few spiritual giants such as Enoch and Elijah have ever attained permanent communion.

Despite this clear distinction between God and the created soul, there are also pantheistic elements in the Zohar. Interestingly, as in the case of the Rhineland mystics, these are more often found in popular expositions of the Kabbalah than in the learned tracts. Yet the Zohar, too, can say that 'God "is everything" and that everything is unified in him, "as is known to the mystics"' (144). This is not to say that everything is God. It reflects, rather, the Neoplatonic principle that all things proceed from a single first cause, participate in it by virtue of their being caused by it, and find their fulfilment through returning to their original unity in it. The pantheistic elements of the more philosophical 'speculative Kabbalah' represented by the main parts of the Zohar were intensified in the 'practical Kabbalah', which had to do with the practice of magic through the esoteric manipulation of the divine Names. Both these versions of Kabbalah were to prove attractive to those Renaissance thinkers who were already enthusiastic students of Hermes Trismegistus.

CHRISTIAN HERMETISTS AND KABBALISTS

The intense interest in the Hermetic writings and the Kabbalah that began in the late fifteenth century was largely due to the fact that they were considered to be much more ancient than they really were. The Hermetic writings (until correctly dated by the great Hellenist, Isaac Casaubon, in 1614) were thought to have been contemporary with Moses, and thus to have preceded Plato. The Kabbalah was also regarded as contemporary with Moses and indeed as the secret spiritual teaching communicated by him to his inner circle of disciples. For their fifteenth-century Italian readers, these texts enshrined the *prisca sapientia*, the most ancient, and therefore the most profound, surviving wisdom relating to the divine. The study of Hermetic teaching by Western scholars, however, began earlier than the discovery of the Greek Hermetic Corpus and its translation by Marsilio Ficino. Like the renewed study of Dionysius the Areopagite, it goes back to the pivotal figure of Albert the Great.

In Albert's time (the mid-thirteenth century), the only Hermetic texts that were available in Latin were the *Asclepius* and a few associated works, including magic and astrological texts and the important compilation, the *Liber de XXIV philosophorum*. Albert makes use of these (Sturlese, 1980) but it is only in the following century, with Berthold of Moosburg (also a Dominican), that they contribute significantly to theological thought.[19] Berthold is a fascinating figure who only began to attract scholarly attention in the twentieth century after his *Expositio super Elementationem Theologicam Procli*, a massive commentary on Proclus's *Elements of Theology*, was discovered in the Vatican Library.[20] In the Byzantine East, Proclus was much read but usually treated with suspicion. The only comprehensive work in Greek on the *Elements of Theology* is a mid-twelfth-century refutation by Nicholas of Methone. Berthold has the distinction of being the only Western theologian to have written a step-by-step commentary on the *Elements*, which he treats as the work of 'the Euclid of theological wisdom'.[21] Among the main authorities he draws on for his commentary are the *Asclepius* and the *Liber de XXIV philosophorum*.

Like Lactantius, Berthold treats Hermes Trismegistus as a pagan prophet of the truth revealed in Christ. Hermes is therefore useful in validating the statements Berthold finds in Proclus that concur with Hermetic teaching (as most of them do, of course, because the thought-

---

[19] For a survey of Berthold's thinking, see de Libera, 1984: 317–442; on his use of the Latin Hermes, see Sannino, 2000 and 2003.

[20] A second copy was later discovered in the library of Balliol College, Oxford.

[21] Sannino, 2000: 243. The only Eastern commentary was composed in Georgian by the Neoplatonist, Joane Petrizi, in the twelfth century. In the mid-thirteenth century, Petrizi's commentary was translated into Armenian.

world in which both Proclus and the Hermetic authors were operating was Neoplatonic). On the topic of deification, however, Berthold encounters a difficulty. A notorious passage in the *Asclepius* (already denounced by Augustine in the *City of God*) describes how the statues in the Egyptian temples are endowed with divine life by rituals that draw down divine power into them (*Asclepius* 23–24; Schiavone, 2018: 334; Augustine, *City of God* VIII, 23–24). As a result, man is a maker of gods (*homo fictor est deorum*) and illuminates the divine as well as being illuminated by it. Some authors tried to give a symbolic meaning to this,[22] but Berthold roundly condemns it. Although normally most reliable, he says, Hermes slips up badly here (*prudentissimus vir in multis sapiens sed in hoc desipiens supra modum*).[23] Only the First Cause can make gods. As Proclus taught, the divine character is acquired progressively through participation in higher levels of being (*Elements of Theology*, prop. 129 [ed. Dodds, 1963: 114)]). Such participation makes matter the 'receptacle' (*receptaculum*) of the divine. For Berthold, the Neoplatonic metaphysics of unity through participation, a metaphysics that makes the attaining of divinity by created being conceivable, receives its imprimatur from the Hermetic writings, judiciously interpreted.

The retrieval of Hermetism during the Renaissance was based on a much broader range of Hermetic texts than those available to Berthold. The key figures in this retrieval are Marsilio Ficino and Giovanni Pico della Mirandola, both of them members of Cosimo de' Medici's Florentine Platonic Academy. It is through them that a great interest in natural magic developed in the fifteenth century. What made this possible was the much more positive view taken of the *Asclepius* in the light of the Greek Hermetic material translated by Ficino.[24] This material enabled the magical drawing down of divine power in the *Asclepius*, too, to be seen as the beneficent work of the great pagan prophet of the Son of God.[25] The Christian Magus was one who, in turn, drew down the divine powers in

---

[22] For example, Thomas Bradwardine (c. 1295–1349), who died as archbishop of Canterbury.

[23] Berthold, *Propositio* 115B, cited by Sannino, 2000: 250. Berthold is commenting on Proclus, *Elements of Theology*, prop. 115 (Dodds, 1963: 100–102).

[24] According to Frances Yates, 'The rehabilitation of the *Asclepius* through the discovery of the *Corpus Hermeticum* is one of the chief factors in the Renaissance revival of magic' (2002: 43).

[25] Yates points out that the commentary on the *Asclepius* in Ficino's collected works with its 'strong disapproval of the "god-making" passage' is not in fact by Ficino but by the French Hermetist Lefèvre d'Etaples (2002: 42).

order to transform the material world and regenerate it in Christ. Music was part of this. Ficino himself (a Catholic priest) is known to have sung Orphic songs, accompanying himself on a lyre. 'To complete our view of Ficino's natural magic', says Frances Yates, 'we thus have to think of him drawing down the stellar influences by musical incantations as well as by sympathetic arrangement of natural objects, talismans, exposing oneself to the air, and so on, for the *spiritus* is caught by planetary songs as well as in the other ways described' (2002: 85). Everything in the universe belonged to a complex interrelated system endowed with soul. 'The magician was one who knew how to enter into this system, and use it, by knowing the links of the chains of influences descending vertically from above, and establishing for himself a chain of ascending links by correct use of the occult sympathies in terrestrial things, of celestial images, of invocations and names, and the like' (48). By harnessing these divine forces, the Magus himself could rise up through the chain of ascending links to the One who is the All.

Pico combined Ficino's Hermetism with the Kabbalism he had been studying with Samuel ben Nissim Abul Farag (Flavius Mithridates), integrating them with the angelic hierarchies of Dionysius the Areopagite. The result was a complex religious system, a *prisca theologia*, that Pico (taking for granted the supposed great antiquity of his sources) believed represented the original unity of all true religion. He was so excited by this that in 1486 he went to Rome armed with nine hundred theses, his *Conclusiones*, which were meant to prove the truth of his convictions before the Church's highest authorities. While he was in Rome, he gave his famous *Oration on the Dignity of Man*, in which he emphasises that 'man is a great miracle ... for he passes into the nature of God as if he himself were a god' (*hoc enim in naturam dei transit, quasi ipse sit deus*), quoting not a father or doctor of the Church but Hermes Trismegistus.[26] Not everyone was impressed by this. Indeed, Pico came very near to being indicted for heresy during his time in Rome and was only saved by the accession in 1492 of the Borgia Pope, Alexander VI, who was himself fascinated by Hermetism.[27] This period marks the high point of Hermetic influence in official Church circles. In the next century, the tide was to turn against the Magi, driving Hermetism underground.

---

[26] Cited by Yates, 2002: 119. The quotation is from *Asclepius* 6 (Schiavoni, 2018: 298).
[27] Hence the cycle of 'Egyptian' frescoes that Alexander VI commissioned from Pinturicchio for the Appartamento Borgia.

The dreams of Ficino and Pico of a reform of Catholicism through Hermetism were taken up in the sixteenth century by Francesco Patrizi (1529–1597), Giordano Bruno (1548–1600), and Tommaso Campanella (1568–1639).[28] All three hoped for an end to the murderous religious wars of their time and the unification of Catholics, Protestants, and even Muslims through a return to the *prisca theologia* with its perennial and universally valid philosophy. Patrizi wanted Hermes Trismegistus taught in the universities instead of Aristotle. Bruno was even more radical, wanting to replace Christianity with the 'Egyptian' religion of Hermes – and being burnt at the stake in the Campo di Fiori in Rome on refusing to recant. Campanella wanted to see a harmonious world state established with a priesthood of Catholic Magi administering a religion in accord with modern Copernican science and therefore with natural magic. And all three saw the world as a living organism held together by occult sympathies through the manipulation of which modern Hermetists could imitate their ancient counterparts and ascend to union with the divine:

For as the divinity descends in a certain manner inasmuch as it communicates itself to nature, so there is an ascent made to the divinity through nature. Thus through the light which shines in natural things one mounts up to the life which presides over them . . .. Whence with magical and divine rites they ascended to the height of the divinity by that same scale of nature by which the divinity descends to the smallest things by the communication of itself.[29]

For the Hermetists, this is more than a simple ascent. Just as lead can be transmuted into silver and thence into gold, so too the Magus can become divine through an ontological transformation of his being.

It is only now in the sixteenth century that we can speak of 'esotericism'. The term itself dates from the early nineteenth century,[30] but the major elements were already in place by the end of the Renaissance. These are listed by Antoine Faivre, the leading scholar on esoteric spirituality, as the following (1998: 119–20): (1) a conviction of the interconnectedness of the entire universe, with a correspondence between the exterior world and the interior world of the human person; (2) an understanding of the natural world as a single living being held together by a network of sympathies and antipathies; (3) an emphasis on the imagination as a faculty of the soul that gives access to different levels

---

[28] On Patrizi, see Leijenhorst, 1998. On Bruno, the classic study is Yates, 2002; Campanella is discussed on pp. 394–432.

[29] Giordano Bruno, *Spaccio della bestia trionfante*, dial. 3, trans. Yates, 2002: 233.

[30] First used by Jacques Matter in 1828, as noted by Laurant, 1992: 19, 42.

of reality and functions through the mediation of 'rituals, symbolic images, numbers, mandalas, intermediate spirits, and the like' (119); (4) the experience through the acquisition of gnosis of a 'second birth', a transformed state of being in which the illuminated person 'participates in the process by which the universe is born and moves towards its fulfillment' (120); (5) the praxis of concordance, which is the search for the common element in the traditions of wisdom of different cultures, the central feature of the *philosophia perennis*; and (6) the necessity of a spiritual guide because 'a person cannot arbitrarily choose to initiate him/herself but must pass through the regular channel of an authorized initiator' (120). The first four of these elements are described by Faivre as 'fundamental' and the last two as 'relative'. Perennialism and spiritual discipleship are not always found in the European esoteric traditions, but the correspondence of the exterior and interior worlds, the living unity of the whole of nature, the mediatory function of the imagination, and the experience of transformation or divinisation are core ideas that they all share.

ESOTERICISM AND THE BEGINNING OF THE THEOSOPHICAL MOVEMENT

Early in the seventeenth century, the centre of gravity moves from Italy to Germany. A notable event marking this transition is the publication in 1614 of the manifesto of a group calling itself the Fraternity of the Rosy Cross under the ambitious title Allgemeine und General Reformation der gantzen weiten Welt (Universally Applicable and General Reformation of the Whole Wide World).[31] The fraternity was supposed to have been founded by one Christian Rosencreutz, who had travelled widely and studied alchemy, magia, and the Kabbalah. Borrowing ideas from Giordano Bruno and other Hermetists, the Rosicrucians sought to establish a universal religion that would overcome the hatred of the religious and dynastic wars that had convulsed Europe in the sixteenth century and were about to enter an even more catastrophic phase with the Thirty Years War (1618–1648). Also important were the publications of Paracelsus, the pseudonym of Theophrastus von Hochenheim (1493–1541), a remarkable physician whose ideas anticipate many of

---

[31] On the Rosicrucians, see Yates, 2002: 443–51.

those of modern holistic medicine. But most influential of all were the writings of Jakob Boehme (1575–1624), the true founding father of the modern theosophical movement.

Boehme was a native of Görlitz, a largely Protestant town in Saxony lying today on the border with Poland. He was not a university man but earned his living as a cobbler. Yet despite his lack of a formal education, his voluminous writings, 'based in a fusion of alchemical, Paracelsian, and Hermetic expressions and concepts with what we may call High German mysticism' have been hailed as 'a uniquely modern revelation of virtually inexhaustible depth and range' (Versluis, 1998: 219). His house became a centre for people with esoteric interests, which aroused the ire of the local Lutheran pastor but did not prevent the circulation of his writings in manuscript form. Many of these were only published after his death, including the nine treatises assembled under the title *The Way to Christ*, which aroused immense interest and were translated into English as early as 1648.[32]

It is in *The Way of Christ* that we encounter, for the first time since the Christian Gnostic texts of the second and third centuries, the figure of Sophia. Virgin Sophia has many facets: she is the humanity of Christ, yet she is also the bride of Christ; she crowns the soul after its judgement, yet she is also the soul's spouse. Boehme's discussion of her is reminiscent of the *Brautmystik*, the bridal mystical language, of Bernard of Clairvaux and thirteenth-century Flemish mystics such as Hadewijch of Antwerp. There are substantial differences, however, due perhaps to a reaction against the austere masculinity of orthodox Lutheranism. In Boehme it is not the feminine soul that seeks union with the male Christ but the male believer (even if in German, as in Latin, the soul is feminine) who seeks union with the feminine element in the divine. Boehme addresses the soul in the following terms:

Dear soul, you must always be in earnest, without relenting. You will obtain the love of a kiss from the noble Sophia in the holy Name JESUS for She stands immediately before the soul's door and knocks and warns the sinner of [his] godless ways. If he desires Her love She is willing and kisses him with a beam of Her sweet love, by which the heart receives joy. But she does not immediately enter the marriage bed with the soul, that is, She does not immediately awaken the corrupted heavenly image that was lost in Paradise in it [the soul]. (*The Way to Christ* I, 33; trans. Erb, 1978: 43–44)

---

[32] Translated by John Sparrow (1615–1670), a barrister of the Inner Temple, who with his cousin, John Elliston, went on to translate all of Boehme's works.

And a little later, Sophia addresses the soul:

My noble bridegroom, be comforted. I have engaged myself to you in my highest love, and in my faith [have I] bound myself to you. I shall be with you in all the days to the end of the world. I shall come to you and make my dwelling in you in your eternal choir. You will drink from my fountain, for I am now yours and you are mine, and the enemy shall no longer separate us. Work in your fiery characteristic [and] I shall give you my love-beams in your activities. We wish to build Christ's vineyard. You give the essence of fire; I shall give the essence of light and growth. You be fire; I shall be water. We shall bring about in this world what God has foreordained us [to do]; we shall serve Him in His temple which we ourselves are. (*The Way to Christ* I, 51; trans. Erb, 1978: 62)

Heaven is within the believer. Union with the divine is described, in erotically charged imagery, as taking place when the heavenly image lost by the fall is restored by the kiss of Sophia, who 'kisses [the soul] completely inwardly with her sweet love and presses love into its desire as a sign of victory' (*The Way to Christ* I, 38; trans. Erb, 1978: 45). This is the spiritual rebirth, the *Wiedergeburt*, that lies at the heart of Boehme's teaching. Elsewhere, Boehme speaks of this as the third birth (after physical birth into fleshly life and astral birth through spiritual struggle) in which, without leaving the flesh, the believer 'must strive with his soul to "press through the firmament of heaven to God, and *live* with God." In this way, then, one must unite all three realms – body, soul, and spirit – in this lifetime, pressing beyond the astral to the transcendent spirit' (Versluis, 1998: 219, citing Boehme's *Aurora*). In the second passage from *The Way to Christ* quoted above, the union of fire and water resonates with Nicholas of Cusa's coincidence of opposites. But Boehme is not a theorist of the mystical life. His entire emphasis is on direct spiritual experience, and the fervour of his evocations of such experience was to make his writings enormously influential.

Boehme's influence was particularly strong in the Protestant world of north-western Europe and the American colonies. In England, his chief exponent was John Pordage (1608–1681), the founder of the Philadelphian Society, who wrote a treatise on Virgin Sophia in which he insists that union with Sophia is attained not through ascending to the celestial realm but 'through descending and sinking into one's own inward ground'.[33] Pordage encountered much hostility in England from

---

[33] From John Pordage, *Sophia: The Graceful Eternal Virgin of Holy Wisdom, or Wonderful Spiritual Discoveries and Revelations that the Precious Wisdom has Given to a Holy Soul* (London, 1675), cited by Versluis, 1998: 222.

the Anglican establishment. He found it difficult to publish his writings but many of them were soon translated into German and became popular with German readers. German spiritual writers deeply influenced by Boehme include Johann Georg Gichtel (1638–1710), who lived most of his life in Amsterdam and founded a lay community known as the Angelic Brethren; Gottfried Arnold (1666–1714), who published a scholarly treatise entitled *The Mystery of Holy Sophia*; and Angelus Silesius, the pseudonym of Johann Scheffler (1624–1677), whose epigrammatic *Cherubinic Wanderer* has attracted serious attention from modern philosophers such as Martin Heidegger and Jacques Lacan.[34] The reception of Boehme's influence further east, however, had to await the Russian Religious Renaissance of the late nineteenth and early twentieth centuries. When Quirinius Kuhlmann (1651–1689), a member of Gichtel's Angelic Brethren, tried to propagate Boehmenist ideas in Moscow in the 1680s, he was burnt at the stake for his pains.

THE THEOSOPHICAL MOVEMENT IN THE LATE NINETEENTH AND EARLY TWENTIETH CENTURIES

In the late nineteenth century, the esoteric movement gained strength, partly as an alternative to the Victorian era's scientific positivism and dogmatic materialism.[35] There is a break, however, with the earlier tradition. The second half of the nineteenth century saw the rapid colonial expansion of the Western powers in Africa and the Far East. For the first time, Western spiritual seekers encountered the traditions of India and Tibet. One of the most influential of these seekers was Helena Petrovna Blavatsky (1831–1891).

Helena Blavatsky (Madame Blavatsky, as she was generally known) was born to an aristocratic German family in the Russian imperial service, the von Hahns. At a very early age (just before her seventeenth birthday) she was married to a much older man, Nikifor Vassilievich Blavatsky,

---

[34] On Angelus Silesius and his influence on Heidegger and Lacan, see Gale, 2020. Gale cites Heidegger's quotation of Silesius in his *Der Satz vom Grund* 'in relation to the notion of the foundational, primal ground (*Ur-grund*) or underlying ground (*zu-grunde liegend*) of being' and Lacan's description of the *Cherubinic Wanderer* in *The Seminar of Jacques Lacan, Book I* as 'one of the most significant moments in human meditation on being, a moment richer in resonances for me than the *Dark Night* of St John of the Cross, which everyone reads and no one understands'.

[35] Spiritualism also became very popular at this time for the same reason. For an introduction to this counter-culture, see Van Egmond, 1998.

vice-governor of Erivan in Armenia. The marriage failed within three months; but instead of returning to her father near St Petersburg, as arranged by her maternal grandparents living in nearby Georgia (her grandmother was a Princess Dolgoruki), she took a boat to Constantinople and began a ten-year period of wandering around the globe. A chance meeting in London with a member of the Nepalese delegation to the Great Exhibition of 1851 led to her visiting Tibet, which she claimed marked the beginning of her initiation into Buddhist mystical teaching. In 1873, she arrived in New York, where she met a lawyer and journalist with a strong interest in spiritualism called Henry Steel Olcott (1832–1907), and two years later founded with him the Theosophical Society. Convinced that although all religions contained a common basis of truth, the traditions of Indian spirituality were superior to all others, she moved to India, and soon afterwards, in 1882, the Theosophical Society moved its headquarters to Adyar, near Madras (today Chennai) in India. There she came under a cloud after accusations were made of charlatanism,[36] was expelled from the Theosophical Society, and ended her days in London living in the house of another famous theosophist, Annie Besant (1847–1933). She wrote a number of books, the best known of which are *Isis Unveiled* (1875) and *The Secret Doctrine* (1888). The first of these vast works is a comprehensive, if unsystematic, history of the occult, the second an esoteric account of the generation of the cosmos and the races of humanity. Both are extraordinary tours de force, an amalgamation of ancient gnosis with Kabbalah, Hermetism, the Upanishads, and the teachings of Mahayana Buddhism, to name only a few of the traditions that Blavatsky draws upon. Among the fundamental ideas that emerge is the conviction that everything in the universe is conscious – there is no such thing as dead matter – and that human beings, whose higher selves alone are divine and god, become co-workers with nature in the cyclic task of evolution towards divinity.

Madame Blavatsky's relevance to a discussion of the place of theosis in the Christian tradition, however, rests not only on her writings but also on the influence she exerted on her disciples and successors. This remarkable woman, despite recurring accusations of charlatanism, attracted gifted followers. Some of them, like the artist George Frederic Watts

---

[36] By Richard Hodgson, who was sent to India by the London-based Society for Psychical Research to investigate the claims coming from Adyar and published his findings in the *Proceedings of the Society for Psychical Research* 3 (1885), pp. 207–380. The accusations were retracted by the Society in 1986.

(1817–1904) and the poets William Butler Yeats (1865–1939) and George William Russell (1865–1935) found in Blavatsky something that resonated strongly with ideas they already held about the inability of either dogmatic materialism or conventional Western religion to account for the richness of the interior life. Watts first discovered theosophy on his return to London in 1887 from his honeymoon in Egypt with his second wife, Mary.[37] Madame Blavatsky had only just moved to London but was already attracting interest. Watts never became a fully committed theosophist, but according to Mary Watts he found Blavatsky's ideas 'far more Christian than many'.[38] His core conviction was that the world is not something inert and exterior to ourselves but that it is in fact created by human consciousness. It is the defining of the world by the mind that gives it meaning. This relationship between the inner and the outer worlds was also a central concern for Yeats and Russell.

W. B. Yeats and George Russell were friends from their student years at the Dublin Metropolitan School of Art. Yeats, of course, is celebrated as one of the greatest poets of the twentieth century – he won the Nobel Prize in Literature in 1923 – but Russell was also a major figure in the Irish Literary Revival of the late nineteenth and early twentieth centuries.[39] Yeats moved to London in 1887, the same year as Madame Blavatsky. By 1888, he was a regular member of her circle in Holland Park and, in December 1889 (having previously joined the Theosophical Society in Adyar), was admitted to the Esoteric Section of the Theosophical Society in England. He had already encountered theosophy through A. P. Sinnet's *Esoteric Buddhism*, an influential work first published five years earlier, which purports to present the teaching of two Indian spiritual adepts but in fact is a distillation of the thinking of Madame Blavatsky. On his return to Dublin, Yeats gave a copy to Russell, who was thus also introduced to theosophy. The two friends found it a convincing systematisation of intuitions that they both shared and were to maintain throughout their lives.

Chief among Russell's convictions was that we are gods in exile. 'The gods are still living', he says, 'They are our brothers. They await us. They beckon us to come up and sit upon equal thrones' (Æ, 1990: 84). Clement of Alexandria had said something similar, but in his case the gods were

---

[37] On Watts's relationship to theosophy, see Stewart, 1993.
[38] From Mary Watts's diary entry for 13 July 1890, quoted by Stewart, 1993: 300.
[39] A cousin of my paternal grandfather, he wrote under the pseudonym Æ.

the saints;[40] in Russell's, they are the ancient Celtic deities. Some of his statements, however, are perfectly consonant with Christian orthodoxy. For example: 'If in the being of the Ancient of Days there is power, as there is wisdom and beauty, we must liken ourselves to that being, partake, as our nature will permit, of its power, or we can never enter it. The Kingdom is taken by violence' (80). This is not very different from the participation in the divine attributes, or divine energies, in accordance with our capacities and through ascetic discipline, that is taught by the later Greek tradition on deification. Yet Russell was also a believer in multiple reincarnations of the human soul: 'From long pondering I have come to believe in the eternity of the spirit and that it is an inhabitant of many spheres, for I know not how otherwise I can interpret to myself the myriad images that as memories or imagination cling to it' (85). What has priority is personal experience. It is this that also convinces him of the truth of the 'perennial philosophy' of the writers of the ancient sacred books, 'whether Syrian, Greek, Egyptian or Hindu', who 'had all gazed upon the same august vision and reported of the same divinity' (Æ, 1990: 87).

Blavatsky's ideas, although treated with great deference in the British Isles, did not obtain the same hold on the continent of Europe. This was largely because Blavatsky's Austrian disciple, Rudolf Steiner (1861–1925), broke away from her movement in 1913 and founded his own variation of theosophy, which he called anthroposophy. Steiner was much more of a philosopher than Blavatsky – his *Philosophy of Freedom* (1894) is still respected – but his fundamental ideas concerning karma and multiple reincarnations seem to owe much to hers. Where he does differ significantly from her is in the central role he gives to 'the Christ event', as 'the single most significant event in human history' that 'made it possible for humanity as a whole to achieve a new participation in spiritual worlds' (Lachman, 2007: 130–31). In keeping with this conviction, Steiner regards the Indian tradition, although very interesting, as specific to its own culture. Despite his commitment to the Indian notions of karma and reincarnation, he prefers, by his own account, to be guided by Eckhart, Boehme, Paracelsus, and Giordano Bruno. Yet his teaching differs from theirs, too. As a thinker in the German idealist tradition, he held that matter was produced by consciousness, not the other way round. Consciousness is not passive, for the content of reality is the reflection of our own minds. He therefore saw anthroposophy as

---

[40] Clement of Alexandria, *Stromateis* VII, 56, 3–6; cf. Russell, 2004: 133.

correcting and completing the one-sided materialism of his age. This element of philosophical idealism is combined with a grand cosmological theory that sees the whole universe in evolutionary terms as descending into increasing materiality until it reaches its lowest point and then, after the decisive 'Christ event', ascending in decreasing materiality to union with its spiritual origin. Human beings through their successive reincarnations have participated in this process from the beginning. Their deification (although Steiner does not use the term) consists in their return after many lives to their source.

THE IMPACT OF ESOTERICISM ON MAINSTREAM CHRISTIAN THINKING ON THEOSIS

The esoteric traditions have had a greater influence on Christian thinking than is often admitted. In the early centuries of the Church, there is a firm tradition of hidden knowledge handed down by Christ, which is not to be revealed to the uninitiated. This tradition was appropriated with particular enthusiasm by groups that were branded by ecclesial Christians as heretical gnostics and therefore eventually disappeared.[41] Its heyday was in the second century, when it was combatted fiercely by Irenaeus of Lyon and Hippolytus of Rome. Clement of Alexandria, however, was less hostile to it. He studied it sympathetically – we have a collection of notes he made on the work of the Gnostic, Theodotus – and it has left its mark on his teaching on theosis.

Clement believed that there was an authentic gnosis accessible to the advanced Christian. At the beginning of the Renaissance, with the discovery of the Hermetic Corpus and its translation into Latin, the same conviction resurfaced. This was because Hermes Trismegistus was believed to have preceded Christ and indeed to have been a contemporary of Moses. As a pagan prophet of Christianity, he merited theological respect. For a while he was influential in high Church circles. Upon the Reformation and the outbreak of the wars of religion, his devotees thought that he could unify the warring factions under a common interpretation of Christianity, or in the case of Giordano Bruno, a new religion. But the attitudes of Rome and the Reformers hardened against those they saw as magicians and heretics. Esotericism went underground.

---

[41] There is a fascinating collection of essays by Guy G. Stroumsa on this topic: Stroumsa, 1996.

It resurfaced again in Russia in the eighteenth century. Jakob Boehme was widely read in Russia from the time of Peter the Great (Zdenk, 1962; O. Smith, 2014). In the next century, Helena Petrovna Blavatsky attracted a great deal of interest, particularly in view of her Russian origin. Mikhail Nikiforovich Katkov (1818–1887), a leading journalist and literary editor, who first published Turgenev's *Fathers and Sons*, Tolstoy's *Anna Karenina*, and Dostoevsky's *Crime and Punishment* in his journal *Ruskii Vestnik (Russian Messenger)*, gave Blavatsky an important platform, publishing two articles by her in his newspaper *Moskovskie Vedomosti (Moscow News)*. When her *Secret Doctrine* was issued in French in 1904, it circulated widely in Russia, especially in artistic and literary circles. During Russia's brilliant Silver Age (the decade or so before the First World War), Rudolf Steiner (whose second wife, Marie von Sivers, was Russian) also enjoyed considerable influence. His intuition that Russia, as the meeting-place of Eastern and Western cultures, had a global role to play resonated profoundly with Slavophile ideas concerning Russia's messianic destiny. Leading figures on the Russian cultural scene, such as the symbolist poets Maksimilian Voloshin (1877–1932) and Andrei Bely (1880–1934), the composer Aleksandr Scriabin (1871–1915), and the painter Wassily Kandinsky (1866–1944) were all immersed in Steiner's anthroposophy. Among theologians, Vladimir Soloviev (1853–1900), Pavel Florensky (1882–1937), and Sergius Bulgakov (1871–1944) also read Steiner with respect and were sympathetic to some of his ideas. It was precisely these theologians who were to develop the Russian Silver-Age version of theosis.

In Greece, theosophy began to be taken up towards the end of the nineteenth century (Ferentinou, 2016). The first theosophical lodge, 'The Ionian Theosophical Society', was founded in 1876, significantly in Corfu, which had never been part of the Ottoman Empire and was more Western-oriented than the rest of Greece. A decade later, articles on theosophy began to appear in Athenian newspapers. The name most closely associated with the spread of theosophical ideas is that of Platon Drakoulis (1858–1934), who also belonged to the London Theosophical Society. His book *Light from Within* (Φῶς ἐκ τῶν Ἐνδῶν, 1894) became the standard work in Greece on theosophy. As in Russia, it was principally artists, poets, and journalists who tended to be attracted by the new syncretistic spirituality. The work of the artist Frixos Aristeus (1879–1951) and the poets Kostis Palamas (1859–1943) and Angelos Sikelianos (1884–1951) is deeply imbued with theosophy, as is also that of the novelist Nikos Kazantzakis (1883–1957), the creator of Zorba the

Greek. Besides its relevance to the private spiritual outlook of individuals, theosophy in Greece, as in Russia, also had a broader cultural and political dimension. On the one hand, it emphasised Greece's continuity with the religious culture of ancient Greece (an important nation-building concern in the early twentieth century); on the other, it universalised modern Hellenism as something of interest and of value to the whole world. The ecclesiastical establishment was very hostile to theosophy but, through the poets and intellectuals of the last century, theosophy did contribute, as in Russia, to the cultural climate that facilitated the flowering of modern Greek thinking on theosis in the latter half of the century.

An interesting figure bridging Greece's literary and theological cultures in this period is Philip Sherrard (1922–1995). As a young British officer in Athens in 1946 he came across the poetry of George Seferis (1900–1971), which fired him with a vision of the unity of the temporal and the transcendent, the natural and the supernatural, as a quintessential part of Greek experience down through the centuries. He made Greece his home and joined the Orthodox Church in 1956. He wrote a number of books on Modern Greek poetry, admiring the way both Kostis Palamas and Sikelianos brought together the world of the spirit and the natural world – 'everything that lives is holy', he said, silently quoting William Blake. He also wrote books on theological topics, many of which were translated into Greek, but his influence on Greek theology has been marginal. This was mainly because of the perennialist cast of his thinking. Although he was profoundly Orthodox and a frequent pilgrim to Mount Athos, he did not believe that any one tradition had an exclusive hold on the truth but was convinced that a universal wisdom underlay all sacred traditions. One of the things for which he is best known is his project, together with Metropolitan Kallistos (Ware) and Gerald Palmer, of translating the Greek *Philokalia* into English. I knew Philip Sherrard and had collaborated with him on his translations for a number of years before the *Philokalia*. It is characteristic of his unfanatical spirit that it was he who brought me on to the *Philokalia* project as an initial translator even before I became Orthodox. The publishing success of the *Philokalia* in English has been a further step in disseminating more widely what Fr Andrew Louth has called a 'philokalic tenor of theology', a theology that 'initiates us into a participation in the divine life, the divine energies, by ... a process of purification, illumination, and perfection' (2012: 59).

To return from perennialism to theosophy in the narrow sense, in the West the latter has been treated with contempt by most intellectuals but not all. Jung, for example, whose interest in the esoteric led to part of Nag Hammadi I being named 'the Jung Codex',[42] has said that the hostile critics of theosophy 'overlook the fact that such movements derive their force from the fascination of the psyche, and that it will express itself in these forms until they are replaced by something better' (Jung, 1964: 187; cited by Tacey, 2004: 69). That replacement by something better is taking place in contemporary popular spirituality – 'New Age' spirituality – by the appropriation of a version of theosis from the esoteric traditions, or from modern Orthodox texts related to them such as the *Philokalia* and the Russian *Way of a Pilgrim*. 'In the future', a modern psychologist has said, 'theology will need to develop into *theopoiēsis*, that is, a recognition of the living God and the mystery of the spirit at the very core of our universe' (Tacey, 2004: 165). Academic theologians need to take note.

---

[42] Forty leaves of Nag Hammadi I, containing, among other treatises, *The Gospel of Truth*, were exported illegally from Egypt and acquired in 1952 by the Jung Institute of Zürich, which named them 'the Jung Codex' (a naming which Jung himself is known to have resisted). The leaves were returned to Egypt, to the Coptic Museum in Cairo where the rest of the Nag Hammadi Codices are kept, in 1975.

5

'People Will Be Gods'

Russian Versions of Theosis

In 1905, the Russian religious thinker Nicolas Berdyaev (1874–1948) published an article in one of the leading journals of the time, *Voprosy zhizni* (Questions of Life),[1] entitled 'The New Religious Consciousness'.[2] The article celebrates the new developments in Russia's religious experience that were discernible in the last decades of the 'long' nineteenth century – Russia's Silver Age – and were to be accelerated by the revolution of 1905. Commenting on the 'new religious consciousness' promoted by the founders of the Symbolist Movement, Dmitry Merezhkovsky (1866–1941) and his wife Zinaida Gippius (1869–1945),[3] Berdyaev presents the core of the Merezhkovsky's version as the union of opposites, the union of spirit and flesh, with the attempt to create a non-ascetical spiritualism that does not kill the flesh but unites heaven with 'moist mother-earth'. According to the Merezhkovskys, sexual energy (the religion of Dionysus) must be united with the spirit (the religion of the incarnate suffering God) if the union of heaven and earth is to be accomplished. The Merezhkovskys set up a 'new Church of the Holy Spirit' to embody their ideas of adjusting a reformed, de-monasticised Orthodoxy to the spiritual needs of the Russian intelligentsia. Berdyaev is sympathetic but critical: 'What needs grounding is not spirit or flesh', he says, 'but

---

[1] *Voprosy zhizni* has been described by Catherine Evtuhov as 'one of the most significant publications of the Silver Age' (Evtuhov, 1997: 117). Founded by Dmitry Merezhkovsky, it was originally called *Novyi put* (The New Way) but in 1905 was relaunched as *Vosprosy zhizni* under new editors, Sergius Bulgakov and Berdyaev himself.

[2] N. A. Berdiaev, 'Novoe religioznoe soznanie'; Eng. trans. by Boris Jakim in Berdyaev, 2015: 7–45.

[3] On the Merezhovskys' religious and political programme, see Coates, 2019: 82–109.

personhood in the fullness and specificity of its being, transcendent indi-
viduality which is both "incarnate spirit" and "spiritual flesh"' (Berdyaev,
2015: 26, emphasis orginal). For what our religious striving is fundamentally concerned with is victory over death – the overcoming of the horror
of non-being – which can only be attained through the union of the whole
person with God (15–16).

The Merzhekovskys' 'new religious consciousness', a movement within
what has been called the 'Russian Religious Renaissance',[4] did not of
course come out of nowhere. The yearning to unite the human with the
divine, to divinise the human, is a notable feature of the Greek philokalic
spirituality that entered Russia in the late eighteenth century, in Church
Slavonic dress, as the *Dobrotoliubie* of St Paisii Velichkovsky
(1722–1794).[5] Paisii's compilation of patristic texts attained a broad
readership in the last decades of the nineteenth century when it was
translated into Russian and augmented by Bishop Theophan the
Recluse (1815–1894).[6] The same yearning as that of the *Philokalia*
received philosophical expression in the idea of Godmanhood developed
by Vladimir Soloviev (1853–1900). On a more popular level, it was
central to the esoteric writings that were widely read in the same period.
Finally, it was the subject of authoritative academic treatment in a set of
influential essays on deification in the patristic tradition published by Ivan
Popov (1867–1938) from 1903 to 1909. We need to consider each of
these different strands that contributed to the Russian understanding of
deification before we examine the major philosophical/theological expositions of the theme in Florensky, Bulgakov, and Berdyaev.

PHILOKALIC SPIRITUALITY

The Philokalia of the Neptic Fathers, compiled by St Nikodemos of the
Holy Mountain under the direction of St Makarios of Corinth and

---

[4] The origin of the phrase 'Russian Religious Renaissance' is attributed to Nicolas Zernov
(1898–1980), himself a participant in it, who published an influential book under that title
in 1963. Berdyaev had already spoken of 'the Russian renaissance' but it was more a
cultural renaissance that he had in mind.

[5] The Slavonic version of the *Philokalia* (the *Dobrotoliubie*) was first published in Moscow
in 1793. For more details, see Tachiaos, 1995: 240–41; Louth, 2012: 53.

[6] For a brief overview of Russian religious developments in the nineteenth century, see
Russell, 2017a: 540–48, and for more detailed discussions, Emerson, Pattison, and Poole,
2020: Part II, The Nineteenth Century, and Part III, The Religious-Philosophical
Renaissance, 1900–1922.

published by them in Venice in 1782, is a collection of Greek patristic
writings from the fourth to the fifteenth century that was designed to
deepen the spiritual life of both monastics and laypeople in an era of
social and intellectual ferment among the Greeks of the Ottoman Empire
when increasing emphasis was being placed on the responsibility of the
individual for his or her own inner life.[7] In his preface to the work,
Nikodemos makes it very clear that the fundamental purpose of this
collection of texts is to bring out the importance of deification in God's
preordained plan for humanity.[8] As Metropolitan Kallistos Ware has
said, 'the ideal of *theosis* is the most decisive of all the connecting threads
that bind the *Philokalia* into a unity' (Ware, 2012: 31). Yet the densely
printed folio volume that issued from the press of Antonio Bortoli in
Venice had little impact in the Greek-speaking world until very much
later. The importance of the *Philokalia* in the nineteenth century derives
chiefly from the Slavonic version of St Paisii Velichkovsky.

Paisii's work, the *Dobrotoliubie*, is not in fact a translation of the
Greek *Philokalia* but a parallel work with the same title (*dobrotoliubie*
being a Slavonic calque on the Greek word *philokalia*, 'love of beauty'),
which circulated in manuscript for many years until it was printed in
Moscow in 1793 (eleven years after the Greek *Philokalia*) at the instigation of Gabriel, Metropolitan of Novgorod and St Petersburg.[9] Both
Nikodemos and Paisii seem to have drawn independently on the same
philokalic collections that already existed in manuscripts on Mount
Athos.[10] Four-fifths of the contents of the two compilations are in fact
the same. The material that appears in Nikodemos, however, but not in
Paisii is telling. It consists mainly of texts by St Macarius the Great,
St Maximus the Confessor, and St Gregory Palamas – precisely the texts
in the Greek *Philokalia* that are richest in teaching on deification. Paisii
owned a copy of the Greek *Philokalia*,[11] but he did not choose to add
Nikodemos's material from Macarius, Maximus, or Gregory to his own
collection. As Andrew Louth has noted, Paisii's version 'is more

---

[7] The *Philokalia* project is of a piece with Nikodemos's adaptations of contemporary
Western spiritual manuals, on which see Russell, 2017b.

[8] For an English translation of the preface (omitted from the translation of the Greek *Philokalia*
by Palmer, Sherrard, and Ware), see Cavarnos, 2008. Gavrilyuk, 2022, points out that
Nikodemos uses the Greek terms for deification twenty times in a dozen pages.

[9] For accounts of the relationship between the *Philokalia* and the *Dobrotoliubie*, see Ware,
2012: 19–25; Louth 2012: 52–55; and especially, Louth, 2018.

[10] Paisii was on the Holy Mountain from 1746 to 1763. Nikodemos did not arrive until 1775.

[11] The British Library copy bears his signature.

straightforwardly ascetical' (2012: 53). In fact, unlike Nikodemos, Paisii did not intend his collection of texts to circulate beyond a monastic readership. It remained in manuscript for nearly three decades before it was printed. Paisii did, however, add a translation of Nikodemos's preface at some stage before publication in which he rendered the Greek terms for deification, *theopoiēsis* and *theōsis*, by the Slavonic word *obozhenie*. But deification is not a theme that features anywhere in the body of the book. The importance of the *Dobrotoliubie* lies not in the dissemination of the idea of deification but rather in the encouragement it gave to the development of spiritual fatherhood, or *starchestvo*.

The movement of spiritual renewal that followed upon the *Dobrotoliubie*'s publication was centred on the monastery of Optino, a hundred miles south-west of Moscow, which became a magnet for laypeople of all classes seeking to deepen their interior life through taking counsel from the *startsy*. Among educated visitors to Optina Pustyn, as the hermitage attached to the monastery was called, were the Slavophils Alexei Khomiakov (1804–1960) and Ivan Kireevsky (1806–1856) and the novelist Feodor Dostoevsky (1821–1881). Although Paisii had intended his *Dobrotoliubie* only for monks, its influence through the *startsy* extended to lay Russian intellectuals. But just as deification did not feature in the *Dobrotoliubie*, neither did it enter into the teaching of the *startsy*. The concern of the *startsy* was to give practical spiritual guidance rather than elucidate the theology that underpinned the goal of the Christian life. The best known of the *startsy*, for example, Amvrosii of Optina (1812–1891), famously Dostoevsky's model for the *starets* Zosima in the *Brothers Karamazov* and later glorified among the saints, saw a stream of people every day from early in the morning to late at night.[12] Each visitor received a few well-directed words of wisdom, drawn from the ascetical tradition, on how to confront the specific problems of their personal life. Amvrosii's own rule of life, he once declared, was based on the Jesus Prayer – 'Lord Jesus Christ have mercy on me, a sinner' – the prayer in the gospels of the blind beggar (Mark 10.47; Luke 18.38) and the tax-collector (Luke 18.13) (Bolshakoff, 1976: 191). The practice of the Jesus Prayer was an important feature of the *Dobrotoliubie*. In Louth's words, 'the use of the *Philokalia* and the

---

[12] For a brief overview of Optina Pustyn, see T. A. Smith (2012); on the *startsy* of Optina in more detail, Dunlop, 1972, and Bolshakoff, 1976: 164–95; and on the rise of *starchestvo*, Kenworthy, 2010.

restoration of the institution of *starchestvo* seem to go hand-in-hand' (2018: 109).

A remarkable work in this connection, which attracted much attention on its publication at the beginning of the 1880s, was the anonymous *Candid Tales of a Wanderer to his Spiritual Father*, known in English as *The Way of a Pilgrim*.[13] The work is cast in the form of stories related by a wandering pilgrim (in Russian, a *strannik*) to his spiritual father, recounting his experiences as he walks immense distances from one monastic shrine to another, with the *Dobrotoliubie* in his knapsack, seeking to discover the meaning of the Apostle Paul's 'pray without ceasing' (1 Thess 5.17) and through the practice of the Jesus Prayer master the inner prayer of the heart. The *strannik*'s goal is the sanctification – the transformation – of the heart, the very core of his being. Again, the word 'deification' (*obozhenie*) is nowhere used, but the spiritual labour needed to attain this goal is the subject of the tales.

The most widely circulated edition of the *Candid Tales* was published by Bishop Theophan the Recluse in 1884.[14] At the time, he was also working on his Russian translation of the *Dobrotoliubie*, which was published in five volumes from 1877 to 1890. Theophan's translation was based on Paisii's *Dobrotoliubie* but with the addition of a great many patristic texts mostly, though not entirely, from the Greek *Philokalia*.[15] Two of the authors translated from the Greek *Philokalia* are selections from Maximus the Confessor (in vol. 3) and Gregory Palamas (in vol. 5). Only four of the passages from Maximus, however, and none from Palamas, touch on deification.[16] Writings by Palamas dealing more fully

---

[13] The latest translation, by Anna Zaranko, edited with an introduction by Andrew Louth, was published by Penguin Books in 2017.

[14] The textual history of the *Candid Tales* is complex. *The Way of the Pilgrim* in its present form consists of seven tales. The first four are now known to be the work of Mikhail Koslov (1826–1884), a convert from the Old Believers, who became an archimandrite in the Russian Orthodox Church. Kozlov's work was supplemented by an otherwise unknown writer called Arsenii Troepolskii (1804–1870) and published in 1881. The first two editions sold out quickly. A third edition, edited by Bishop Theophan the Recluse, was published in 1883, and again with some additions in 1884. The 1884 edition, despite the later addition of three further tales, became the classic version.

[15] For a table comparing the list of authors in the Greek *Philokalia*, Paisii's *Dobrotoliubie*, and Theophan's Russian version, see Kadloubovsky and Palmer, 1954: 416–18; and for a full synopsis of all the versions (Greek, Slavonic, Russian, Modern Greek, Romanian, French, English, and Italian), see Conticello and Citterio, 2002. Cf. Louth's comments on Theophan's principle of selection in Louth, 2018: 104–5.

[16] These passages are Maximus's *Centuries on Love* III, 6 and his *Various Texts* I, 32, 42, and 62.

with deification, such as the *Hagioretic Tome* and the *One Hundred and Fifty Chapters*, are omitted altogether by Theophan on the grounds of the difficulty both of understanding them and of expressing their contents. Theophan also wrote a new preface, discarding the original one by Nikodemos (although it had been included by Paisii in the printed Slavonic version of the *Dobrotoliubie*) with its emphasis on deification. In Theophan's view, the fundamental purpose of the *Philokalia* was the 'interpretation of life hidden in the Lord Jesus Christ'.[17]

Not all spiritual writers were as reserved with regard to deification (or at least its terminology) as Bishop Theophan. His contemporary, the controversial Archpriest John of Kronstadt (1829–1908), although a married man, lived like a *starets* and attracted huge numbers of people in search of spiritual advice and consolation. His spiritual autobiography, *My Life in Christ* (published in 1894), draws on the eucharistic dimension of deification prominent in the fourteenth-century hesychast writer Nicholas Kabasilas (in Christ 'we have all been deified')[18] but develops it in a moral direction, for it was chiefly moral guidance that his numerous disciples sought from him. '*My Life in Christ*', as Paul Gavrilyuk remarks, 'does not present a systematic treatment of deification, but nevertheless provides a noteworthy link between spiritual life and deification terminology, which was otherwise lacking in the Russian spiritual writers of the nineteenth century' (Gavrilyuk, 2022: 105). John of Kronstadt thus does something to mitigate the absence of attention to deification – perhaps even the suspicion of deification – in Russia's appropriation of philokalic spirituality in the late nineteenth century.

SOLOVIEV AND RUSSIAN PHILOSOPHY

An important younger contemporary of Bishop Theophan was the religious philosopher Vladimir Soloviev (1853–1900). A precocious and brilliant student, Soloviev entered the University of Moscow at the age of fifteen to study physics and mathematics, transferring in his third year to the Faculty of History and Philosophy. During his third year (1871), he

---

[17] Theophan the Recluse, cited by Gavrilyuk, 2022: 103, who refers to vol. 1, p. iii, of the five-volume edition of the *Dobrotoliubie*, published in Moscow in 1895 by Tipo-Litografiia Efimova (reprinted in 1992). Gavrilyuk draws attention to Theophan's avoidance of the term 'deification' (*obozhenie*) and his preference for expressions such as 'communion with God' (*Bogoobshchenie*) – see Gavrilyuk, 2022: 103–4, 113.

[18] John of Kronshtadt, *Moia zhizn' vo Kriste* (Moscow: Sovietsakaia Rossia, 1991), para. 450, cited and translated by Gavrilyuk, 2022: 105.

also attended lectures at the Moscow Theological Academy, by then having abandoned the atheism he had embraced in his early adolescence. In 1874, he defended his master's thesis, *The Crisis of Western Philosophy*,[19] at the University of Moscow with such brilliance that at the age of twenty-one he was appointed to a teaching position at the university. It was recognised even then that a new genius had appeared upon the Russian scene.[20]

In *The Crisis of Western Philosophy* it is apparent that Soloviev had not only acquired a mastery of the Western philosophical tradition but was already proposing an alternative to the currently dominant positivism through a synthesis of science, philosophy, and religion that drew mainly on Spinoza and the German Idealists (Copleston, 1988: 11–12). In the year after the publication of his dissertation, he went to England to carry out research at the British Museum. He particularly wanted to deepen his knowledge of Gnosticism and other esoteric traditions that would help him articulate his intuition about the unity of all things. These esoteric traditions were to play an important part in his later writings.

In the year after his return to Russia, Soloviev obtained a new post at the University of St Petersburg, where in 1877 he delivered a series of public lectures, published in 1877–1880 under the title *Lectures on Godmanhood* (*Chteniia o bogochelovechestve*). The word 'godmanhood' (*bogochelovechestvo*) is significant both theologically and philosophically. Theologically, the Russian word is a calque on the Greek *theanthrōpia* (θεανθρωπία) or *theanthrōpotēs* (θεανθρωπότης), which in the sixth century had been used to characterise the heretical monophysite position (a confusion of divinity and humanity in Christ) but by the late Byzantine period had become acceptable as a term for the transformed humanity of Christ.[21] Philosophically, *bogochelovek* (god-man) is a

---

[19] The full title is *The Crisis of Western Philosophy. Against the Positivists* (*Krizis zapadnoi filosofii. Protiv pozitivistov*), published in Moscow in 1874. Eng. trans. Soloviev, 1996.

[20] Semyon Frank reports that a distinguished St Petersburg historian declared at the time of the defence: 'Russia may be congratulated upon a new genius' (Frank, 2001: 9).

[21] It is usually claimed, on the basis of the appearance of the expression 'deus-homo' in Rufinus's Latin translation of Origen's *On First Principles* (2.6.3) that the term θεάνθρωπος (*theanthrōpos*, God-man) was coined by Origen in around AD 230. This does appear to be the case, Origen holding that Christ's soul mediates between God and the flesh in the God-man of the Incarnation. But the term then drops out of sight, only to reappear three centuries later in quite a different theological context, when θεανθρωπία (*theanthrōpia*) was anathematised as a monophysite expression in a *Letter of Quintianus, bishop of Asculum to Peter, bishop of Antioch* (Peter the Fuller) that was read out and approved at the anti-monophysite Council of Constantinople of 536 (Schwartz, ACO III,

reversal of *chelovekobog* (man-god), a term first used by Nikolai Speshnev (1821–1882), a utopian socialist, as a translation of Nietzsche's *Übermensch* (superman).[22]

Soloviev begins his lectures with the declaration that he intends to discuss the neglected truths of positive religion, defining religion in broad terms as 'the connection of man and the world with the unconditional beginning, which is the focus of all that exists', and dismissing contemporary religion as 'a pitiful thing', more a personal mood that depends on the taste of the individual.[23] The first three lectures focus on philosophical issues and define some of his key terms. Both socialism and positivism attempt to realise moral truth, in the former case social justice, in the latter the rights of human reason. Both, however, when their principles are followed through logically, lead to 'a demand for religious principles in life and in knowledge' (Solovyov, 1948: 74), for if justice is not to become simply the assertion of the self-interested claims of one group over another, or positivism the elevation of reason, which is only an instrument of knowledge, to the status of the actual content of knowledge, an unconditional principle is needed that integrates all things, and that which unites the phenomenal world with this integral principle is religion. Religion is thus the realisation of the Kingdom of God, the spiritualisation of human society, the 'free internal union between the unconditional divine beginning and the human personality' – or at least it ought to be (79). Historically, however, religion, in the form of the Church, has sought to dominate society. The reaction to this, understandably, was eventually to replace faith in God with faith in man. Yet the two may be synthesised, or rather, the two come down to the same thing, for the human personality in its unity of spirituality with materiality possesses the

17.13). In the eighth century, John Damascene regarded 'Godmanhood' (θεανθρωπότης, *theanthrōpotēs*) as a monophysite opinion implying a passible Godhead (*On the Two Wills in Christ* 8, col. 2. 87). John's contemporary, Anastasius of Sinai, however, was already speaking of Christ as θεάνθρωπος (*theanthrōpos*) in contrast to ψιλάνθρωπος (*psilanthrōpos*), a mere human being (*Hodegos* 13.4). By the time of the fourteenth-century Hesychast Controversy, all parties were happy to speak of Christ as *theanthrōpos*. It is this late Byzantine sense of *theanthrōpia* freed from any monophysite associations, rather than Origen's usage (although Soloviev had a great respect for Origen), that is taken up in the *Lectures on Godmanhood*.

[22] The usual Russian word for *Übermensch*, however, is *sverkhchelovek*, as in Soloviev's article on Nietzsche, 'Ideia sverkhcheloveka' – see Kornblatt, 2009: 23.

[23] Solovyov, 1948: 67. He later rephrases his definition, 'Religion is the reunion of man and the world with the unconditional and integral principle' (74), equating 'religion' with 'reunion' in a manner that recalls Augustine's etymological definition of religion from *re-ligo* ('I bind together' or 'I unite again').

whole of being. Thus 'faith in oneself, faith in human personality, is at the same time faith in God; for Divinity belongs to man as well as to God – with this one difference, that God possesses it in eternal reality, whereas man can only attain to it' (84).

How, then, does man attain to divinity? After a hundred densely argued pages, Soloviev arrives in his tenth lecture at a detailed consideration of *theosis* (*obozhenie*). This is fundamentally the divinisation of all that exists through the incarnation of 'the divine idea', the metaphysical first principle (178). A key term for Soloviev is 'all-unity' or 'pan-unity' (*vseedinstvo*), which designates the original absolute unity of everything in God. This unity was compromised by the cosmogonic process for the sake of a supreme good, that of freedom: All that exists was made to be united with Divinity not by necessity but in reciprocal freedom. The world is animate, endowed with soul. But 'the world soul as a passive force, as a pure aspiration, does not know originally towards what it should aim, i.e., does not possess the idea of all-unity; whereas the divine Logos as the positive beginning, as the active and formative force, has the idea of all-unity in Himself, and bestows it upon the world soul as the determining form' (178). The human being is the end of the cosmogonic process. 'In man the world soul for the first time is internally united with the divine Logos in consciousness, as in the pure form of all-unity' (181). The historical development of religion follows the emergence of man as humanity struggles to recover a dimly perceived all-unity, first in astral religion (the despot of the skies, a desolate unity), then in solar religion (Krishna, Osiris, Apollo) and the worship of the God of earthly organic life (Shiva, Dionysus), and finally in a spiritualised religion that goes beyond the worship of cosmic forces – the religion of the Hindus, the Greeks, and the Jews, of which the highest expressions are Buddhism, Platonism, and the preaching of the Hebrew prophets, respectively. Lastly comes the incarnation, or rather, the inhomination of the divine Logos, who in the person of Jesus Christ unified the spiritual and the material through overcoming the spirit's will to dominate (in his temptation by the devil) and through forcing the sensual will to conform to the divine will (in his passion and death on the cross). It is by participation through the Christian Church in this new unified (and therefore deified) humanity that man attains to Divinity.

For a while in the late 1880s and early 1890s, Soloviev was driven by a passion for the historical realisation of his vision of the new unified humanity. His book published in French, *La Russie et l'église universelle*,[24] sets out his proposal for a Christian world united under the Russian emperor and the Roman pope, a theocracy in which the Jewish people with their prophetic tradition also had a role, a messianic kingdom in which the yearned-for all-unity would be achieved on earth. A little while before his death, however, Soloviev abandoned this project as impractical, although not wrong in principle.

It is remarkable how modernist Soloviev is. He integrates insights from German idealist philosophy, particularly Schelling, and from the contemporary philosophy of religion within an overall framework that is personally constructed yet nevertheless fundamentally Orthodox. For his notion of the unifying force in the cosmos, which he calls Sophia, he draws on the Wisdom tradition of the Bible, on Gnosticism, on the Kabbalah, and on the esoteric teaching of Jakob Boehme.[25] Sophia is a feminine principle with a dual aspect, one active, which is the Divine Wisdom,[26] the other passive, which is the world soul, the receptive character of the natural order, both of which are contained and unified in Jesus Christ (Solovyov, 1948: 163). Soloviev invested considerable emotional energy in Sophia – he records three visions of Sophia as a female figure,[27] which he experienced first as a child in Russia, then as a researcher in the Round Reading Room of the British Museum, and lastly as a visitor to Egypt before returning to Russia in 1876 – but the theological elaboration of Sophia was not to take place until later, in the thinking of Florensky and Bulgakov.

THE ESOTERIC MOVEMENT

It was in Soloviev's time that the ideas of Madame Blavatsky started to receive attention in Russia.[28] The first notices concerning the Theosophical Society appeared in the early 1880s in the spiritualist journal *Rebus*, which published letters from her and advertised her journal,

---

[24] The first edition was published in Paris in 1889, and the book was frequently reprinted. For the full publishing history, see Valliere, 2000: 177 n. 11.

[25] For an excellent analysis of Soloviev's notion of Sophia together with an anthology of relevant texts, see Kornblatt, 2009.

[26] Solovyov, Lecture 7: 'Sophia is God's body, the matter of Divinity [used as relative categories], permeated with the beginning of divine unity. Christ, who realized that unity in Himself or is the bearer of it, as the integral divine organism – universal and at the same time individual – is both Logos and Sophia' (1948: 154).

[27] Soloviev recounts these in a poem called *Three Meetings*.

[28] The history of the theosophical movement in Russia is discussed by Maria Carlson in fascinating detail in Carlson, 1993. See also Carlson, 1996.

The Theosophist (Carlson, 1993: 44–45). In 1887, the popular monthly, *Russkaya mysl'* (Russian Thought), published a critique of Madame Blavatsky's ideas by the philosopher V. V. Lesevich that was dismissive but nevertheless made her known to a broad public. In 1890, Soloviev himself reviewed her *Key to Philosophy*, published by the Theosophical Society in New York earlier that year, in the journal *Russloe obozrenie* (Russian Review). Less hostile than Lesevisch, who castigated Blavatsky for 'babbling out a tremendous lot of all kinds of rubbish', he still regarded her ideas as 'shaky and vague' (46). Within two years, however, Soloviev's attitude had hardened. He now saw her as a complete charlatan, no doubt confirmed in this view by his brother, the novelist Vsevolod Soloviev, a former follower of Blavatsky, who published a damning exposé of her in 1892 in the influential literary journal *Ruskii vestnik* (Russian Messenger) (47–48). Vladimir Soloviev's considered opinion of Blavatsky was set out in the same year in an article for a biographical dictionary edited by S. A. Vengerov.[29] Subjecting her teaching to rigorous analysis, he concluded that her anti-philosophical and incoherent adaptation of Buddhism, based on the doctrines of fictitious Mahatmas supposedly living a hidden life in the Himalayas, was manifestly 'untenable and false' (Carlson, 1993: 47). Despite her Russian roots and her desperate anxiety to be taken seriously in Russia – she got her sister Vera Zhelikhovskaia to mount a vigorous defence of her – Madame Blavatsky never succeeded in establishing a solid following among the intellectual elite of her native land.

Such was not the case with Anthroposophy, Rudolf Steiner's variant of Theosophy, which had an early entrée into Russia through his Russian wife, Marie von Sivers.[30] Steiner's philosophical work, published in German, a language widely known among Russian intellectuals, commanded respect.[31] Moreover, Steiner was not encumbered by a lurid past, as Madame Blavatsky was. Although the Anthroposophists remained a smaller group than the Theosophists, they were well educated and interacted more deeply with the leaders of the Russian religious renaissance.

---

[29] For the bibliographical details, see Carlson, 1993: 216 n.26.

[30] Von Sivers organised a Russian lecture tour for Steiner in 1905, but it had to be cancelled because of the revolution in October of that year. In 1906, however, well before his break with theosophy and his founding of anthroposophy, he lectured to an audience of Russians and Germans in Paris (Lachman, 2007: 156–57).

[31] Not from Berdyaev, however, who describes Steiner's *The Philosophy of Freedom* (1894) as 'of little or no value' (Berdyaev, 1951: 193).

Steiner is cited as an authority by both Florensky and Bulgakov. In his discussion of the symbolism of sky-blue in appearances of Sophia in *The Pillar and Ground of Truth* (1914), Florensky appeals to Steiner as a witness to the religious significance of a blue aura. According to Steiner, when a blue aura is seen surrounding a human body, it indicates a devout and self-renouncing religious nature.[32] Florensky finds this helpful and goes on to discuss the three further auras distinguished by theosophists within the overall blue aura. For him there are evidently aspects of theosophy that can enrich our understanding of Sophiology.

Bulgakov, in a work of the same period, *Unfading Light* (1917), engages with Steiner more critically. He begins the book with a consideration of religious consciousness in which he analyses the concepts of the transcendent and the immanent, 'a pair of correlative concepts', he says, that 'plays a most substantial role in the definition of religion' (Bulgakov, 2012: 20), the immanent being that which lies within the confines of human consciousness and the transcendent that which lies beyond them. 'Does the transcendent exist?' he asks. In answering the question, he distinguishes between two paths of investigation, that of 'mysticism' and that of 'occultism'. He defines the latter in Steiner's words as 'the science of how to attain cognition of higher worlds' (21). But this application of Steinerian scientific positivism to religion leads, in his view, to a dead end. Occultism for Bulgakov is 'a replacement for religion, its Gnostic surrogate, and in such a case it changes into a vulgar pseudoscientific mythology' (37). Only the mystical path, the recognition of the Transcendent in religious *experience*, can open one's eyes to the transcendent in the world (23).

Nicolas Berdyaev is also critical of theosophy and its Steinerian variant but is much more willing than Bulgakov to see a positive side to it. In an essay entitled 'Theosophy and Anthroposophy in Russia', published in *Russkaya mysl'* in November 1916,[33] he sets out with admirable clarity both the weaknesses and the strengths of theosophy from the point of view of the Russian religious renaissance. Like Bulgakov, he sees one of its main weaknesses as the pedagogical emphasis on knowledge, as if one could arrive at an experience of the divine merely through study.

[32] Florensky, 1997: 400–401, citing Steiner, *Theosophia*, translated from the 2nd German edition by Anna Mitslova, 154–58. In this connection, Florensky also mentions C. W. Leadbeater (1847–1934), a leading theosophist of the generation that succeeded Mme Blavatsky.

[33] English translation by Boris Jakim in Berdyaev, 2015: 141–62.

Moreover, the education that theosophy offers is not of a high level. It adapts and simplifies the wisdom of India, combining it with features drawn from nineteenth-century positivism, chiefly Darwinism, with the result that 'theosophy is compelled to naturalistically divinise the fact of cosmic evolution' of which 'man is only a transitory instrument' (Berdyaev, 2015: 143, 148). The philosophical characteristics of theosophy, says Berdyaev, are immanentism and monism. God is identified with nature, with the result that everything proceeds by an inexorable evolutionary process. Moreover, the doctrine of karma means that there is no forgiveness or mercy, no doctrine of grace; there is only 'the nightmare of the unredeemed past' that descends upon us (146).

Although with Steiner theosophy moves westwards, taking a more positive view of Christianity (Steiner refers to the 'Christ impulse'), the essentials of theosophy – the doctrine of cosmic evolution, of different planes, of karma and the transmigration of souls – remain the same.[34] Freedom and creativity are precluded, for 'creativity presupposes the overcoming of Karma'.[35] Again like Bulgakov, Berdyaev distinguishes between mysticism and occultism,[36] but he is not as severe on the occult path as Bulgakov is. 'For many people', he says, 'theosophy is the only bridge by which they can cross into the spiritual life, by which they can leave the soulless and meaningless life of the contemporary world' (Berdyaev, 2015: 144). Accordingly, although personally not attracted by theosophy,[37] he welcomed its spread in Russia because of the inroads it was making on the then dominant positivism and materialism, thus 'raising the average spiritual level' and preparing the ground for the rebirth of religion (159).

---

[34] Berdyaev, 2015: 152. Carlson, 1993: 149 points out that Steiner attempted to mitigate the implacability of karma by introducing the concept of grace through the 'Christ impulse'.

[35] Berdyaev, 2015: 160. The Symbolist poet Andrei Bely (a keen Steinerian) is excluded from this rule by Berdyaev as an exception. But Berdyaev's judgement is still too sweeping. Among prominent theosophists were also the painters N. K. Roerich and W. Kandinsky, the composer A. K. Scriabin, and the poet A. M. Voloshin.

[36] Berdyaev, 2015: 147: 'Mysticism always knows this victory over time and over the world, for it is directed at the depths of divine life. Occultism does not know this victory, for it is directed at the infinitude of cosmic life.'

[37] See Berdyaev's account of the course of lectures by Steiner that he attended in Helsingfors (Helsinki) in 1912 (Berdyaev, 1951: 192–93). 'This experience,' he says, 'confirmed my worst anticipations. Steiner himself made an extremely painful impression, although he did not strike me at all as an impostor' (192).

ACADEMIC THEOLOGY

For the rebirth of religion to become fully integrated with the Russian tradition, the professional theologians of the Theological Academies needed to engage with the mystical and philosophical trends current in Russia's Silver Age. The turn to religion in general and to Orthodoxy in particular, however, by members of the intelligentsia was largely independent of the work of the Academies.[38] This was to change in the early years of the twentieth century. Until then, academic theology had for the most part ignored the patristic teaching on deification.[39] But from 1903 to 1909, Ivan Vasilevich Popov (1867–1938), professor of patristics at the Moscow Theological Academy, published a series of articles entitled 'The Religious Ideal of St Athanasius of Alexandria' (1903–1904), 'The Mystical Justification of Asceticism in the Works of St Macarius of Egypt' (1904–1905), and 'The Idea of Deification in the Ancient Eastern Church' (1909).[40] These articles, totalling more than 200 pages, revolutionised the Russian approach to deification. They are in effect, as Paul Gavrilyuk has said, the first monograph to appear on the subject since Gregory Palamas's treatise, *On Divine and Deifying Participation* (Gavrilyuk, 2022: 111).

What prompted the articles? At the turn of the century, Popov took study leave to go and acquaint himself with the latest theological developments in Germany. In Berlin, in 1902, he attended the seminars of Adolf von Harnack (1851–1930), where he encountered Harnack's Ritschlian views on the patristic doctrine of salvation. We may guess the tone of the seminars from Harnack's *Dogmengeschichte* published less than a decade earlier. What troubled Harnack was the Fathers' casting of salvation in terms of deification, with a distorted emphasis, as he saw it, on the *physical* transformation of human nature brought about by the Incarnation, which resulted in the separation of salvation from the

---

[38] Both Soloviev and Florensky, however, had followed courses of lectures at the Moscow Theological Academy.

[39] Gavrilyuk draws attention to the exception provided by Aleksandr Brilliantov in a study on Dionysius the Areopagite's influence on John Scotus Eriugena published in Moscow in 1898 (Gavrilyuk, 2022: 108).

[40] For the Russian titles and publication details of these articles, see Gavrilyuk, 2022. The last article, 'Ideia obozheniia v drevne-vostochnoi Tserkvi', is translated by Boris Jakim in Kharlamov, 2012: 42–82. Popov's work and its context are the subject of Gavrilyuk's important article (Gavrilyuk, 2022) on which my discussion is based.

moral dimension of the Christian life.[41] The Greek conception of salvation has the advantages, says Harnack, of compactness and clarity. 'But these advantages are purchased, first, by abandoning any attempt to establish an inner unity between the supreme notions of "moral good" and "blessedness" (imperishableness); secondly, by the depreciation of positive morality in favour of asceticism; thirdly, by completely caricaturing the historical Christ.'[42] The first of the representative passages selected by Harnack to illustrate his contention is Athanasius's classic statement of the exchange formula: 'He was inhominated that we might be deified.'[43] This patristic understanding of deification as a 'hyperphysical process', was deplorable in Harnack's view but although still officially Greek Orthodox dogma, he said, was now happily moribund (Harnack, 1958: vol. 3, 162).

When Popov returned to Moscow, he immediately set about writing his own account of Athanasius's idea of deification.[44] The moment was opportune. In 1902–1903, the works of St Athanasius were published in Russian translation in two volumes by the Trinity-St Sergius Lavra in Moscow. The materials were therefore readily available to a broad audience. Popov's achievement was twofold: first, he showed how Athanasius's presentation of deification (*theopoiēsis*) was not an extraneous embellishment but 'a *structurally indispensable* element of [his] theology';[45] second, by going on to discuss Athanasius's *Life of St Antony*, he connected the 'physical' aspect of deification (the transformation of human nature by Christ) with the 'moral' aspect (the appropriation of this transformed nature by the believer through faith and ascetical practice). The two aspects were not, as Harnack thought, in opposition to each other but closely linked.

[41] Harnack sets out his views on deification in the second chapter of the second part of his *Lehrbuch der Dogmengeschichte* (Harnack, 1958: vol 3, 163–90).
[42] Harnack, 1958: vol. 3, 178. The historical Christ for Harnack, a liberal Lutheran theologian, was not the God-man of the patristic tradition (post Origen) but a moral exemplar who reconciled sinful humankind to God by his atoning death. In his view, the Orthodox doctrine of Christ was inherently Monophysite.
[43] Athanasius, *De Incarnatione*, 54; cited by Harnack, 1958: vol. 3, 164 n. 2.
[44] Gavrilyuk points out that 'prior to Popov's study in Germany, there is nothing in his scholarship to indicate an interest in deification' (2022, 110). Harnack was correct in regarding the patristic doctrine as moribund in the Orthodox Church.
[45] Gavrilyuk, 2022: 111, my emphasis. Gavrilyuk's expression 'structurally indispensable' is the key to understanding the theological role of deification in Athanasius and his successors right through to Maximus the Confessor and beyond. Harnack did not disagree that deification was structurally indispensable to the Alexandrian Christological tradition; he was simply glad that by his own time it was a dead letter.

By the time he came to write his third essay in 1909, Popov had arrived at further insights into the nature of deification, which he now sees as a *symbolic* conception uniting hitherto disparate areas of Russian religious life:

In its religious life, every nation usually consists of several strata. The refined conceptions of Dostoevsky, Khomiakov, and Solovyov, the products of school theology, and the old woman trudging with a satchel on her back to a miracle-working *raka* – these are different modes of understanding one and the same symbol.[46]

The different modes of understanding listed here are concrete expressions of the same fundamental idea that do not exclude one another. Not restricted to the use of the word *obozhenie* (deification), they include what I have called the Philokalic, philosophical, esoteric, and academic modes, along with the intensely devotional mode of the great mass of the Russian people. Moreover, they enable Popov to articulate for the first time a taxonomy of deification in order 'to clarify the essence and significance of this idea in the history of dogmas' (Popov, 2012: 45).

Popov distinguishes in his article between 'realistic' and 'idealistic' forms of deification. The realistic form focuses on the transformation of human nature. Relying on the Stoic conception of reality, it assumes that there is not a sharp distinction between spirit and matter: 'spirit is simply matter that is extremely subtle and rarified' (45). Within this framework, the Stoic terms *mixis* (mingling) and *krasis* (blending) explain how two substances can become united by a mechanical interpenetration without any change in the essential properties of either. These conceptions were utilised in a Christological context to explain how the divine and human natures are united in Christ without confusion and in a soteriological context to explain how God becomes united with the individual Christian believer without a merging of identities. The idealistic form of deification, by contrast, draws on the Platonic concept of God. Free from any materiality, the Platonic God is more like an impersonal force diffused throughout the world. In the Christian version, however, God is personal, operating through his will, not by necessity. All goodness, beauty, and life originate in the will of God and seek in freedom to return to him. A vital role is played by the mind, or soul, which mediates between the spirit and the flesh. The soul's task is to elevate and transform matter,

---

[46] Popov, 2012: 44. Jakim (the translator) explains in a footnote that a *raka* is a raised tomb in a church containing the relics of a saint.

with the soul becoming for the body what God is for the soul.[47] This transformation is not physical, as in the realistic form of deification, but spiritual, being expressed as the attainment of moral likeness to God.

The greatest patristic exponents of the idealistic form of deification are Gregory of Nyssa and Dionysius the Areopagite, who both present the attainment of moral likeness in terms of intellectual ascent towards God. Popov discusses Dionysius at some length. The first stage of the Christian who has embarked upon the path of intellectual ascent is to penetrate the concrete symbols of nature and Scripture (to see behind the beauty of the created world and the allegories and divine names of Scripture). The second stage is to master abstract thought (to arrive at perfect conceptions of being, unity, goodness, and so on, by abstracting from the data given to us by our sense perceptions). The third stage is to ascend above reason (to enter into direct union with God through transcending our own nature). In its idealistic form, deification is thus the fruit of a state of ecstasy, when 'all that is sensuous and intelligible, all that is and all that is not' is left behind and the soul penetrates 'into the invisible and unknowable and there see God'.[48]

Having discussed the idealistic form of deification, Popov emphasises that the path to union with God is not simply an intellectual process. It is accompanied by a state of intense feeling (as we may see in Gregory of Nazianzus's account of Christ the beloved drawing the soul after him in *Oration* 38.7 or in the erotic mode of union in Gregory of Nyssa's *Commentary on the Song of Songs*), which Popov describes as 'a process that is completely parallel to the cognitive one' that focuses one's whole being in love on God (Popov, 2012: 81). Thus, in his trilogy of articles on deification, Popov not only answers Harnack's complaint that the patristic doctrine of deification is entirely physical, lacking any moral content but provides his readers with a conceptual framework that is able to unite the Philokalic, mystical, ascetical, and academic approaches to deification, along with popular piety (whether the term *obozhenie* was used or not) within a single narrative comprising different registers. This was to bear fruit not only in the generation that came to maturity before the Revolution of 1917 but even more so in the next generation of Russian theologians in exile.

---

[47] Popov, 2012: 63, citing Gregory of Nazianzus, *Or.* 2.17, PG 35, 425.
[48] Popov, 2012: 73–74, citing Dionysius, *Mystical Theology* 1.1 (PG 3, 997) and Gregory of Nyssa, *Life of Moses* (PG 44, 376–77).

DEIFICATION IN THE RUSSIAN SILVER AGE

On the academic level, Popov's trilogy of articles on deification influenced several important patristic studies. Popov's student, Anatoly Orlov (1897–1937), who had based his master's thesis (published in 1908) on Hilary of Poitiers, followed it up in the following year with an article drawing attention to Hilary's use of the deification theme.[49] In 1913, Sergei Epifanovich (1886–1918) also made use of Popov's work on deification in his dissertation on Maximus the Confessor, published two years later as his groundbreaking study, *St Maximus the Confessor and Byzantine Theology* (1915), a work that is still of value (Gavrilyuk, 2022: 119–20). With regard to the relationship of deification to religion, however, we need to move outside the academy to examine the use made of deification by some representative leaders of Russia's early twentieth-century turn to religion.

It was another of Popov's students, Pavel Florensky (1882–1937) who, in Gavrilyuk's words, 'injected Popov's account of deification into the bloodstream of the Russian religious renaissance' (117). In Florensky's massive work, *The Pillar and Ground of the Truth* (1914), there only two endnotes that mention Popov (Florensky, 1997: 525 n. 479, 553 n. 520), but Popov's 'realistic' and 'idealistic' taxonomy of deification is evident in Florensky's conviction, on the one hand, that the 'holy sacraments are sources of deification' (94) and, on the other, that deification is the fundamental idea of asceticism (213). It is a deliberate decision of Florensky not to quote academic authorities except in the endnotes. His intention is to offer the reader the fruits not so much of scholarship (although the evidence of his scholarship both in the main text and in the notes is impressive) but primarily of experience.[50] This experience, which he does not claim as his own but attributes to the hesychasts and *startsy* of the Orthodox tradition, and even to the *strannik* of the *Way of a Pilgrim*, is focused almost entirely on ascetic effort (*podvizhnichestvo*).[51] As a recent convert to Orthodoxy from his adolescent hostility to religion (he was brought up in an agnostic family),

---

[49] On Orlov's work, see Gavrilyuk, 2022: 116–17. This stimulated Popov himself to produce a monograph on Hilary in 1930.

[50] Florensky, 1997: 236: 'Only do not think that my cold words, are metaphysical speculation, "gnosticism." They are only poor schemata for what is experienced in the soul.'

[51] He published a hagiographical memoir of his own *starets*, Isidor. For bibliographical details, see Coates, 2019: 186.

Florensky has the rationalism of the late Tolstoy and the symbolism of God-seekers of the Merezhkovsky type in his sights.[52] A de-monasticised, modernised Orthodoxy such as theirs is anathema to him. His models are the spiritual fathers of the *Philokalia*; his favourite teachers are St Macarius of Egypt and St Isaac the Syrian (Coates, 2019: 182); his modern heroes are St Seraphim of Sarov and the *startsy* of Optina. At the heart of the Russian religious renaissance lay a desire to reconnect with the faith of the Russian peasant but in a manner that went beyond the proprieties of the state religion. Florensky's way was chiefly through the exaltation of the ascetic tradition.

It is difficult to summarise such a rich work as *The Pillar and Ground of the Truth*.[53] Cast in the form of twelve letters addressed to a 'radiant friend' (Christ himself?), it ranges over a variety of topics from the nature of the triune divinity to chaste friendship as the union of souls, with long quotations from the Fathers and much analysis of the etymology of words and the symbolic significance of images on the way. The mood is elegiac, *fin-de-siècle*, the tone often precious by modern standards. On the third page of the first letter, for example, we read: 'On quiet autumn nights, in the holy hours of silence, when a tear of rapture sparkles on my eyelashes, I will secretly begin to write down for you schemata and pitiful fragments of those questions which we so much discussed together' (Florensky, 1997: 13). Yet the personal, confessional emphasis of the work is essential to its fundamental argument: one cannot arrive at certitude in matters of faith by means of logic; one needs through direct experience to arrive at a knowledge that is mystical and intuitive.[54]

Deification is rarely mentioned by name in the text but it underlies the whole work.[55] It is described by Florensky in the tenth letter as 'the fundamental idea' of asceticism, for asceticism purifies the heart and sanctifies both the body and the soul (Florensky, 1997: 213). The intelligentsia seem ashamed of bodily functions. Asceticism, however, is not life-renouncing but life-enhancing. 'Thus, the goal of the ascetic's

---

[52] For a very fine biography of Florensky, see Pyman, 2010. Both Tolstoy and Merezhkovsky, whose meetings Florensky had attended in St Petersburg, were people he had formerly admired.

[53] For a brief but excellent analysis of the work, see Coates, 2019: 174–207.

[54] Ruth Coates notes that Florensky deliberately plays down the significance of school theology: 'He is interested in deification not primarily as a doctrine, but as an experience' (2019: 206).

[55] For a detailed, but ultimately hostile, analysis of Florensky's understanding of deification, rejecting the essence/energies distinction, see Borysov, 2012.

strivings is to perceive *all* of creation in its original triumphant beauty', which is to attain 'the deification of the flesh through the acquisition of the Spirit' (226).[56] The contemplation of the triumphant beauty of creation leads Florensky in the next letter to a consideration of Sophia, 'the Great Root of the whole of creation' by which creation enters into 'the intra-Trinitarian life and through which it receives Life Eternal from the One Source of Life' (237). What Florensky does by this raising of creation in the form of Sophia to union with God is to restate the patristic doctrine of deification in the sophiological language he has derived from Soloviev: 'Sophia takes part in the life of the Trihypostatic Divinity, enters into the interior of the Trinity, and enters into communion with Divine Love' (252). Yet the Fathers and early ecclesiastical writers are not left behind. Many of them are invoked for their praise of Sophia under various guises, for example, as the Church in the figure of a woman clothed in a brilliant garment (Hermas), as the Divine Wisdom, who enables people to know that they are created in the image of God (Athanasius), or as the Mother of God, who is the bearer and manifestation of Sophia (Andrew of Crete).

Within weeks of the appearance of *The Pillar and Ground of the Truth*, Berdyaev published a hostile review in *Russkaya mysl'*.[57] He objects to what he calls Florensky's 'stylized Orthodoxy', his burying of himself in an imagined past: 'I do not doubt the authenticity and significance of the religious experiences of the author of *The Pillar and Ground of the Truth*; but the expression of these experiences in the form of an archaic Orthodoxy constitutes a stylization' (Berdyaev, 2015: 176). The narrowness of this backward view is exemplified for Berdyaev by Florensky's confining of ecclesial mysticism to St Macarius of Egypt and St Symeon the New Theologian and his rejection of such figures as Meister Eckhart and Jakob Boehme and even St Francis of Assisi and St Catherine of Siena. This is the result, says Berdyaev of Florensky's 'transcendental gnoseology', which leads him to a flawed philosophy of religion and conception of the Church. 'On the one hand, dogmas are revealed by spiritual experience'; on the other, the same dogmas 'are transcendentally imposed on spiritual experience' by Orthodoxy (183). The Church is tasked with the authoritarian imposition of dogma, yet at the same time Orthodox ecclesiality is defined as 'new life, life in the

---

[56] To illustrate this, Florensky appeals to the experience of the Desert Fathers and of the *strannik* in *The Way of a Pilgrim*.

[57] Eng. trans. by Boris Jakim under the title 'Stylized Orthodoxy: On Father Pavel Florensky' in Berdyaev, 2015: 175–95.

Spirit', the criterion of which is beauty (184). Florensky, it seems to Berdyaev, is trying to have his cake and eat it too.

Berdyaev was able to respond to Florensky at some length so quickly because between 1912 and 1914 he was working on his own book centred on the idea of deification: *The Meaning of Creativity*.[58] Writing about his book many years later, he says that most of the spokesmen of the Russian renaissance were preoccupied with cosmology, whereas he was concerned with anthropology. They looked for 'signs of divine glory and wisdom in this world', whereas he 'saw man relegated to the cosmic cycle, in which he is paralysed and crushed by inexorable necessity and reduced to the semblance of a "thing" or "object"' (Berdyaev, 1951: 167). Berdyaev was strongly opposed to Schleiermacher's definition of religion as a 'sense of dependence' (*Abhängigheitsgefühl*). For him religion was a sense of *independence*: 'If God does not exist, man is a being wholly dependent on nature and society, on the world or the state. If God exists, man is a spiritually independent being; and his relation to God is to be defined as freedom' (179–80). Freedom entails the synergistic character of humanity's relation to God, our collaboration with God in his creative activity, for the universe is in a state of constant evolution towards a preordained end and we have a vital part to play in this.

Berdyaev in the *The Meaning of Creativity* derives his leading idea from Boehme. Fundamental to this idea is the view of reality as a creative process. Berdyaev accepts Boehme's notion of the divine *Urgrund*, the mysterious impersonal source of divinity that has evolved out of non-being. From the *Urgrund*, the personal Trinitarian God of Christianity emerges, who then out of himself (not out of nothing) produces the universe as the 'other' that is consequently shot through with divine energy. That is why much later, in *Spirit and Reality*, Berdyaev is able to say:

There is no gulf between the Creator and the creature such as exists in the Catholic and Protestant West. Theosis bridges this gulf. The sensible world is symbolical of the spiritual world (St. Maxim the Confessor). Through the Divine image the creature participates in the Divine qualities. Man's ideal nature is revealed in Christ. Human nature is consubstantial with the human nature of Christ. In the East the human element is permeated by the Divine; while in the West the human element ascends towards the Divine. (Berdyaev, 1939: 156)

In her illuminating analysis of *The Meaning of Creativity*, Ruth Coates judges that Berdyaev 'betrays a great deal of ignorance about the doctrine

[58] Published in 1916. Eng. trans. by Donald A. Lowrie (Berdyaev, 2009).

of deification and its expression in the Orthodox tradition' (Coates, 2019: 139). Certainly, he seems unaware of Popov's articles. But, as Coates also says, after his conversion to Christianity, which followed his move from St Petersburg to Moscow, he professed a 'sincere desire to share in the life of the Orthodox Church' (138, citing Berdayev, 2009: 164). He declares in fact that 'the Moscow period coincided with a serious attempt on [his] part to study and to relate [his] thinking to, the theological traditions of the Orthodox Church' (Berdyaev, 1951: 165). In Moscow, he joined the Religious-Philosophical Society, founded in memory of Vladimir Soloviev, of which Sergius Bulgakov was a leading member. In Bulgakov's company he attended gatherings of the ex-Tolstoyan convert to traditional Orthodoxy, Mikhail Novoselov (1864–1938).[59] There he encountered a devout liturgy-centred Orthodoxy, and with Novoselov visited the Zossimova Hermitage in the province of Vladimir in order to experience *starchestvo* for himself. Although one of the two *starsty* there impressed him, he was not attracted to surrendering his entire will to a *starets*. The visit only confirmed his love of freedom, he says. He read the spiritual and ascetic writings of the *Dobrotoliubie*, but the moral teachings of Theophan the Recluse repelled him. He explored the world of Steiner's anthroposophy and even frequented the meetings of the religious sects – Bessmertniki (who regarded themselves as immortal), Baptists, Dukhobors, Tolstoyans, and Khlysty (heterodox ecstatics) – at a Moscow inn called 'the Pit'. He did not like the proselytising Baptists but found the mystical sects interesting, even though some of them were 'of a distinctly Manichaean and Bogomilian character' (Berdyaev, 1951: 197). He could not overcome his resistance to official Orthodoxy yet he did read early ecclesiastical writers and particularly liked Origen and Gregory of Nyssa (whom he calls Doctors of the Church) and was greatly moved by Isaac the Syrian (165).

Ruth Coates believes that *The Meaning of Creativity*, based as it is on a Boehmian perspective, 'belies [Berdyaev's] claim that he had "no wish to break from the church, or assert [himself] in some sectarian independence"' (Coates, 2019: 139, citing Berdyaev, 1951: 172). I think this is too harsh a judgement. *The Meaning of the Creativity* was written at a time, Berdyaev says, when he was reacting strongly against Moscow's Orthodox circles and had left both the Novoselov group and the

---

[59] Glorified as a saint in 2000.

Religious-Philosophical Society.[60] Berdyaev was committed to free religious thought but had no wish to set himself up against the Church as the alternative repository of truth. Nicolas Zernov rightly describes his Christianity as 'more prophetic than traditional' (Zernov, 1963: 152), but to the end of his life he never broke with Orthodoxy. His understanding of deification was of a theandric creative act that comes about when 'man awaits the birth of God in himself, and God awaits the birth of man in himself' (Berdyaev, 1951: 209). Creativity and freedom are synonymous. They belong properly to God and when human beings come to share fully in them, they share in the life of God.

Sergius Bulgakov, in this period still a friend of Berdyaev, was not impressed by *The Meaning of Creativity*.[61] He came to his mature understanding of deification as a result of his own personal spiritual journey that took him from Marxist materialism (although he was to deny that he had ever been an atheist), via German philosophical idealism, to the recovery of the Church's faith in a version strongly coloured by Soloviev's sophiology. Unlike his mentor Pavel Florensky, Bulgakov was not a graduate of one of the Theological Academies. His early work was in economics, as a result of which he was appointed professor of political economy in 1901 at the Kiev Polytechnical Institute. Yet already he was moving away from Marxism under the influence of Neo-Kantianism. By 1902, he had discovered Soloviev, who showed him a way of integrating the spiritual realm with the material, and began later to immerse himself in the study of the Greek Church Fathers.[62] This spiritual evolution gave rise to the two books with deification as a major theme that were published before Bulgakov was expelled from the nascent Soviet Union in 1922: *Philosophy of Economy* (1912)[63] and *Unfading Light* (1917).[64]

---

[60] Berdyaev, 1951: 211. It may also be mentioned that this was the period of the *Imiaslavie* Controversy, which concerned Russian monks on Mount Athos who maintained that the name of Jesus was itself divine. The monks were condemned on that account by the Holy Synod in Moscow and some 800 of them were arrested and brought by force to Russia in the summer of 1913. Berdyaev wrote an article protesting the arrests and denouncing the sanctimonious worldliness of the Holy Synod. He was charged with blasphemy, which carried the penalty of exile to Siberia for life, but was saved from trial by the outbreak of the revolution (202–3).

[61] In *Unfading Light* (1917), his only reference to Berdyaev is to say: 'The disclosure of the disharmonies of creativity in various respects is the chief worth of N. A. Berdiaev's book, *The Meaning of Creativity*' (Bulgakov, 2012: 501 n. 91).

[62] He does not seem to have encountered Popov's work – at least he never mentions him.

[63] Eng. trans. by Catherine Evtuhov: Bulgakov, 2000.

[64] Eng. trans. by Thomas Allan Smith: Bulgakov, 2012.

The first of these books came at a stage when Bulgakov had already abandoned Marxist materialism. His growing dissatisfaction, however, with the Neo-Kantianism that replaced it was leading him to re-engage with the Orthodoxy of his youth (he was from a priestly family) in an attempt to give spiritual and philosophical meaning to economic endeavour beyond the nineteenth-century idea of 'progress' or the pragmatic pursuit of power through wealth. Deification lies at the centre of this enterprise, because to seek deification and to engage in economic activity are both concerned, on different levels, with the struggle for survival, with the assertion of life against death.[65] In articulating this conviction, Bulgakov draws principally on the philosophy of F. W. J. Schelling (1775–1854), which, on the model of Vladimir Soloviev, he combines with insights derived from the Greek patristic tradition.[66]

Two elements of Schelling's philosophy in particular are important to Bulgakov: the identity of spirit and matter and the ontological status of nature as animate being that realises itself by producing subjectivity. The first element is a counter-proposal to Kant's dualism (things as they are in themselves contrasted with their appearance, which is all we actually know); the second combats the monism that results from the denial of dualism (the problem of how the One is also the many). Nature in Schelling becomes an absolute producing subject, a unified organism that Bulgakov adopts and correlates with Sophia, the hypostatised divine Wisdom of the Greek Old Testament: 'Sophia reconciles the world to the Absolute by restoring the unity-in-difference of matter and spirit.'[67] The world is in need of reconciliation because the original unity of the divine Ideas was broken by the emergence of finite particulars through the exercise of freedom by the Ideas. This is correlated by Schelling with the Fall, which he sees not as a historical but as a metaphysical event, the Incarnation then taking place historically in order to restore the broken bond between spirit and nature. Bulgakov believed that 'Schelling expressed one of the most fundamental truths of Christianity in the philosophical language of his time',[68] namely, the unity of flesh and spirit

---

[65] Coates, 2019: 152–55. The whole of Coates's chapter on Bulgakov (140–73), is important. For a brief introductory essay, see Jakim, 2007: 250–58.

[66] Coates remarks that 'it is crystal clear in *Philosophy of Economy* that Bulgakov does not rely on Soloviev as an intermediary but draws directly from Schelling and Greek patristics. Soloviev is an intellectual ally, not an intellectual source' (Coates, 2019: 142 n. 5).

[67] Coates, 2019: 146. Coates points out that the first appearance of the concept of Sophia in Bulgakov is in his *Philosophy of Economy* (originally published in 1912) (146 n.17).

[68] Bulgakov, 2000: 87; cited by Coates, 2019: 155.

that 'is the basis for the doctrine that the human incarnation of God brought about a potential divinisation of the flesh'.[69] Bulgakov thus sees Schelling's principal insight as a philosophical restatement of the 'exchange formula' that we find in the Greek patristic tradition (and also in Augustine): God became human that we might become divine, which for Bulgakov is the realisation of the potential divinity in humanity through our participation in Sophia.

When Bulgakov returns to the theme of deification five years later in *Unfading Light*, he shows a greater familiarity with the patristic tradition. The Russian Silver Age was an era of impressive achievements in patristic study, mainly through work carried out in the Theological Academies of St Petersburg, Moscow, Kiev, and Kazan. All the important Church Fathers had by then been translated into Russian. Landmark publications cited by Bulgakov in *Unfading Light* include A. Brilliantov, *The Influence of Eastern Theology on Western Theology in the Works of John Scotus Eriugena*;[70] Bishop Aleksii, *Byzantine Church Mystics of the Fourteenth Century*;[71] and S. L. Epifanovich, *St. Maximus the Confessor and Byzantine Theology*.[72] Curiously, Bulgakov does not mention Popov's 'Idea of Deification in the Early Eastern Church', but its influence is not absent. In Popov's terms, Bugakov's focus in *Unfading Light* is squarely on the idealistic form of deification, with its emphasis on the Platonic notion of participation.

Unfading Light is divided into three sections, each considering from a different angle how the transcendent and the immanent are bridged in human experience. The first section, on 'divine nothing' is on negative theology, which alone can express the transcendent with any adequacy. The second, on 'the world', discusses how divine Sophia, in virtue of her dual nature, mediates between the absolute and the contingent, making the transcendent immanent. Turning to the contingent, Bulgakov sees creation as 'the self-bifurcation of the Absolute ... the sacrifice of the Absolute for the sake of the relative, which becomes for it "other" (*thateron*), a creative sacrifice of love' (Bulgakov, 2012: 185). Creation thus entails a self-renunciation by God in order that the relative, while remaining relative, may come to participate in the freedom of the

[69] Bulgakov 2000: 87; cited (modified) by Coates, 2019: 155.

[70] A. Brilliantov, *Vliianie vostochnago bogosloviia na zapadnoe v proizvedeniiakh Ioanna Skota Erigeny* (St Petersburg, 1891).

[71] Bishop Aleksii, *Vizantiiskie tserkovnye mistiki 14-go veka* (Kazan, 1906).

[72] S. L. Epifanovich, *Prepodobnyi Maksim Ispovednik i vizantiiskoe bogoslovie* (Kiev, 1915).

Absolute. In the third section, on 'the human being', Bulgakov turns to the biblical account of creation with a commentary on the first chapter of Genesis. He opens his account with a citation of John 10.34, where the Saviour quotes Psalm 81(2).6: 'I said, you are gods and all of you sons of the Most High.' Bulgakov interprets this as a programmatic statement of the divine origin of humanity and its ultimate return to union with God. Adam before the Fall represents the human being as simultaneously a creature and not a creature: 'the absolute in the relative and the relative in the absolute' (286). It is the divine potential in humanity that makes it capable of divinisation. This also has implications for the incarnation of the Word. As Bulgakov puts it: 'Neither the inhominization of God nor the divinisation of the human would be possible if the very nature of the human was not deiform and receptive of God' (286). This is the truth encapsulated in the assertion of Genesis 1.26 that humanity was created in the image and likeness of God.

Following Maximus the Confessor and John Damascene, Bulgakov makes a distinction between the image and the likeness. In a sense 'the world is God *in process*' (196) as the initial image develops to become the full likeness. The details of Adam's life in Paradise stand for stages in the growth of self-awareness. The first stage, the prohibition to eat of the tree of the knowledge of good and evil (Gen 2.17), is God's awakening in the creature of the recognition of its creaturely freedom. The second, the naming of the animals, is the establishing of self-definition with regard to all living things. The last, the temptation of Adam, is his being prompted to misuse his 'theophoric dignity', to seize divinity by an act of will before the proper time, for humanity was not yet ready to participate in the freedom of the Absolute, which is the full realisation of the likeness.

The Fall inhibited but did not annul the destiny of human beings to become 'gods by grace'. The creation of the world was a kenotic act of love, God's free limitation of his own omnipotence that included the kenotic act of divine incarnation as a pre-eternal decision to recreate humankind in Christ in order that it might come to share in the life of the Godhead. Christ became 'the deep foundation, the most intimate essence of humankind' (348), and through his obedience to the Father, even to the Cross, raised it by his sacrificial struggle to a level it could not have attained by itself, for 'the divinization of humanity can by no means be achieved through the path of evolution' (351).

In *Unfading Light*, Bulgakov discusses deification principally from a philosophical perspective, which of course in the Orthodox context does not exclude theology. Only after his exile and arrival in Paris was he able to embark on a fuller consideration of the theological dimension. It was in Moscow, however, a year before his ordination to the priesthood, that he laid the foundation for his great Paris trilogy that we shall consider in Chapter 6.

In late imperial Russia, the intelligentsia, for the most part implacable opponents of the tsarist autocracy, were also alienated from the Orthodox Church, which they saw simply as an arm of the tsarist system. In the Silver Age, however, a new current stirred large numbers of the intelligentsia. The spiritual sterility of the dominant materialism and positivism, combined with the highly charged anticipation of far-reaching change after the revolution of 1905, led many to be receptive to a wide variety of intellectual and religious influences ranging from German idealism (Schelling and Nietzsche) and esotericism (Boehme and Steiner) to those aspects of the Orthodox tradition (the *Dobrotoliubie* and *starchestvo*) that were untainted by the dead hand of the state religion. The Greek Fathers also began to be easily available in Russian translation in this period, and Popov (whose influence was to grow among the theologians of the emigration) showed the new converts to Orthodoxy how to read them.

Florensky, Berdyaev, and Bulgakov came to Orthodoxy by different routes, and indeed arrived at different versions of Orthodoxy, but they have a number of things in common. They believed that deification bridges the gulf between God and man; they were convinced that it was not logical analysis but direct experience that brings us to true knowledge; they were reserved (to say the least) towards the Orthodoxy that was the official state religion, although first Florensky and then Bulgakov sought ordination to the priesthood; they valued the same body of authors, chiefly Soloviev, Boehme, and the spiritual teachers of the *Dobrotoliubie*; and the favourite Church Father of all three was St Isaac the Syrian, the father who conveys most powerfully – in non-philosophical terms – the union of the transcendent with the immanent. Yet, as authorities, the Fathers were not especially privileged. Bulgakov, for example, gives as much weight to Soloviev. Nevertheless, for all of them theosis expresses the entire purpose of religious faith. And although theosis is not found exclusively in Orthodoxy, as Berdyaev discovered from his study of Boehme and as Popov pointed out in his articles on the patristic idea of deification, theosis was discovered by them (even by Berdyaev) to be most fully expressed in the Orthodox tradition.

6

'The *Via Regia*'

Deification in the Russian Diaspora

In the 1920s, especially after Lenin's expulsion of non-Marxist intellectuals from what was to become the Soviet Union, Paris rapidly became the intellectual centre of the Russian emigration. Even before the Revolution, Russians had been coming to Paris for a variety of cultural reasons. Myrrha Lot-Borodine (1882–1954), daughter of the director of the Botanical Gardens in St Petersburg, Ivan Parfenievich Borodine (1847–1930), came in 1907 to begin studies at the Sorbonne in French mediaeval literature. Sergei Sakharov, who was to become Archimandrite Sophrony (1896–1993), came in 1922 to further the career he had begun in Moscow as an artist. Vladimir Lossky (1903–1958), son of the famous philosopher Nikolai Onufriyevich Lossky (1870–1965), arrived a little later, in 1924, and like Lot-Borodine enrolled at the Sorbonne.[1] In the following year, Metropolitan Evlogy (Georgievsky) (1868–1946) invited Fr Sergius Bulgakov to come from Prague to head the newly founded Theological Institute of St Sergius in Paris. Bulgakov developed his teaching on deification along the sophianic lines he had already laid down in Moscow but only in Russian-language publications. Sakharov soon left to become a monk on Mount Athos, where his encounter with *Starets* Silouan was to lead to his engagement with mystical theology but not until the 1950s. The Russians who in the early twentieth century did most to introduce the doctrine of deification to Western theologians as an organising principle of Orthodox thought were therefore Lot-Borodine and Lossky, who were initially not theologians at all but Francophile

---

[1] For a good sketch of the life and work of both Lot-Borodine and Lossky, see Louth, 2015b: 94–110.

students of Western mediaeval civilisation. As we shall see, this is not without significance.

RUSSIAN ÉMIGRÉ ENGAGEMENT WITH THE WESTERN TRADITION: MYRRHA LOT-BORODINE

It was at one of the regular Sunday meetings of Russian exiles at Berdyaev's house in Clamart (in the south-west suburbs of Paris) in the late 1920s that Myrrha Lot-Borodine first heard about theosis from a paper read by another visitor, Georges Florovsky (1893–1979).[2] Although brought up in a non-practising family, she had always been interested in religion and since 1920 had been actively investigating the foundations of the Christian faith.[3] What she learned about theosis from Florovsky immediately fired her to immerse herself in the study of the subject.[4] She was already following the lecture courses of Fr Jules Lebreton SJ (1873–1956), Professor of the History of the Origins of Christianity, at the Institut Catholique de Paris.[5] She also began to attend lectures by Henri-Charles

---

[2] Florovsky's paper is likely to have been a version of an article entitled 'Tvar' i tvarnost'' ('Creation and creaturehood'), published in Russian in 1928, in which he discusses the implications for the Father's eternity of the creation of the world out of nothing and the generation of the Son from the Father's essence. For bibliographical details and an analysis of the article, see Gavrilyuk, 2022: 122–23.

[3] These biographical details are from Lot-Borodine's own notes in French published by her daughter, Marianne Mahn-Lot, who says that her mother visited the Dominicans at Le Saulchoir, attended interconfessional meetings at the house of Jacques Maritain and his Russian wife Raissa at Meudon, and often entertained her compatriots to tea at her house in the Paris suburb of Fontenay-aux-Roses. She also followed the lectures of Étienne Gilson, who introduced her to St Bernard's mystical theology (Mahn-Lot, 2004).

[4] In a note published by Marianne Mahn-Lot, Myrra Lot-Borodine says: 'In the course of a meeting at Berdyaev's house, I was struck by a communication of Florovsky's on the theme of deification in the Graeco-Oriental Church, all the more so as I was following at the time the courses of Père Lebreton at the Institut Catholique. I therefore listened to what Florovsky was saying on *Theosis* in the Greek Fathers. I thereupon applied myself with the ardour of a neophyte to our *Theologia mystica* and decided to go more deeply into it' (Mahn-Lot, 2004).

[5] Lebreton, appointed professor at the Institut Catholique de Paris at the height of the modernist crisis, had to steer a very careful line with regard to the ecclesiastical authorities. He was nevertheless able through his important patristic studies to exercise a profound influence on all the subsequent leaders of 'la nouvelle théologie' (Irenaeus was the Father he most valued). In the Preface to his magisterial *Histoire du dogme de la Trinité des origines au Concile de Nicée* (Paris: Beauchesne, 1928), he remarks: 'The living chain of our tradition binds us even more tightly and more securely to the past than the commentaries of exegetes and the dissertations of historians', an opinion that could easily have been voiced by an Orthodox. Lot-Borodine cites her teacher several times early in her article, although she is not entirely uncritical of him, rejecting (correctly), for example, his

Puech (1902–1986), a specialist in Neoplatonism, Hermetism, and Manichaeism, who was then at the beginning of his long career at the École Pratique des Hautes Études. Her research resulted in an essay, 'La doctrine de la "deification" dans l'Église grecque jusqu'au XIe siècle', which was first published in three instalments in the *Revue de l'histoire des religions* (a journal with which Puech was closely connected) in 1932–1933.[6] This essay was the first monograph-length study of deification to appear in a Western language. It immediately attracted attention. The Benedictine Abbey of Beuron in southern Germany contacted her. The Priory of Chevetogne in Belgium, then still at Amay, invited her to contribute to their journal *Irénikon*. To her surprise, she found that she had acquired an international reputation as a theologian.

Lot-Borodine's essay was not only the first in a Western language but also the first to be addressed principally to a non-Orthodox audience. Its purpose was therefore different from that of two studies on deification previously published in France by Lev Karsavin (1882–1952) and Georges Florovsky.[7] Not only did Karsavin and Florovsky write in Russian, but their aim was to educate their fellow Russians about the ultimate goal of their own Orthodox faith. Lot-Borodine's concern, by contrast, was to inform her Francophone readers how, on the fundamental topic of salvation, the

---

claim that Clement of Alexandria shows evidence of heterodox influences (Lot-Borodine, 1970: 74 n. 8) and his opinion that St Maximus the Confessor was basically 'only a compiler without originality' (80 n. 14).

[6] Myrrha Lot-Borodine, 'La doctrine de la "deification" dans l'Église grecque jusqu'au XIe siècle', *Revue de l'Histoire des Religions* 105 (1932), 5–43; 106 (1932), 525–74; 107 (1933), 8–55. Puech became a member of the editorial team (secrétaire de rédaction) of the *Revue de l'Histoire des Religions* in 1934. Lot-Borodine's deification article, along with two others, was republished with a Preface by Cardinal Jean Daniélou in Lot-Borodine, 1970: 19–183.

[7] The philosopher Lev Karsavin was briefly Florovsky's predecessor as Professor of Patristics at the Institute of St Sergius in Paris. In 1926, he published a short book on the Fathers for the use of his students, which although only a rapid survey with little documentation gave prominence to the goal of deification. The following year, he left for Lithuania to become Professor of Universal History at the University of Kaunas. (If he had stayed on at St Sergius, we might not have had Florovsky's 'neopatristic synthesis'. Karsavin was a mediaevalist who valued the Western tradition – before his expulsion from Russia on the 'philosophers' ship' of 1922 he had published a Russian translation of the Revelations of Blessed Angela of Foligno.) In 1949, he was arrested (the Soviets having incorporated Lithuania into the Soviet Union after World War II) and sent to the Gulag, where he spent the remaining three years of his life. For a moving account of his Christian witness there, where he gathered a group of disciples to whom he talked about philosophy as 'the road that leads up to the absolute', see Niqueux, 1996. On the approach to deification in his 1926 book on the Fathers, see Gavrilyuk, 2022: 121–22.

Orthodox version differed from the Catholic and the Protestant. Behind
that, as we shall also see, though in a rather different way, in Lossky's case,
lay the need of Russian émigrés to demarcate the boundaries of their
Orthodox faith with regard to the faith of the Catholic majority among
whom they lived. It is this confessional agenda that accounts for what Paul
Gavrilyuk has called 'the polemical edge in Lot Borodine's presentation of
deification as "Eastern"' (Gavrilyuk, 2022: 124).

The polemics did not put off Lot-Borodine's Western readers. In his
Introduction to the 1970 re-edition of the articles, Cardinal Daniélou
speaks of his excitement at first reading them on the recommendation of
one of his fellow Jesuits – either de Lubac, he says, or von Balthasar: 'The
reading of these articles was for me decisive. They crystallized something
I was looking for, a vision of man transformed by the divine energies.
I don't know if it is because of these articles that I first began to research the
mystical theology of Gregory of Nyssa. But I do know that this book is shot
through with the influence of Myrrha Lot-Borodine' (Lot-Borodine, 1970:
10).[8] Scholars like Daniélou who were struggling to find in the Fathers a
theological resource (*ressourcement*) coherent enough to provide a coun-
terweight to the officially sanctioned (neo-)Thomism that at the time pre-
dominated in the Roman Catholic Church were much encouraged by Lot-
Borodine's synthetic presentation of the patristic teaching on deification.

A critical factor that commended Lot-Borodine's articles to her
Francophone readers was her rich documentation from Western sources.
Besides the Greek Fathers, she also refers to St Augustine, St Bernard,
St Bonaventure, the Rhineland mystics, Hugh of Balma, and Nicholas of
Cusa. The secondary literature copiously cited in the footnotes consists
predominantly of books and articles by French and German authors.
Daniélou refers to Lot-Borodine's 'strange style, laden with Greek
and Latin words and sumptuous neologisms' (10), but her articles could
not be dismissed as particularly exotic or theologically alien. They are
written in the conventional academic style. The scholars most frequently
cited are the Jesuits Marcel Viller (1880–1952) and Irénée Hausherr
(1891–1978).[9] The Russians relied upon are chiefly Epifanovich and

---

[8] The book Daniélou refers to is his classic *Platonisme et la théologie mystique* (1944).
[9] Both were renowned specialists in patristic and Byzantine spirituality. Viller, one of the
founders of the great *Dictionnaire de spiritualité ascétique et mystique*, had just published
(in 1930) his *Aux sources de la spiritualité de saint Maxime: Les oeuvres d'Évagre le
Pontique*. Hausherr, who in 1934 was to become Professor of Christian Spirituality at the
Oriental Institute in Rome, had already published two important works: *La méthode
d'oraison hésychaste* (1927) and *Un grand mystique byzantine: Vie de Syméon le Nouveau*

Bulgakov,[10] but Western scholars predominate, even if some of them are sharply criticised.[11] Lot-Borodine's 'polemical edge' does not reflect a simple East–West division, with the East characterised as orthodox and the West as heterodox, nor is deification simply 'Eastern', even if the Eastern version is to be preferred.

In her preliminary remarks, Lot-Borodine emphasises the limitations of her work. First, she stops in the middle of the eleventh century with Symeon the New Theologian. A new era opens in the fourteenth century with the Athonite hesychasts, she says, but the contentious issues arising out of that era still await resolution.[12] Second, she does not discuss liturgical mysticism or the deifying grace conveyed by the sacraments. Her intention is simply to pass from a discussion of the theological foundations of deification to 'the solitary quest of the soul as it ascends towards God, without ever losing touch with the theology of the Fathers or traditional *ascesis*' (21 n. 1).

For this reason, Lot-Borodine's essay is weak on the ecclesial aspects of theosis. Its strength lies in the illuminating way it traces the Dionysian (apophatic) lineage of thinking on deification in both the East and the West, in the East through Maximus the Confessor and in the West through John Scotus Eriugena. The Western line of this tradition, however, was broken by the dominance of Augustine's theological heritage.[13] After Eriugena, the Dionysian strand was not recovered until Meister Eckhart 'and perhaps Tauler and Ruysbroek' (33–34).[14] Deifying union

---

Théologien par Nicêtas Stêthatos (1928). Neither, however, completely escapes censure. Hausherr, in particular, is chided for not taking late Byzantine spirituality seriously (133).

[10] Epifanovich's groundbreaking book on St Maximus is cited four times (82, 90, 97, 142). Bulgakov, 'an eminent representative of the Russian sophianic doctrine' (43), is cited a further five times (90, 97, 131, 162, 183), but *The Philosophy of Economy* and *Unfading Light* are not mentioned. Popov is cited twice (49, 132), but even though Athanasius is discussed, his articles on deification are not mentioned.

[11] Harnack, who believed that Hellenism had corrupted the biblical faith of the early Christians, 'understands nothing of the Greeks' (55); Reitzenstein's edition of the *Historia Lausiaca* and the *Historia Monachorum* is often referred to, but at the same time Lot-Borodine signals her strong dissent from his views on the contamination of early monastic sources by ideas drawn from the pagan mysteries.

[12] For an account of how these issues were being addressed at the time, see Russell, 2019b: 49–62.

[13] On Lot-Borodine's negative attitude to Augustine, see Gavrilyuk, 2022: 124.

[14] Having earlier (30) strongly commended Brilliantov's study of Eriugena (published in Russian in 1898), Lot-Borodine refers here to Lossky's studies on the Dionysian heritage in the West (Lossky, 1929, 1930). She seems unaware, however, of the tradition of commentary on Dionysius that began with Albert the Great (d. 1280).

cannot be other than the fruit of a final negative knowledge (36). Augustine, however, can only conceive of union in affirmative terms as the *vision* of the divine essence (*visio dei per essentiam*), because for him deification, rather than simply beatitude, would entail divine-human consubstantiality and co-penetration (39–40).[15] What Augustine lacks, in Lot-Borodine's view, through the absence in his thinking of a negative theology, is a mystical anthropology.

The Eastern line of thinking on deification begins with Irenaeus and, passing through Athanasius, comes to fulfilment in Maximus the Confessor. 'Maximus', says Lot-Borodine, 'considers the *nous* (which is the Augustinian *spiritus*, the *mens*, or better, the *apex mentis* of the mediaevals, *the interior man* of Eckhart and Tauler) – this capping of the soul – as naturally *deiform*' (42). There is something implanted naturally in the soul that makes it receptive to God. Writers in the Augustinian tradition, however, prefer to speak of *analogy*, that is to say, of a purely psychological image imprinted in humanity – intelligence, memory, and will – rather than a *real* image of the threefold God. With them the boldness of the Greek doctrine of a real transformation is reduced to a deification *in potentia*. In the Greek Fathers, however, humanity was created in order to share in the life of God – the Incarnation, in a sense, already being Redemption 'because that which Christ has assumed he redeems' (56).[16] 'Then why the Passion?' Lot-Borodine asks. The answer is in order to expiate by divine blood and bring about immortality. The Incarnation and the Redemption are inseparable and together complete the work of recapitulation. In the life of Christ humanity becomes triumphant.

The deiform human soul was thus created in order to attain its fulfilment through being conformed to the glorified Christ. Lot-Borodine draws attention to the contrast between the liturgical reproduction of the life of Christ in Orthodoxy, on the one hand, and the tenderness and sentiment of Catholicism's devotion to the Sacred Heart, on the other. The mediaeval way, the way of St Bernard, was 'per Christum hominem ad Christum Deum' ('through Christ the man to Christ the God'). The Byzantine way, the way that leads directly from St Athanasius's *Life of*

---

[15] For a critique of Augustine's anthropology based on Popov and Gilson, see also 49–50.

[16] This is understood as a corollary of Gregory of Nazianzus's 'What is not assumed is not healed' (*Ep.* 101). There is no part of human nature (except sin) that the Word has not assumed.

Antony to the fourteenth-century hesychasts, was to share in divine glory through the deifying vision of the divine light.

The second part of Lot-Borodine's essay, on the ascent of the mind to union with God, revolves around the title of St Bonaventure's great work, *Itinerarium mentis in Deum* (The Soul's Journey to God). For Lot-Borodine, Bonaventure is 'the Prince of mediaeval mystical theology' (153).[17] Yet even he will not allow God to be seen by the intellect, for intellectual knowledge in Bonaventure's view is trumped by love. The contrasts established in the first part of the essay on the theological foundations are carried through into the second part on the ascent of the soul. The deiform *nous* (mind) of the Greeks is set against the mere *ratio* (reasoning faculty) of the Latins. The role of the Holy Spirit, fundamental to the Greek ascent, is contrasted with the Christomonism of the Western version – 'Even in Eckhart and Tauler nothing intervenes between the soul and Christ' (158 n. 83). The fully Trinitarian mystical theology of the Greeks was 'not content with ecstasy on earth, or even the *visio beata* beyond'. The Greeks thus went much further than the Latins. And to conclude her essay, Lot-Borodine sings the praises of the fourteenth-century hesychasts of Mount Athos:

> For them, the divine essence pouring out its energies on creatures deifies them fully, in their very interior itself, on condition that their wills give themselves there to the hard effort of ascesis and their spirit to the abandon of cognitive love. The *gnôthi seauton* (know thyself) leads to the first spiritual knowledge. The imma-nent God and the transcendent God meet in the solitude of the pure heart, of the 'intelligent heart', the extreme point of the deiform *noûs*. (179)

Lot-Borodine is glad, as a Russian scholar writing in French, to have drawn attention for the first time to 'the spirituality that is such a distin-guishing feature of the Christian East ... the *via regia* of Deification' (183). Her readers, for their part, were equally glad to have been given a comprehensive conspectus of the Eastern theological tradition that establishes theosis as an organising principle of Orthodox thought, dis-cusses the implications of theosis for the ascent of the mind to God in the hesychast tradition, and sets this tradition within a broad context that relates it to the great spiritual currents of the mediaeval and early modern West.

---

[17] On Bonaventure, Lot-Borodine's guide is É. Gilson's 'magisterial' *La philosophie de Saint Bonaventure* (Paris: Vrin, 1924).

THE SOPHIANIC VERSION OF DEIFICATION:
SERGIUS BULGAKOV

Within a few months of the appearance of the last part of Lot-Borodine's essay on deification, Sergius Bulgakov published (in Russian) the first volume of a projected trilogy entitled *On Godmanhood*. The title of the trilogy deliberately echoes that of Soloviev's *Lectures on Godmanhood*, but whereas Soloviev (and indeed Bulgakov himself in *The Philosophy of Economy* and *Unfading Light*) conducted his discussion on the level of philosophy, in this new enterprise Bulgakov turns to the theological dimension of theosis. The first volume, published in 1933, is called *The Lamb of God*.[18] As the title implies, its subject is Christology. It was followed three years later by a volume on the Holy Spirit entitled *The Comforter*.[19] The final volume, on the Church, entitled *The Bride of the Lamb*, was published posthumously in 1945.[20]

Expelled from Russia in 1922, Bulgakov arrived in Paris three years later, via Constantinople and Prague, to join the faculty of the Theological Institute established in Paris in 1925 by Metropolitan Evlogy (Georgievsky).[21] Bulgakov was invited by Evlogy to be Professor of Dogmatic Theology and Dean of the Institute, a post he held until his death in 1944. It was Evlogy's intention that the Institute should carry on the tradition of the Theological Academies of pre-revolutionary Russia, but in a new Western environment, 'in order that Orthodoxy would no longer be hidden under a bushel, but would gradually become the inheritance of all Christians' (Evlogy, 2014: 513). The language of instruction at St Sergius, however, was Russian and the professors published their work in that language, thanks to the Russophile YMCA Press in Paris, so the task of bringing Orthodoxy out from under its bushel, at least in

---

[18] S. N. Bulgakov, *Agnets Bozhyi* (Paris: YMCA Press, 1933), trans. B. Jakim as *The Lamb of God* (Bulgakov, 2008).

[19] S. N. Bulgakov, *Uteshitel'* (Paris: YMCA Press, 1936); trans. B. Jakim as *The Comforter* (Bulgakov, 2004).

[20] S. N. Bulgakov, *Nevesta agntsa* (Paris: YMCA Press, 1945); trans. B. Jakim as *The Bride of the Lamb* (Bulgakov, 2002). Although published posthumously, *The Bride of the Lamb* was completed in 1942.

[21] Metropolitan Evlogy, Archbishop of Volynia and Zhitomir, had been asked by the émigré bishops who formed an informal synod in Serbia, to take charge of the Russian churches in Western Europe. His appointment was later confirmed by Patriarch Tikhon of Moscow. The creation of the St Sergius Orthodox Theological Institute in Paris was one of his most important achievements.

Bulgakov's case, fell largely to translators, whose work only got under way after the Second World War.

The first volume of the trilogy, *The Lamb of God*, reveals that Bulgakov undertook a thorough study of the Christological tradition of the Fathers only to find it wanting.[22] In his view, patristic theology failed to arrive at a coherent doctrine of the Incarnation: 'It knew only God and man, Divinity and humanity, outwardly conjoined but not inwardly united' (Bulgakov, 2008: 210).[23] He reserves his most severe criticism for St John Damascene, whose interpretation of divine-human action is simply 'a variant of monophysitism' (73, 210) and whose discussion of the divine and human wills in Christ is 'a series of nearly incoherent and even divergent propositions' (82). Suspicious of what he calls Cyril of Alexandria's 'obstinate monism', Bulgakov is impressed by Nestorius's understanding of 'bi-unity as a unity not of natures but of their personal centers' (45–46). This leads him to his own 'sophiological' solution to the problem of how divinity and humanity are inwardly united in Christ. By Sophia, with her dual aspect, both created and uncreated, he attempts to give an ontological foundation for the Incarnation. He is attracted to the expression 'theandric energy', which he thinks goes some way to elucidating 'the *mode* of the union of the natures in relation to the one hypostasis' (209).[24] Indeed, given the creation of humanity in the divine image, the human itself is theandric, presaging the Incarnation from the beginning:

Man is created as the god-man in the sense that, in his creaturely psycho-corporeal essence, he contains a spirit of divine origin. In the God-Man this spirit is the Logos Himself. And if the uncreated-created human spirit is open for the reception of divine life, for deification, for communion with the divine nature, then in the God-Man this divine nature exists, from the beginning, without separation from the hypostasis. (230)

In other words, humanity was created in the divine image precisely in order to be a receptacle for the inhomination of God. Humanity is the creaturely Sophia with which the Divine Sophia is able to unite herself

---

[22] 'Wanting' in the sense of at best incomplete and at worst misleading. This why in an essay first published in 1937 he complains about the uncritical reception of a neo-patristic synthesis and warns against an attitude of patristic 'rabbinism'. See Bulgakov, 2003: 70–71.

[23] Bulgakov ignores John Damascene's use of the concept of *perichoresis* as a dynamic interpenetration of the human and divine natures in Christ and, moreover, his innovative application of *perichoresis* to the divine hypostases in the Trinity.

[24] Bulgakov regards 'theandric energy', a term that he has found in John Damascene's *Exposition of the Orthodox Faith* 63, as 'a capital that is yet to be exploited'.

because both are different sides of the same reality. The deification of Christ's human nature is distinguished from the deification of the creature 'by the fact that the creature receives it as the supernatural, grace-bestowing principle of life, whereas the Son only returns to the heaven He voluntarily abandoned, to His proper natural consciousness of Himself' (280).

The second work of the trilogy, *The Comforter*, has little to say about deification beyond the claim that the descent of the Holy Spirit fulfils and continues the work of the Incarnation with the aim of bringing about the deification of all creation (Bulgakov, 2004: 278). The universality of deification is a theme that becomes prominent in the final work, *The Bride of the Lamb*. For Bulgakov, 'the ontological possibility of "salvation" through deification is predetermined by the very creation of man in the image of God' (Bulgakov, 2002: 203). Here Bulgakov distinguishes between natural grace and divine grace. Natural grace is entailed by creation; it is that which keeps creatures from sinking into 'the abyss of *nothing*' (247, emphasis original). Divine grace is 'precisely the power of deification, in which creation surpasses itself in man, transcends the bounds of natural or physico-sophianic being, and acquires the power of new sophianization by receiving the principles of divine life in Divine-humanity' (247–48). The goal is the deification of the whole of human-kind and indeed, through man, the entire cosmos. The descent of the Holy Spirit at Pentecost 'lays the foundation not only for the world's being but also for the world's deification through the penetration of the creaturely Sophia by the Divine Sophia' (425). Eternal life is a dynamic, actualised sophianisation. Bulgakov then (but without discussing the role of human freedom) goes on to refute the idea of eternal damnation: 'Can the sophianization of creation in resurrection fail to be accomplished?' (452). It is not surprising that his most quoted patristic authors in this work are Origen, Gregory of Nyssa, and Isaac the Syrian.

Bulgakov is not directly concerned in his writings with the journey to deification by the individual believer. Theosis is a structural element in his theological vision: the creation of humanity in God's image both as the preparation for the Incarnation – Bulgakov goes so far as to speak of Christ as 'a maximally deified Man, in whom the entire fullness of divinity abided bodily' (Bulgakov, 2011: 88) – and as the condition of humanity's reception by grace of divine life. Bulgakov's preferred way of speaking of this reception is in terms of the sophianicity of creation and of the coming together in deified humanity of the creaturely and the divine Sophia. It is a theological vision of great power (despite some aspects that are questionable from the neopatristic viewpoint), which although ignored for many decades is again receiving serious attention.

THE PATRISTIC VERSION OF DEIFICATION: VLADIMIR LOSSKY

Bulgakov was working almost entirely in a Russian-speaking environment. Yet he was also eager to reach out to his Roman Catholic and particularly his Anglican fellow Christians, which he was able to do from time to time through Metropolitan Evlogy's participation in the nascent ecumenical movement.[25] By contrast, Vladimir Lossky from the start had much closer relations with Western Christians, especially with sympathetic French Catholics. Not only did he write in French, but deeply Francophile, he sought to delineate the differences between Orthodoxy and Western Christianity in a constructive manner. His principal aim, in those pre-ecumenical days,[26] was not simply to protect Orthodox identity from Catholic encroachment, although that was far from unimportant, but also to communicate to Western Christians the wealth of the Eastern tradition. He did so not in a proselytising spirit but for its own sake, in order to help French Catholics enrich their own tradition.[27]

The work Lossky is best known for is his *Mystical Theology of the Eastern Church* (1956), originally published as *Essai sur la Théologie de l'Église d'Orient* (1944) – the only one of Lossky's books actually published in his lifetime. As his son, Fr Nicholas Lossky, relates, it was originally written in the form of twelve lectures delivered in 1944 at the request of a group of Catholic friends, who included the future cardinals Jean Daniélou, Henri de Lubac, and Yves-Marie Congar, to explain Orthodoxy to a non-Orthodox audience (Lossky, 2012: 110). Lossky is widely known as an anti-Westerner on account of his hostility to the *Filioque*, but in fact the *Filioque* is not used by him as a stick with which to beat the Latins but as an example – indeed the only example – of a doctrine that is a diriment impediment to reconciliation, as he says, only because it prevents the Latins from considering that Byzantine theological developments (particularly in the matter of essence and energies) are expressive of the truths of a tradition that has its roots in the earliest

---

[25] See Metropolitan Evlogy's chapter, 'The Ecumenical Movement', Evlogy, 2014: 651–84.

[26] It should be remembered that by the 1928 encyclical of Pius XI, *Mortalium Animos*, Catholics were forbidden from engaging in liturgical worship and prayer with non-Catholics. Orthodox, for their part, were forbidden by their canons from prayer with 'heretics and schismatics'.

[27] This point is very well made by Anthony Feneuil in Feneuil, 2018: 50–51.

centuries of the Church (Lossky, 2001: 95–96). This is the attitude that informs *The Mystical Theology of the Eastern Church*.[28]

Deification is one of the main themes running through *The Mystical Theology*. Lossky begins his book with the statement that '"mystical theology" denotes no more than a spirituality which expresses a doctrinal attitude' (Lossky, 1957: 7). He is opposed to Bergson's distinction between the '"static religion" of the Churches' and the '"dynamic religion" of the mystics', only the latter being considered 'personal and creative' (7). In Bergson's view, the religion of the mystics springs from the *élan vital*. But this is only because Bergson, says Lossky, like many Western thinkers can only see dogmatic religion, expressed in theological formulations, as a lifeless intellectual construct. With Filaret of Moscow (1782–1867), Lossky insists that what dogma expresses is an unfathomable mystery that transcends our understanding but which we can enter into through mystical ascent: 'If the mystical experience is a personal working out of the content of the common faith, theology is an expression, for the profit of all, of that which can be experienced by everyone' (8–9). There are not two different kinds of religion, one for the masses – including academic theologians – the other for an élite. Mysticism is 'the perfecting and crown of all theology' through its personal appropriation (9).

Theology is thus a means, not an end. To treat the possession of knowledge as an end is gnosticism, but the end of the Christian faith is union with God, the theosis of the Greek Fathers. Not that Lossky regards the Greek Fathers as the exclusive teachers of truth:

The Orthodox Church would not be what it is if it had not had St. Cyprian, St. Augustine and St. Gregory the Great.[29] No more could the Roman Catholic Church do without St. Athanasius, St. Basil or St. Cyril of Alexandria. Thus when one would speak of the mystical theology of the East or of the West, one takes one's stand within one of the two traditions which remained, down to a certain moment, two local traditions within the one Church, witnessing to a single Christian truth; but which subsequently part, the one from the other, and give rise to two different dogmatic attitudes, irreconcilable on certain points. (11–12)

It is this conviction that accounts for Lossky's passion to communicate the treasures of Orthodoxy to Western Christians – almost all his theological writings that are not of purely Russian interest were composed for English

---

[28] Lossky, 1957: 56: 'The *filioque* was the primordial cause, the only dogmatic cause, of the breach between East and West.'

[29] Key works from all three had been translated into Greek by the fourteenth century.

or French audiences.[30] He loved France and her ancient Christian trad-
ition. The fall of France in 1940 caused him intense personal anguish.
He longed for the French to rediscover their spiritual patrimony. 'Is
French Christianity', he asks, 'capable of undergoing spiritual renewal?
Of bringing about a total transfiguration which would cause to gush forth
again springs of living water from the parched earth of its Church?'
(Lossky, 2012: 42). Anthony Feneuil puts is well when he says that
Lossky 'was not attempting to replace one theological tradition by
another. On the contrary, he relentlessly sought to understand how the
Eastern Christian tradition might be useful to Western theology *as such*'
(2018: 51). Lossky's *Mystical Theology* was thus not intended simply to
inform Western Christians about the content of Orthodox teaching.
It was meant to stimulate them to rediscover their own spiritual potential.

'The way of the knowledge of God', says Lossky, 'is necessarily the
way of deification' (Lossky, 1957: 39). In the orthodox Christian tradition, in contrast with Gnosticism, the reality of divine knowledge is
transformative. It demands *change* in the believer. Following St John
Damascene, Lossky says that humanity was created 'for deification'
(126).[31] Adam was created not in a state of completion but with an
orientation towards union with God. He had to grow into this union,
not only for his own sake but – as the intelligent tip of creation – for the
sake of the entire cosmos. But Adam failed to fulfil his vocation. Yet the
Fall did not destroy God's plan. It only modified it. The Incarnation of the
Word was always intended; it was not simply a response to the Fall. What
was changed by the Fall was the inevitability of the Lord's passion and
death. The twofold economy of the Son and the Spirit was therefore
intended to open anew for us the way of deification (133–34).

The economy of the Son is described by Lossky as a movement towards
unification, the bringing together of a world that has been fractured by
sin. This movement is more than 'salvation', which Lossky sees as negative term, a term signifying the removal of an obstacle, namely, death and
its root cause, sin (135). The positive term for this movement is 'deification', which is not simply a line of ascent by humanity towards God. This
would have been impossible for human beings unless God had first taken

[30] The exception is his first article, on Dionysius, published in 1929, which was written
in Russian.
[31] Like Lot-Borodine (1970: 43), Lossky calls man 'a created god', attributing this to
Maximus the Confessor. I have not found this phrase in Maximus or in any of the other
Greek Fathers. Lossky must have taken it from Lot-Borodine. He does not repeat it,
however, in his chapter on Maximus in *The Vision of God*.

the initiative through the incarnation of the Son: 'What man ought to have attained by raising himself up to God, God achieved by descending to man' (136). The unifying work of the Son, however, occurred on the level of the human nature that he assumed. What was also needed was the diversifying work of the Spirit. 'The work of both is requisite', says Lossky, 'that we may attain union with God' (156). The Son unifies human nature by deifying it through his enfleshment, through his assumption of a complete human nature, resulting in what the Fathers call the hypostatic union. By baptism, Christians are incorporated into this unified human nature, the Body of Christ, which is also the Church, 'in so far as Christ is her head' (157). Baptism brings about the recovery in Christ of the divine image – an ontological change, which is the same for everyone. The work of attaining the divine likeness then begins – the working out and completion of this ontological change on the moral level in the Holy Spirit, which is different for each person. The way Lossky puts it is this:

The Holy Spirit grants to each person created in the image of God the possibility of fulfilling the likeness in the common nature. The one lends His hypostasis to the nature, the other gives His divinity to the persons. Thus the work of Christ unifies; the work of the Holy Spirit diversifies. Yet the one is impossible without the other. (167)

Subsequently, Lossky attracted criticism, from Orthodox as well as Catholics, for positing two distinct and parallel economies, that of the Son and that of the Spirit. If we bear in mind, however, the French Catholic audience to whom he first delivered the lectures that resulted in the *Mystical Theology*, we can understand how this emphasis – perhaps overemphasis – on distinction arises from his conviction that the Western *Filioque* resulted in an undervaluing of the role of the Spirit (through not according the Spirit a full hypostatic reality) and his desire to help Western Christians bring the Spirit's role back into focus as equal and complementary to that of the Son.[32]

It was also for a Western audience that Lossky wrote his *Vision of God*, first delivered as a series of lectures given at the École Pratique des Hautes Études in Paris in 1945–1946. These lectures adopt a historical perspective taking us in nine chapters from 'The tradition of the Fathers and scholasticism' to 'The Palamite synthesis'. Their purpose is to

---

[32] On this topic, see Lossky's lecture, 'The Procession of the Holy Spirit in Orthodox Trinitarian Doctrine', translated in Lossky, 1974: 71–96.

demonstrate a consistent patristic tradition on the mode of union with God leading (not without significant developments) from Irenaeus right up to Gregory Palamas. Their approach, as is appropriate for a university series of lectures, is scholarly and based on a close study of the texts. The vision of God, says Lossky, is the vision of Christ in glory, 'the vision by which man participates in the light of the Invisible God, receiving in this way the state of incorruptibility or deification' (Lossky, 1963: 35). The deification of created beings is fundamentally their participation in divine life. The best image for this is the vision of light. Deification is thus realised by contemplation, which is perfected when knowledge is united with love. The soul is already in the image of God. By attaining the vision of God through contemplation it also acquires the likeness of God. This is not a process that bypasses the Son and the Spirit: it is fully Trinitarian, for 'in the Holy Spirit we see the image of the Son, and through Him we see the Archetype, the Father' (67). At this point, Lossky introduces the notion of 'perichoresis' (mutual interpenetration), a notion that was developed by Maximus the Confessor to explain how the human and the divine in Christ are fully united without either becoming the other and was then applied by John Damascene to the relations between the persons of the Trinity: 'To participate in the divinity of the Son, in the communal divinity of the Trinity, is to be deified, to be penetrated by divinity – just as red-hot iron in the fire is penetrated by the heat of the fire – allowing the beauty of the inexpressible nature of the Trinity to shine in us' (81). This brings Lossky to 'Byzantine theology proper', which he defines as the body of thought that 'makes distinctions between God's unknowable οὐσία [*ousia*, essence] and his manifestations (dynamic attributes, δυνάμεις [*dynameis*, powers] or energies), a distinction which, instead of limiting the mystical flight by placing the human being before a closed door, opens up an infinite path beyond knowledge' (110). Byzantine theology, with its distinction between the unknowable divine essence and the participable divine energies, is the crowning point of a theology that surpasses the 'dualism of the sensible and the intelligible within created being' and enables the vision of light to draw the whole of the human person into an ever-deepening union with God (136). This is the path of deification.

It was probably also for a Western audience, this time Anglican, that Lossky first made the principle of theosis the subject of a special study. At the 1947 summer conference of the Fellowship of St Alban and St Sergius, he seems to have delivered a paper entitled 'Redemption and Deification', for this was the title of an article published in *Sobornost*, the

Fellowship's journal, in the winter of the same year in an English translation by Edward Every.[33] In addressing a Western audience, Lossky concentrates on the aspects of the Latin teaching on redemption that fall short of the Greek patristic vision. The Greeks play with a broad pattern of ideas: κατάβασις (katabasis, decent) followed by ἀνάβασις (anabasis, ascent), κένωσις (kenōsis, emptying of self) followed by θέωσις (theōsis, filling with God), the divine condescension making possible and eliciting the human ascension. When the dogma of the redemption is treated in isolation, insists Lossky, 'there is always a risk of limiting the tradition by interpreting it exclusively in terms of the work of the Redeemer' (Lossky, 1974: 98). Anselm of Canterbury provides a case in point. Lossky regards Anselm's *Cur Deus Homo*, written in 1098, as an impoverishment of the work of Christ. There is too much emphasis here on original guilt and its reparation and nothing about the triumph over death. Moreover, the dispensation of the Holy Spirit is lacking (99). Redemption is not simply retrospective, undoing the effects of the Fall, but looks ahead to its ultimate goal, our deification, which 'cannot be expressed on a Christological basis alone, but demands a Pneumatological development as well' (103).[34] The lack of a Pneumatological dimension is the result of the doctrine of the *processio ab utroque*, the procession of the Spirit from the Father and the Son as from one principle, which denies the Spirit a properly hypostatic existence. These critiques of Western doctrine are not offered in a spirit of confessional point-scoring but to encourage Western theologians to correct the one-sidedness of their own tradition.

A MONASTIC MODEL OF DEIFICATION: ARCHIMANDRITE SOPHRONY (SAKHAROV)

With Archimandrite Sophrony (Sakharov), we move to an altogether more experiential version of deification. The young Sergei (Sophrony's baptismal name) was brought up in Moscow in a pious Orthodox family where daily prayer was the norm. Like many of his contemporaries in the bourgeoisie, he broke with the Church in his adolescence only to return to it in later life. In his case, it was not atheistic materialism that drew him

---

[33] V. Lossky, 'Redemption and Deification' *Sobornost* 12 (1947), 47–56. The French version was published in the *Messager de l'Exarchat du patriarche russe en Europe occidental* 15 (1953), 161–70. Every's English translation is reproduced as chapter 5 of Lossky, 1974.

[34] Lossky comes back here to one of his key ideas: Baptism (the sacrament of unity in Christ) needs to be completed by chrismation (the sacrament of diversity in the holy Spirit).

away in his youth but a spiritual quest for meaning: 'As a young man I was constantly tormented by an urgent need to understand why I had been born into this world. Where are we all going? What could we attain to? Where is our "end"?' (Sophrony, 1988: 64). His nephew and biographer tells us that for a time he embraced Indian mysticism, convinced that Christianity's personal Absolute was inferior to the supra-personal Absolute of the Upanishads (Sakharov, 2015: 17).[35] When Sakharov left Russia in 1921 to develop his art in Western Europe, he had still not returned to Orthodoxy. Yet all the time he was searching, hoping through art to capture the transcendent, the 'wholly other'. Then in 1924 came a turning point. He had an experience that he interpreted as a vision of uncreated light.[36] He enrolled at the newly established Institute of St Sergius, taking Bulgakov as his spiritual father and learning from him about the kenoticism that was to become a central feature of his own spiritual teaching. In the same period, Berdyaev's personalism also exercised an important influence on him. The academic curriculum at St Sergius, however, did not satisfy his spiritual yearning. Within a few months, he left Paris to follow a monastic path on Mount Athos.

At the Russian monastery of St Panteleimon on the Holy Mountain, Sakharov became a disciple of *Starets* (now St) Silouan, whom he came to revere as a model of Christ-like humility. From the *starets*, he learned much that was to be fundamental to his spiritual life. Two things stand out: how to face the sense of abandonment when instead of God all one experiences in prayer is desolate emptiness and how to cope with the anguish that accompanies intense prayer for the suffering world. The first was given meaning by the concept of Godforsakenness that Sakharov was later to develop more fully, the second by the injunction revealed in prayer to the *starets* and communicated by him to his disciple: 'Keep your mind in hell and despair not!'

After the death of his *starets* in 1938, Sophrony, as Sakharov now was, retreated to the 'desert', an area of isolated hermitages on the south-west edge of Mount Athos, where he was ordained and subsequently sought out as a confessor and spiritual father. The Second World War was a period of anguish for him that undermined his health. On top of that, the

---

[35] Sophrony tells us that his '"eastern" phase' lasted seven or eight years (Sophrony, 1988: 33). He does not say whether this came about through an encounter with theosophy (as in the case of other artists of the period) or whether it was through an independent study of Indian religious thought.

[36] Interestingly, like Florensky and Bulgakov, Sophrony has a theosophic view of auras: 'Azure-blue is the colour of transcendency' (Sophrony, 1988: 166).

situation of Russians in Greece became difficult in the Greek civil war that began as the Second World War came to an end. In 1947, Fr Sophrony returned to Paris where he joined Vladimir Lossky (both of them belonged to the jurisdiction of the Moscow patriarchate, whereas St Sergius had been placed by Metropolitan Evlogy under the patriarchate of Constantinople) and assisted him with editing the *Messager*, the Russian patriarchate's journal in France. In the 1950s, Fr Sophrony became well known through his publications on the life and teaching of *Starets* Silouan and began to attract disciples. This led to his founding a monastery in England in 1959, the Monastery of St John the Baptist at Tolleshunt Knights in Essex, where he was to spend the rest of his life.

Fr Sophrony founded his monastery the year after Lossky died, but it was not Lossky's death that prompted the move to England. His ideas had begun to diverge from Lossky's long before, so Paris was coming to hold less attraction for him. Lossky was not impressed by his writings on *Starets* Silouan. Moreover, Fr Sophrony's tendency to bare his soul, which became more pronounced in later life, did not go down well with the Russian community. Yet it is in his autobiographical writings, especially in *We Shall See Him As He Is* (first published in French in 1984) that he gives us his mature thinking on deification.[37]

We Shall See Him As He Is was well received by Western theologians, less so by Orthodox, especially Russians (Sakharov, 2015: 36). Westerners are accustomed to spiritual autobiography – there are examples from almost every century from Augustine's *Confessions* to Pope John XXIII's *Journal of a Soul* – but Russians are not. Fr Sophrony's work appeared to many Russians to be somewhat boastful and self-promoting,[38] yet for the Western reader the personal testimony can be compelling. From the point of view of modern thinking on deification, the way in which Fr Sophrony connects kenosis ('emptying of self') with theosis ('filling with God') is of great interest.

There is a strong Russian tradition of thinking on God's self-limitation in the act of creation, the Incarnation, and the historical life

---

[37] For an illuminating discussion of Fr Sophrony's teaching on deification, see R. Williams, 2021: 98–111.

[38] One of Fr Sophrony's strongest critics was Archbishop Basil Krivochéine (1900–1985), who knew him well from the time when they were both monks at St Panteleimon. Indeed, their years on Mount Athos (1925–1947) coincided exactly. Metropolitan Kallistos of Diokleia once told me that he heard the archbishop say to Sophrony: 'Fr Sophrony, we know you, and it's not true!'

of Christ.[39] In his influential sermons, Metropolitan Filaret (Drozdov) of Moscow (1782–1867) made the humiliation of Christ central to the doctrine of redemption as 'the expression of the crucifying, crucified and triumphant love of the Triune God'. 'God approaches man and partakes of his humiliation', says Filaret, in order to restore in him the hope of the glory that he had tried to seize for himself by eating of the forbidden fruit (Gorodetzky, 1938: 108–9). The topic was treated for the first time in a scientific manner with copious references to patristic sources by Mikhail Tareev (1866–1934), Professor of Moral Theology at the Moscow Theological Academy.[40] Tareev sees kenosis as the self-limitation of God, beginning with the act of creation, in order to make the 'other' – humanity – capable of participating in God's glory and making it its own. The self-limitation of God and the deification of man go hand in hand (145).[41] This is taken up by Bulgakov, who says that 'the creation of the world was in its very foundation a sacrificial act of Divine love, a voluntary self-depletion or self-effacement of Divinity... [that] pre-eternally included a concrete kenosis, the incarnation of the Son of God and the sacrifice on Golgotha' (Bulgakov, 2012: 343). It was no doubt from Bulgakov that Sophrony derived the fundamentals of his kenotic teaching. Sophrony, however, takes its implications further by connecting kenosis with the attainment of 'hypostatic' existence, or true personhood, with living not in the egocentric human mode but in the self-giving divine mode. Rowan Williams sums it up helpfully: 'When the created subject receives the revelation of divine hypostatic being through relation with Christ in the Spirit, that subject is radically altered: our existence begins to become hypostatic in the divine mode, that is, to be structured by, defined by, kenosis, the dissolution of the ego's defence and individual interest' (2021: 98–99).

There is also another dimension of kenosis, which comes out of Sophrony's experience of Godforsakenness (*bogoostavlennost'*) and his meditation on the significance of Gethsemane. This is not quite the same as St John of the Cross's 'dark night of the soul', although there are some similarities. For the Spanish mystic, the dark night of abandonment (*derelictio*), a concept deriving from Dionysius the Areopagite and

---

[39] The classic study on this, which has still not been superseded, is Gorodetzky, 1938. The humiliated Christ is also the subject of an iconographical tradition.

[40] On Tareev, see Gorodetzky, 1938: 139–56.

[41] See the important passages she cites from Tareev, *Foundations of Christianity*, iii, 229, 230.

referring ultimately to Moses's ascent to God through the dark cloud on Mount Sinai, is a stage that must be endured because it leads to divine illumination. For the Russian, the sense of being forsaken by God (and vulnerable to diabolic attack) is an ordeal calling for repentance and spiritual weeping, yet it is also a necessary stage of spiritual growth. 'No one genuinely seeking salvation can escape the experience of being bereft by God' (Sophrony, 1988: 129). But we are not to accept Godforsakenness passively. The Spirit draws us into the prayer of Gethsemane and the more we struggle to make this prayer our own, the more complete our self-emptying becomes and the closer we come to the realisation of the hypostatic principle within us.

What does 'the realisation of the hypostatic principle within us' actually mean? Williams has described it as 'the dissolution of what is not yet personal in the full and theologically determined sense' (2021: 103). Perhaps more simply, it means attaining experiential knowledge of God, which is not a matter of intellectual information about God but a knowledge that makes us personal participants in his being. Such participation does not absorb us into an undifferentiated Absolute (this is precluded by the word 'hypostatic'). Nor does it empower us as deified superhumans, which is the Luciferian deification promised to Adam and Eve (Gen 3.5). 'Our divinization', says Sophrony, lies in perfect God-like humility' (1988: 67). Or in Williams's words, 'the "divinized" subject is the undefended subject', a vulnerable self with its defences down (2021: 101). Yet this vulnerable self is so joined to uncreated grace that the two become one. Theosis is 'the wondrous process of the creation by God from nothing of gods like Himself' (Sophrony, 1988: 224) even to the point of their sharing in uncreatedness.[42]

THEOSIS AND RELIGION IN THE RUSSIAN DIASPORA

All the Russian émigré writers discussed in this chapter were convinced that religion must be experiential yet at the same time rooted in dogma understood as the collective expression of the faith of the Christian community from earliest times. In Russia before the Revolution, a distinction was often made between the Church as an institution – the 'ecclesiastical administration, the creed and rites of worship', in Tareev's

---

[42] Sakharov (2015: 26) quotes a passage from a letter of Fr Sophrony to David Balfour: 'We long for participation in eternal life. What actually happens is that man becomes not only immortal but without beginning also.'

words – and religion as something that was personal and intuitive. Such a distinction was not acceptable to the theologians of the diaspora. Lossky explicitly rejects Bergson's thesis that distinguishes 'the "static religion" of the Churches from the "dynamic religion" of the mystics; the former social and conservative in character, the latter personal and creative' (1957: 7). For the Russian émigrés religion was the faith of the Orthodox Church, not something distinct from it.

That is not to say that the religious truth expressed by Orthodoxy was regarded as its exclusive possession. In none of the writers we have been considering do we find a simple East/West divide. Karsavin, Lot-Borodine, and Lossky, for example, were mediaevalists with a deep appreciation of Western culture. Even before leaving Russia, Karsavin published a Russian translation of the Revelations of the Umbrian mystic, Angela of Foligno (c. 1248–1309). Lot-Borodine was a noted scholar of the French mediaeval tradition.[43] Lossky's doctoral dissertation, published posthumously in 1960, was on the greatest of the Rhineland mystics: *Negative Theology and Knowledge of God in Meister Eckhart.* Both Lot-Borodine (who in 1909 married the distinguished French mediaevalist, Ferdinand Lot) and Lossky were disciples of the great historian of mediaeval philosophy, Étienne Gilson (1884–1978). Moreover, Lossky and Bulgakov were both active in the early days of the ecumenical movement, with annual visits to the conferences organised in England by the Fellowship of St Alban and St Sergius. Metropolitan Evlogy, who famously wanted to bring Orthodoxy out from under its bushel (cf. Mt 5.15), greatly admired Cardinal Mercier (1851–1926), the Belgian prelate who did much to foster ecumenical relations at a time when Rome was deeply suspicious of them. None of these writers sought to proselytise. Certainly, they wanted to define the boundaries of Orthodoxy. But more than that, they wanted to share with Westerners their insights into Orthodox mystical theology – in Lossky's case to help the Western Church forsake her aberration (there was only one, the *Filioque*) and become herself.

On the experiential level, the emphasis of all our writers is on the mystical. 'In a certain sense', says Lossky, 'all theology is mystical' (1957: 7). Even the more academic theological treatments, such as that of Lot-Borodine, take this for granted. For Bulgakov, the mystical also embraces the intuitive: 'only an immediate sense of God grants one to see

---

[43] Her dissertation, *Womanhood in the Work of Chrétien of Troyes* was published in 1909 and her later research, *Lancelot and the Quest for the Holy Grail*, in 1919.

the divine in the world, to come to know the world as a revelation of God' (2012: 23). In this perspective, it was natural that the main focus should be on the goal of mystical theology, namely, deification or theosis.

Popov's taxonomy of deification ('realistic' and 'idealistic') helps us to position our authors in relation to each other. Bulgakov and Lossky are exponents principally of the *realistic* mode. They present deification as a structural element of the theology of salvation that explains first how the human and divine natures are united in Christ and then how, by virtue of humanity's creation in the divine image and Christ's divinisation of humanity through his Incarnation and Passion, human beings become receptive of divine life. Lossky makes a useful distinction between salvation *from* (looking back to humanity's alienation from God through sin) and deification *to* (looking ahead to participation in divine glory). The *idealistic* mode is explored by Lot-Borodine in patristic texts as the ascent of the deiform human soul to union with God and by Archimandrite Sophrony, with the accompaniment of striking autobiographical testimony, as the hypostatisation in the ascetic struggler of the divine attributes, even the attribute of uncreatedness. 'In the act of divinization', says Fr Sophrony, 'grace exalts man from the dimensions and patterns of the earth to the dimensions and the patterns of Divine Life' (Sophrony, 1988: 192). Christians 'live on two planes simultaneously, the temporal and the eternal. And time itself we apprehend as a wondrous process of the creation by God from nothing of gods like himself' (224). Theosis is thus the means by which through attaining God-like humility – 'God-like' because it mirrors God's kenotic acts of creation, incarnation, and acceptance of death – we paradoxically attain a community of being with him who is beyond being through his willingness to share himself with the 'other'.

7

One with God

From Academic Re-engagement with Theosis to Its Popular Reception

For all the main Christian communions today, including the Orthodox, re-engagement with theosis on the academic level has been the result of the retrieval of an important but neglected aspect of biblical and patristic teaching. In both Russia and the West, the beginning of this retrieval was stimulated by the assertion of members of the Ritschlian school that the patristic notion of the Christian's deification was a corruption of the original faith of the Apostles under the pernicious influence of pagan Greek thought. It was in reaction to the Ritschlian school and particularly to Adolf von Harnack that both Ivan Popov in 1909 and Jules Gross in 1938 produced their seminal studies of deification in the early Greek Fathers. In Gross's case, he was also reacting to Myrrha Lot-Borodine's classic 'La doctrine de la "déification" dans l'Église grecque jusqu' au XIe siècle' (first published in 1932–1933), with its hostility to Augustine and its emphasis on deification as characteristically 'Eastern'. Towards the end of the Second World War, Lot-Borodine's essay was followed by Vladimir Lossky's *Essai sur la théologie mystique de l'Église d'Orient* (1944). The work of Lot-Borodine and Lossky, in turn, contributed to a revival of interest in deification in the Orthodox world, especially in Greece. The translation of some of the resulting Greek publications into English, particularly works by Georgios Mantzaridis and Panayiotis Nellas translated in 1984 and 1987 respectively, gave a powerful impetus to the renewed study of deification already under way in the Anglophone world. Thus the modern re-engagement with theosis is not principally a matter of Catholics and Protestants appropriating a theological tradition native to the Orthodox Church – although on one level that is also true – but a reciprocal enrichment of both East and West through a return to patristic sources. This enrichment has taken place chiefly on the level of academic research but it has spread from there to considerations of how Christians can be transformed by Christ on the practical level – to the relationship between theosis and religion.

RE-ENGAGEMENT WITH THEOSIS IN THE
TWENTY-FIRST CENTURY

The 2004 colloquium on theosis/deification organised at Drew University by two members of the university's Caspersen School of Graduate Studies, Vladimir Kharlamov and Jeffery Wittung, raised the question of what precisely constitutes theosis. The editors of the book that resulted from the conference describe theosis as a 'compelling vision of human potential for transformation and spiritual perfectibility' (Christensen and Wittung, 2007: 11). What precisely that vision consisted in varies greatly in the essays presented in the book. Two contributors call for greater precision or, better perhaps, for a maximalist interpretation. Andrew Louth, drawing on the cosmic dimension of Orthodox theology (prominent in Maximus the Confessor), sees deification as encompassed by a great arch stretching from creation to the consummation of God's intention in the eschaton, within which 'deification witnesses to the rooting of theology in the transforming encounter with God, now known most fully in the Incarnation, and approached through "the gates of repentance"' (2007: 35, 43). Gösta Hallonsten is more blunt about where deification in the maximalist sense is to be located, insisting that a 'real *doctrine of theosis* is to be found only in the East' (2007: 292 n. 43, author's emphasis). Protesting at the interpretation of similarities in different traditions as identities, Hallonsten proposes a threefold taxonomy of theosis: (a) as a theme, like adoption and filiation, closely associated with the 'exchange formula'; (b) as an integral part of patristic teaching on progress from the image to the likeness; and (c) as 'a comprehensive doctrine that encompasses the whole economy of salvation' (287). Hallonsten's distinction between 'theme' and 'doctrine' is a valuable one. The theme is found widely in patristic and later literature. With regard to the doctrine, Hallonsten sees the Palamite essence/energies distinction as an integral part of it. This ties theosis strongly to its developed form in the Byzantine tradition, even though it may be argued that Palamas is simply explicating a distinction that is implicit in the Cappadocian Fathers and is not adding anything substantial to patristic doctrine.[1] Certainly, Hallonsten is right to complain about arbitrary exclusions from the content of theosis, such as the setting aside of the sacramental dimension by the Protestant authors of the introduction to the English translation of Gross's book, Kerry Robichaux and Paul Onica, who reject this dimension so as to make theosis supposedly 'more universally Christian' (Gross, 2002: xii). Yet even in the East, we find a writer such as Nicholas Kabasilas (c. 1322/3 to after 1391) maintaining a doctrine of theosis in his spiritual treatises *An Explanation of the Divine Liturgy* and *The Life in Christ* without making use of the essence/energies distinction; while in the West, Meister Eckhart's comparable distinction between *gotheit* and *got* enables him to enunciate a doctrine of total transformation into God (*got*) without becoming God as he is in himself (*gotheit*), though he comes perilously close to that. The example of Nicholas Kabasilas shows that the doctrinal dimension of theosis does not necessarily require that participation in the energies should be a sine qua non, even though the Constantinopolitan council of 1351 gave dogmatic approval to the essence/energies distinction and Gregory Palamas himself made it central to his account of deification.

Other taxonomies have been suggested besides that of theme and doctrine. Paul Gavrilyuk distinguishes between a broad definition and a more developed one, favouring the more developed one, which takes the 'ontological concepts of participation, divine likeness, and union with God' as properly 'constitutive of the notion of deification', a notion that also includes the acceptance of the essence/energies distinction (Gavrilyuk, 2009: 651). Most Orthodox theologians take a similar line. In his distinction between a 'lesser arch' leading from the Fall to redemption and a 'greater arch' leading from creation to deification, Andrew Louth suggests that the greater arch corresponds to the Orthodox doctrine of theosis, whereas 'a concentration on the lesser arch at the expense of the greater arch has been characteristic of much Western theology' (2007: 35). Dumitru Stăniloae distinguishes similarly between 'deification in a broad sense', which begins with baptism and covers the whole of the believer's spiritual ascent, and 'deification in a strict sense', which takes place 'when the operations or energies of human nature cease' and 'are replaced by the divine energies', the believer's natural attributes being 'overwhelmed by divine glory' (Stăniloae, 2003: 362–74). Deification in the strict, or maximalist, sense is thus the

---

[1] As I argue in Russell, 2019b: 169–77.

experience of hesychast contemplatives such as St Seraphim of Sarov who anticipate even in this life the glory of humanity's eschatological fulfilment.

There are further taxonomies that seek to accommodate non-maximalist versions of deification. In my survey of the many allusions to deification found in Greek patristic literature, I suggested a broad fourfold classification (nominal, analogical, ethical, and realistic) (Russell, 2004: 1–3), which Daniel Keating has critiqued and refined, identifying three 'core elements' of deification, a notion (a) grounded in the Scriptures, (b) embedded within Christian doctrine as expressed in 'creedal confession and liturgical prayer', and (c) reliant on the concept of participation in order to maintain a clear distinction between Creator and creature (Keating, 2015: 281–82). Keating's three core elements may conveniently provide us with headings under which to consider in more detail some important aspects of the modern re-engagement with theosis, mainly but not exclusively in its thematic, or non-maximalist, form.

'GROUNDED IN THE SCRIPTURES'

The detailed work of identifying the roots of theosis in the Scriptures has been the achievement principally of Protestant scholars – 'principally' because there is an engaging study by a British Orthodox, Stephen Thomas, which aims to remedy the impression given by books on the Greek Fathers (including my own) that 'the Bible is but the antechamber to greater vistas' (Thomas, 2007: 2). Thomas seeks to interpret the Bible according to patristic principles – the sober principles of St John Chrysostom rather than the mystical flights of Origen – in order to show that as a whole (not just in select passages) it conveys a theology of glory. Glory is also identified by the Baptist author, Ben Blackwell, as the key to the interpretation of Paul's soteriology. 'Thus, the experience of glory', he concludes, 'is not merely the experience of new life but a participation in divine life' (Blackwell, 2016: 244), a divine life that is not something that simply awaits us at the end of time but 'fulfils the original creational intent' and in fact 'also surpasses it' (Blackwell, 2016: 248). For the Methodist New Testament scholar Michael Gorman, it is Paul's emphasis on holiness (a fundamental notion in the Wesleyan tradition) that comes to the fore, and because the call to holiness in Paul is a call to participatory fellowship (*koinōnia*) with Christ, 'the term "theosis" is especially appropriate to characterize [Paul's] view of holiness' (Gorman, 2009: 106). Another Protestant author, Andrew Byers, an Evangelical, examines the Gospel of John in the light of the patristic notion of theosis and finds that John teaches a participatory ecclesiology that christifies believers by the action of the Holy Spirit – not as isolated individuals but as members of the ecclesial community, because 'divinity is a category that is *social*' (Byers, 2017: 238). An important feature that characterises these authors is their willingness to interpret Paul and other New Testament writers within the hermeneutic traditions of the early Church (Blackwell and Byers) or even later Orthodoxy (Gorman), in Blackwell's case specifically through a detailed consideration of Paul in the thinking of two of his patristic interpreters, Irenaeus of Lyon and Cyril of Alexandria.

A dissenting voice in this respect is that of David Litwa, who sees Paul's soteriology as fitting more closely 'the basic pattern of deification in the Graeco-Roman world' (Litwa, 2012: 282). Litwa does acknowledge major differences between Christian and non-Christian forms of deification but for him 'such differences ... do not wash away structural similarities' (287). Litwa's arguments have recently been challenged convincingly by another Evangelical, Eduard Borysov (2019: 149–76). In my own view, the structural similarities discernible between Paul and non-Christian thinking are to be sought not so much in his pagan cultural environment as in Judaism's Merkavah mysticism. Christian deification is rooted not only in a scriptural but, more broadly, in a Jewish matrix.

'EMBEDDED WITHIN CHRISTIAN DOCTRINE'

Orthodox Writers

The embeddedness of deification within Christian doctrine is a striking rediscovery in the twentieth century in all the Christian communions, Orthodoxy not excepted. Russian Orthodox writers may have led the way in the first years of the century in the re-appropriation of patristic teaching on deification (following the development of the earlier sophiological version), but in Russia itself the Bolshevik seizure of power in 1917 put a stop to new theological work, while in the Orthodox-majority countries of South-East Europe a Western-style scholasticism remained dominant until well after the Second World War. In Greece, the standard work of dogmatic theology was a manual by Christos Androutsos, *Dogmatikē tēs Orthodoxou Anatolikēs Ekklēsias* (Dogmatic Theology of the Eastern Orthodox Church), first published in Athens in 1907 and translated into Romanian in the late 1930s by Dumitru Stăniloae, which relies on abstract argument rather than patristic teaching to support its

theses. Even the three-volume dogmatic theology by Panagiotis Trembelas
that began to replace Androutsos at the end of the 1950s, *Dogmatikē tēs
Orthodoxou Katholikēs Ekklēsias*, translated into French in 1966–1968
as *Dogmatique de l'Église Orthodoxe Catholique*, only quotes the
Fathers as occasional proof texts.[2] In Greece and the Balkans, dogmatic
theology (itself a Western category) was long taught along strictly
Western lines.

A change began to occur in the mid-1950s, prompted by the first signs
of a turn in Western Europe towards the study of the Fathers. Greece led
the way because at that time it was the only Orthodox-majority country
whose institutes of theology were not under Communist control (Russell,
2006). The first fruits of this change were surveys of deification in Greek
patristic literature up to the time of John of Damascus by Andreas
Theodorou, published in Greek in 1956, with a summary in German in
1961, and by Panagiotis Bratsiotes, published in German in 1961,
German at the time being the language in which most of the theologians
of the University of Athens, including Theodorou and Bratsiotes, pursued
their higher studies. The admittedly rather dry texts they produced were
mainly for academic use. A new departure in a new style came about
through acquaintance in Greece not only with the work of the Paris
Russians, Georges Florovsky, Vladimir Lossky, and John Meyendorff,
but also with the patristic *ressourcement* movement initiated by the Lyon
Jesuits, Henri de Lubac and Jean Daniélou, along with Yves Congar and
Hans Urs von Balthasar. Florovsky and Meyendorff made a deep impression at a congress held in the northern Greek city of Thessaloniki in
1959 to mark the sixth centenary of the death of the city's great archbishop, Gregory Palamas. This congress stimulated a revival of Palamas
studies in Greece, a notable fruit of which was Georgios Mantzaridis's *Ē
peri theōseōs tou anthrōpou didaskalia Grēgoriou tou Palama* (1963),
published in English translation as *The Deification of Man: St Gregory
Palamas and the Orthodox Tradition* (1984). The influence of the French
ressourcement movement had already begun to penetrate Greece by a
different route through a remarkable layman who, although he never held
any official teaching position, shaped the thinking of a whole generation
of talented young theologians: Demetrios Koutroubis (1921–1983).
In Athens as a young man, Koutroubis had wanted to be a doctor but,
when a severe injury forced him to give up his medical studies, he turned

---

[2] See the devastating review of this work by Kallistos Ware (Ware, 1971: 477–80).

his mind to spiritual matters. Just after the Second World War, he became a Roman Catholic and studied with the Jesuits, first in England at Heythrop College in Oxfordshire and then in France at La Fourvière on the heights above Lyon. It was at Fourvière that he encountered Henri de Lubac and Jean Daniélou, who had recently launched the series *Sources Chrétiennes*. Later in Lebanon, where he was sent to teach at the Catholic University in Beirut, he met Lev Gillet (1893–1980), under whose influence he returned to Orthodoxy. In 1954, he went back to Greece, becoming a 'lay elder', as Metropolitan Kallistos has called him, living just outside Athens 'in a discreet and hidden manner', yet exercising a profound influence on a number of young theologians who were to become highly influential in Greece and beyond (Ware, 1984: 71, 1987: 10). Christos Yannaras says of Koutroubis:

He was the first who spoke the 'new' language. It was he who wrote the earliest articles in Greece about the theology of St Gregory Palamas and St Nicolas Kabasilas, he who translated for the first time the texts of the great theologians of the Russian diaspora, and – above all – he who gathered around himself a new generation of theologians and trained them by means of the discreet humility of his Socratic method (Yannaras, 1984: 72).

One of this new generation was Panayiotis Nellas (1936–1986), whose anthropological study of deification, *Zōon theoumenon* (1979), translated as *Deification in Christ: Orthodox Perspectives on the Nature of the Human Person* (1987), has been much cited by Western theologians. Nellas shows how theosis is embedded in Christian doctrine (within the 'greater arch' in Louth's terms) under four main headings: image of God, garments of skin, spiritual life as christification, and union with God. The creation of humanity in the image of God (Gen 1.26) means that 'the essence of man is not found in the matter from which he was created but in the archetype on the basis of which he was formed and towards which he tends' (Nellas, 1987: 33). The meaning of human life ('the ontological truth of man') is therefore not to be sought in our empirical circumstances but lies in the goal set for us from the beginning: man is a 'theological being' whose 'ontology is iconic' (34). The 'garments of skin' (or 'leather tunics' in the Septuagint's version) were provided by God for Adam and Eve after the fall in order to enable them to cope with the conditions of postlapsarian life (Gen 3.21). Drawing particularly on Gregory of Nyssa, John Chrysostom and Maximus the Confessor, Nellas unpacks the rich symbolism of these garments. He rejects the Origeneian interpretation that sees the 'dead skins' as representing the body. They are, rather, the mortal nature assumed by humanity after the fall, intended not merely to enable us to survive, or even to return to our prelapsarian state 'according to the image', but to attain to the archetypal image itself. The fall deprived us of the 'deiform characteristics and tendencies of the "in the image"' but the replacement bestowed by God, the 'garments of skin', may become the 'means of making the new journey towards God'[3] – that is to say, if they are not made *autonomous* (situating our goal within creation, either on the material or the moral level) but are oriented towards the image itself, namely, Christ. The task of contemporary Christian theology and philosophy, says Nellas, 'should be to liberate whatever good exists among the fruits of scientific research, technological development, and so on, from lawless autonomy' and to fill it with 'the glory of the Image, transforming and saving it' (103). The goal is theosis, or deification, but with 'christification as its real anthropological content' (121). Following Nicholas Kabasilas, Nellas insists that there is no need to go to ascetical extremes: christification is not only, or even principally, the fruit of monastic struggle; it is not necessary to abandon one's secular profession in order to practice the spiritual life. The more important task is to transform our world into ecclesial communion.[4] It is this that leads us to union with God.[5]

Another influential theologian of the same generation as Nellas is Christos Yannaras (b. 1935). Unlike Nellas, Yannaras is a philosophical theologian rather than a patristic exegete. His emphasis is on the existential transformation that believers experience within the eucharistic life of the Christian community, which transfigures their mode of existence, changing it 'into a participation in the triadic fulness of life' (Yannaras, 1991: 129). Such participation takes place through the divine energies. In Yannaras's view, the West's denial of the essence/energies distinction makes theosis, or 'the participation of human beings in the divine life', impossible (Yannaras, 2007: 65). Yet Yannaras does not expound theosis explicitly on the basis of Palamite theology. What concerns him most is the relational goal of human life. The transformation of 'the corruptible

---

[3] Nellas, 1987: 91. As examples of these means, Nellas mentions learning, work, science, the arts, and politics.

[4] There are similarities here with Byers's emphasis on the social character of theosis. The fact that Byers never mentions Nellas shows how thoroughly the latter's ideas have become common currency in modern thinking on deification.

[5] I have confined my attention in this section to the 'Greek theological renaissance' of the 1960s. For a broader treatment of the place of theosis in modern Orthodox theology, see Russell, 2009, and for an excellent study of theosis in the thinking of Dumitru Stăniloae, see Bartos, 1999.

time of atomic existence into the incorruptible time of personal relation' is what the mystical life is about. This transformation is the restoration of the person to integrity – which for Yannaras is the fundamental meaning of theosis (293).

One of the most interesting Greek theologians of the younger generation is Fr Nikolaos Loudovikos (b. 1959). Like Yannaras, he gives pride of place in his thinking to relational ontology: 'Human beings can only fulfil their essence in a dialogue that discloses step by step, as their proper eschatological vocation, their mode of existence as becoming-in-communion, as a likeness to their Creator' (Loudovikos, 2010: 215, modified). This achievement of the goal of one's being by means of a dialogical relationship – by means of attaining likeness to the Creator through eucharistic communion – is deification, but Loudovikos does not use the word *theōsis*. Instead, he makes a distinction between *theopoiia* and *theopoiēsis* (two further Greek patristic terms for deification, the one more active, the other more passive) precisely in order to emphasise the dialogical reciprocity between Christ's embodiment through his Incarnation and other charismata in our world (his *theopoiia*) and our participational embodiment in him (our *theopoiēsis*). In a sense (with a continuing play on these words, all deriving from *poiein*, 'to make'), the world is co-created by us as a poem (*poiēma*) written by at least two poets (*poiētai*). Deification is not a mechanical process but an 'inexhaustible erotic surprise' (238–41).[6]

In the Anglophone Orthodox world, most of the work on theosis has been produced by historical theologians. A notable exception is David Bentley Hart (b. 1965), whose recent essay in theological metaphysics, *You Are Gods: On Nature and Supernature* (2022), seeks to push the idea of participation in God, given his premises, to its logical conclusion. Having argued in his previous book, *That All Shall Be Saved* (2020), for a universalist position on salvation,[7] he now turns to the ontology

---

[6] For a useful reflection on Orthodox thinking on theosis in the ecumenical context, see Asproulis, 2021. There have also been some important discussions of theosis in works of historical theology by Greek scholars, especially Yangazoglou, 2001 and Chouliaras, 2020.

[7] With regard to universal salvation, I remain unconvinced that human failure is impossible (appearing, as it does, to extinguish human freedom), but Hart argues his position vigorously and he does have some patristic support, especially in St Isaac of Nineveh (on whose Evagrius-inspired teaching, see Fokin, 2015). Among other Anglophone Orthodox theologians, Metropolitan Kallistos Ware was sympathetic but more cautious. He used to say: 'We may hope for the salvation of all, but we may not teach it'.

implied by this. The premises set out at the beginning of *You Are Gods* may be reduced to two fundamental convictions that drive the argument, the first that *creatio ex nihilo* means that there is nothing that is fundamentally not-God, the second that there is no 'pure nature' that is not already filled with divine grace. Hart's *bête noire* is the Thomist 'two-tier' conception of natural and supernatural, characteristic of the old manuals and now apparently making a come-back, which he believes to be irreconcilable with the truth revealed by the Incarnation (more so, he suggests, than the metaphysics of classical Vedanta). He argues persuasively that an *ontological* transformation (by deification) from a natural being to a supernatural being raises serious questions about the continuing identity of such a being. But whereas the classic solution in modern Orthodoxy is to propose an *existential* transformation as encapsulated by Maximus the Confessor in his expression 'mode of existence' (*tropos hyparxeōs*), an expression taken up by thinkers such as Yannaras and Loudovikos, Hart's solution, by abolishing the distinction between natural and supernatural *tout court*, is to deny that transformation is necessary at all: 'we are nothing but created gods coming to be, becoming God in God, able to become divine only because, in some sense, we are divine from the very first' (34).[8] It follows that 'nothing can exist that is not always already, in eternity, divinized, plunged ecstatically into the fire of the divine life' (105), nothing can be excluded from the return of all things, nothing can exist that is not already redeemed and divinised in eternity, and the 'church is simply a corporate and historical expression of Christ's affirmation that "You are gods"' (111). Hart's ideas move on the same wavelength as Meister Eckhart, Nicholas of Cusa, Jacob Boehme, Nicolas Berdyaev, and Sergius Bulgakov.[9] He stands at a slight angle to today's neopatristically oriented Orthodoxy but is nevertheless highly regarded by many Orthodox (and not only Orthodox) theologians, including, apparently, Patriarch Bartholomew I himself. It cannot be denied that Orthodoxy is a broad Church.

Roman Catholic Writers

Deification has never been entirely forgotten in the Roman Catholic world but – setting aside the mystical tradition – it did not become the

---

[8] The implications of 'transformation' had already troubled Jean Gerson (see *De Mystica Theologia, Consideratio* XLI, discussed above, pp. 90–91), but Gerson's solution is to take transformation in a metaphorical sense.

[9] He quotes the same patristic authorities as Berdyaev and Bulgakov (Berdyaev's 'Doctors of the Church'): Origen, Gregory of Nyssa, and Isaac of Nineveh.

subject of book-length academic treatment until the nineteenth century, when Matthias Scheeben (1835–1888), a German professor of dogmatic theology at the Catholic seminary in Cologne, published his monograph *Natur und Gnade* (1862), translated as *Nature and Grace*, followed a year later by a more popular and widely read version, *Die Herrlichkeiten der göttlichen Gnade* (1863), translated as *The Glories of Divine Grace*, and then in 1865–1897 by *Die Mysterien des Christentums*, translated as *The Mysteries of Christianity*. Scheeben is surprisingly modern. With regard to the rival systems of grace first proposed in the sixteenth century by the Dominican Domingo Bañez (1528–1604) and the Jesuit Luis de Molina (1535–1600), with their distinctions between 'actual or sufficient grace' and 'efficacious grace' causing the human will to pass from a potential state to a free act (Banezianism), or between 'prevenient grace' and 'helping grace' becoming efficacious according to God's foreknowledge of how a person will choose (Molinism), in *The Glories of Divine Grace* Scheeben follows Bañez in distinguishing between prevenient grace, actual grace, and sanctifying grace but goes well beyond Bañez's scholastic distinctions to define grace fundamentally as 'a participation in the divine nature' (Scheeben, 2000: 47, 204). Citing 2 Peter 1.4, Dionysius the Areopagite, and Basil the Great, he characterises deification in thoroughly patristic terms:

The participation in the divine nature, then, which we enjoy by grace, consists in this: Our nature assumes a condition peculiar to the divine nature and becomes so similar to the Deity that, according to the holy Fathers, we may truly say that it is deified, or made deiform . . .. We do not speak of a dissolution of our substance in the Divine Substance, or even of a personal union with it, as in the Incarnation. We speak only of a glorification of our substance into the image of the Divine Nature. Neither shall we become new gods, pretending independence of the true God, but in truth we are made, by the power and the grace of God, something which God alone is by nature; we are made like Him in a supernatural way. Our soul receives a reflection of that glory which is peculiar to Him and above all creatures (26).

Scheeben contrasts this with the likeness to God that was arrogated to himself by Lucifer (Isa 14.14) (29). To partake of the divine nature is not to become what God is; it is 'to partake of the divine cognition' (33, 189), 'to partake of the holiness of the divine nature' (38, 183), to be transformed and glorified (41). The Holy Spirit is in us not simply by reason of his gifts but 'by his very being' (72). Our transformation and glorification are the result of the outpouring of divine love, which enables us to participate in this love and thus leads 'not only [to] the greatest possible similarity with God, but also [to] an intimate union with him' (157). For over four hundred pages, Scheeben argues passionately for a faith that is not a merely intellectual assent but consists in seeking God with all one's powers and nurturing the perfect love that actually attains God. This whole endeavour is tied to the work of grace understood as participation in the divine nature.

Scheeben was regarded with awe in his own lifetime and is still considered one of the greatest theologians of modern times (Kelly, 2016: 199). His thesis, however, is not immune to criticism. In the judgement of Daniel Keating, Scheeben undervalues how we are already children of God in consequence of having been created in God's image and likeness but become so in a more profound way through Christ the true Son. Scheeben assumes that God can only love us after he has first implanted himself in us. His principle that God loves us because of the grace he has given us implies that in loving us God is only loving his own grace.[10] His talk about degrees of grace (the more we have, the more pleasing we are to God) also quantifies grace in a problematic way.[11] In my own view, the individualism of Scheeben's thinking aligns him with the mystical tradition of the Rhineland. Despite his insistence in *The Mysteries of Christianity* that it is baptism and the Eucharist that elevate us to true participation in God (214–18), the ecclesial dimension is strangely absent.

In the following century, deification is not given the prominence that Scheeben accords it, but we do find the notion embedded in the theology of two of the twentieth century's most important Catholic theologians, Karl Rahner (1904–1984) and Hans Urs von Balthasar (1905–1988), even if neither makes much use of its terminology. At the centre of Rahner's theological project is a concern (like Scheeben) to define the relationship between nature and grace. Grace is God's self-communication to humanity, not by overwhelming and annihilating human nature but by raising human beings to participate by grace in the life of the Trinity. This self-communication takes place through Jesus Christ in the Holy Spirit, incarnation and divinisation being considered correlative to each other as God's free act of giving himself to the creature.[12] In Balthasar's case, his project is specifically to investigate the

---

[10] Interestingly, Meister Eckhart had already said that in loving me God is loving himself. Cf. *Sermon* 43 (Quint, *Sermon* 41); trans. Walshe, 2009: 238–39.

[11] Daniel Keating in a personal communication dated 15 March 2020.

[12] For a good essay on Rahner's thinking on divinisation, see Caponi, 2007, and for a brief summary, see Russell, 2004: 316.

nature of the beatific vision.[13] Convinced that this is not 'a spectacle in which we enjoy endlessly the vision of the Divinity',[14] he situates it within what Sigurd Lefsrud regards as his most important contribution to the theology of deification, namely, 'his illumination of the fullness of the nature of love itself' (Lefsrud, 2020: 209). This fullness is manifested paradoxically by the Son's kenotic self-emptying through his acceptance of the limitations of human nature in order to raise that nature to communion with God.[15] 'For Balthasar, deification is about relationship, movement and autonomy – in short, a vibrancy of existence opened up though encounter with the living God' (53–54).

There are some aspects of the Byzantine teaching on deification about which Balthasar has reservations, especially the distinction between the essence and the energies, which he thinks 'results in a bifurcation of God – that there is a hidden, unknowable entity beyond the face that God presents to humanity' (59). But with regard to the Byzantine emphasis on synergy (humanity's active collaboration with God), Balthasar shows himself to be closer to Orthodoxy than to some Western positions.[16] Synergy is to be understood not as a 'joint venture' but as 'our incorporation into Christ's life that alone brings fruition to human endeavors' (164). In other words, 'synergy' is equivalent to 'christification'. Although Balthasar does not use the term, it summarises very well his understanding of how divine grace operates in concert with the human will, if we will allow it to do so, to produce in us a love that is Christlike.

Another Catholic theologian who has drawn attention to Christian deification as an integral element of Christian doctrine is Louis Bouyer. Very influential in the second half of the twentieth century but now somewhat neglected (though not in France),[17] Bouyer was among the first, in his *Spirituality of the New Testament and the Fathers* (1968), to insist on a profound difference between the deification of the pagan Neoplatonists and that of Dionysius the Areopagite, and indeed on the difference between pagan deification and its Christian counterpart more

---

[13] There is now a valuable essay on Balthasar's theology of deification: Ciraulo, 2019, and also a fine book-length study: Lefsrud, 2020.

[14] *Theo-Drama* V, 403, cited by Lefsrud, 2020: 53,

[15] As Lefsrud puts it, kenosis 'is not a "self-emptying" in the sense of the Son *losing* something: it is rather the very manifestation of divinity' (2020: 209–10).

[16] On this topic, the whole of Lefsrud's chapter 11, 'Synergy as the Way of Deification', is particularly interesting.

[17] A congress on Bouyer's theology was held in Paris in 2014 and his books are now being reissued by Éditions du Cerf.

generally.[18] In *The Christian Mystery* (1990), a study of the human impetus towards union with God from the Pauline mystery through to modern mysticism, Bouyer is clear that deification means our becoming *what we already are*, children of God through having been created in his image and likeness: 'In other words, it is perfectly true, as the Greek Fathers so often declare, that that God became man only to divinize us, but we must take care that our salvation is not conceived of as a sort of de-creation' (223). Our transformation through Christ does not leave our humanity behind but brings it to fulfilment.

More recent monographs by Catholic theologians (or collective works edited by them) have focused on identifying the themes of deification in the writings of a variety of historical figures and spiritual movements from Augustine to Pope John Paul II.[19] The incorporation of deification into works of systematic theology is less common, but that will no doubt change. A pioneering book in this respect is Keating's *Deification and Grace* (2007). His aim is a modest one, 'a synthetic account of deification in Christ as the full outworking of grace in the Christian life' chiefly for Catholics puzzled by the sudden appearance of the deification theme in the 1994 *Catechism of the Catholic Church* without any supportive discussion (Keating, 2007: 5). In each chapter, he answers possible objections from Catholic readers as he moves (in Hallonsten's terms) from the theme of theosis as an *admirabile commercium* to that of theosis as the recovery of the divine likeness and places the whole within the larger perspective of the entire economy of salvation. Keating does not shirk the problem of the essence/energies distinction. He sets Aquinas in clear distinction from the Eastern tradition but maintains that although the approaches and the language are different, the intended goal in both traditions is the same: first the communication of the divine attributes to

---

[18] Bouyer, 1968: 400, 416–21 (the original French edition was published in 1960). Bouyer, like many of his Orthodox confrères, rejects the 'Pseudo-' prefix as suggesting something dubious about the thinking of this late fifth-century Syrian mystical writer but puts 'Dionysius' in inverted commas to indicate that it was a pseudonym.

[19] Publications include: Meconi, 2013 (on Augustine); Spezzano, 2015 (on Thomas Aquinas); Meconi and Olson, 2016 (an overview from the early Fathers to post–Vatican II, with valuable chapters covering, among others, the Dominicans, the Franciscans, and the French school of spirituality); Arblaster and Faesen, 2019 (on the Western mystical tradition); Ortiz, 2019b (on the Latin patristic tradition); and Ortiz, 2021 (an ecumenical venture with chapters on the major Christian traditions apart from the Oriental Orthodox).

human beings and then the creature's participation in the intra-divine relationship itself.[20]

Anglican Writers

Anglican interest in deification goes back to Richard Hooker (c. 1554–1600) and the seventeenth-century Cambridge Platonists, becoming particularly intense at the time of the Oxford Movement in the mid-nineteenth century, when theologians such as Edward Bouverie Pusey (1800–1882) and John Henry Newman (1801–1890) sought to affirm the catholicity of the Church of England by leapfrogging Rome to appeal to the authority of the Greek Fathers (Louth, 1983b; Allchin, 1988; Salladin, 2021). In the twentieth century, it was contact with the Russians of the diaspora rather than directly with the Fathers that stimulated interest in deification. An Anglican theologian who came to be very much in sympathy with Orthodox thinking by this route was Eric Mascall (1905–1993). He first got to know the Russians at the Anglo-Russian Student Conferences of the 1920s that led to the founding of the Fellowship of St Alban and St Sergius.[21] Through them, particularly through Sergius Bulgakov, and later Vladimir Lossky, whom he met when the Fellowship conferences were resumed after the Second World War, he became thoroughly acquainted with Orthodox theology. When he first discusses deification, however, it is with reference to St John of the Cross and Jan van Ruusbroec. His intention is to show that 'divinisation' or 'deification', which he defines as a 'participation in the life of God', a 'sharing in the response which the eternal Son makes to the Father's love', is a native Western tradition (Mascall, 1946: 97). At the same time, he counters the individualism characteristic of much of the Western tradition by appealing to Florovsky and Bulgakov (as well as to a striking passage of Hooker) to show that it is through participation in the Church that the individual Christian is elevated into the life of God and so 'participates in God's timelessness in a created mode' (116–17).

---

[20] Keating is thus much more cautious than A. N. Williams, who (not distinguishing between theme and doctrine) declares that the 'ground that Aquinas and Palamas share is vast compared to the points at which they diverge … in most respects, to know and affirm the doctrine of deification in one is implicitly to accept the doctrine of the other' (1999: 175), but fundamentally he agrees with her.

[21] On Mascall's contacts with the Paris Russians, see Russell, 2019b: 81–84, and more fully on the place of deification in his thinking, Russell 2004: 313–15.

More recently, John Milbank (b. 1952) has also drawn on Bulgakov in order to bridge the gulf that has long existed in the Western tradition between nature and grace. In his *Suspended Middle* (2005) he discusses Henri de Lubac's 1946 publication *Surnaturel*, but he does more than simply comment on de Lubac. In the course of his discussion, he develops an argument that there cannot be a third term – the traditional idea of grace – between the natural and the supernatural. The link between the two is deification, which is a gift 'so much in excess of Creation that it entirely includes it' (Milbank 2005: 46). The paradox that confronts us with the created world is 'that God who is in all yet brings about a not-God to share in his nature' (77). Grace is not a divine influence exerted upon us but a gift of something at once both wholly divine and wholly human that transfigures our entire being. When he returns to this idea at a conference held in Cambridge in 2005 that brought together theologians from the Eastern Orthodox Church and the Anglican Radical Orthodoxy movement, Milbank acknowledges the contribution of Bulgakov more explicitly, finding in his Sophiology 'a *metaxu* [an *in-between*] which does not lie between two poles but rather remains both poles at once' (Milbank, 2009: 49). Nature is not a fixed quantity but a dynamic process orientated from the beginning to completion in God. Hence, 'we can become God, because God is constantly becoming us' (78).

The contemporary Anglican theologian, however, who has most fully assimilated the insights that Orthodoxy offers to Western Christianity is Rowan Williams (b. 1950). His thematic collection of essays, *Looking East in Winter* (2021), is an impressive summation of a lifetime's inter-action with Orthodox thinking that began nearly fifty years ago with his 1975 doctoral dissertation on Vladimir Lossky. In *Looking East in Winter*, he touches on deification in a number of places but especially in a chapter that explores Fr (now St) Sophrony (Sakharov)'s struggle to attain the fullest possible realisation of true humanity through the ascetic struggle, the purpose of which is to strip away all the layers of self-interest with which we protect ourselves from the terrifying letting-go that allows us to be penetrated by God.[22] To focus on divine filiation in simple terms, as the acceptance of God as our Father, 'will risk making relation to God a *case* of relation to others – here am I and there is the God I call

---

[22] This entire chapter, entitled 'Participating Divinity, Entering Emptiness', richly repays close study. It was originally given as a lecture at the 2014 Leuven conference on deification at which the twelve papers published in Arblaster and Faesen, 2019 were also given.

"Father" – leaving the self's habits intact' (R. Williams, 2021: 97). Asceticism, again seen in simple terms, as the purification of the self, may result in 'no more than a vastly refined individualism, potentially worse than the unreconstructed individualism of "naïve" filiation' (97). What is needed in order to hold filiation and asceticism in creative tension with each other, as Balthasar saw, is participation in the Son's kenotic self-emptying, which through his acceptance of the limitations of human nature raises that nature to communion with God. 'To attempt to put it in its most basic terms', says Williams, 'there is nothing for the Word to be or to do except to *be from* the Father and towards the Father (the *pros ton theon* of the first chapter of John's Gospel); the Word has no action or subsistence that is not wholly characterized by relatedness to the source' (98). The self-emptying that inserts us into this relationship of the Word to the Father is not self-annihilating but paradoxically fulfils us as persons, making us truly hypostatic. 'To inhabit this reality is to be assimilated to this "hypostatic" world, where there is nothing that is possessed, no solid self that owns, accumulates, gives or holds back according to will: in this sense "deification" is the process of becoming hypostatic, personal in the strictest theological sense' (98). This is what it means to share in the relatedness of the Word to the Father, to participate in the perichoretic life of the Trinity. In the ascetic life of Fr Sophrony, it meant to experience God-forsakenness, to pray the 'Abba, Father' of Gethsemane, to enter into the world's anguish, to descend into hell and fear not. Yet it is in this devastating experience of emptiness that our selfhood is reconstructed because we do not experience it as autonomous individuals. Indeed we *cannot* experience it as autonomous individuals because of 'our ineradicable need for relatedness to God, in which alone we become personal, and thus distinct in a way that is not exclusive, self-asserting and self-protecting' (107).

Protestant Writers

Protestant theologians in recent times have sought to identify the theme of theosis in Martin Luther (Kärkkäinen, 2004 and 2021; Linman, 2007), John Calvin (Billings, 2007; Mosser, 2021b), John Wesley (Christensen, 2007 and 2021), T. F. Torrance (Habets, 2009), and the Baptist tradition (Habets, 2021). Much of this work has been in the field of historical theology, but some of it has also sought to incorporate the theme of deification into a recast systematic theology. This is the thrust of Myk Habets's book on Torrance. Although recognising the fact that in his large corpus of writings Torrance does not deal with theosis systematically or at any length, Habets argues confidently that it is fully in line with Torrance's theology to claim that theosis, which Habets insists is not an individualistic path to God but is attained in community and through liturgical worship, is a reconciliation with God by which 'believers are caught up into the life of the Son's response to the Father and in that communion ... participate in the Divine nature' (Habets, 2009: 192). The reason for this confidence in attributing what amounts to a doctrine of deification to Torrance is clarified by Carl Mosser, who has done valuable work in showing how 'the notion that deification is a distinctly Eastern idea incompatible with the Western theological tradition' was introduced by Albrecht Ritschl (1822–1889) and taken up enthusiastically by Adolf von Harnack and other Ritschlians for the sake of promoting a purified Germanic Christianity but does not represent the earlier Reformed tradition (Mosser, 2020; cf. McInroy, 2021). Mosser has also studied how Torrance abandoned his early negative opinion of theosis as a result of his involvement in the ecumenical movement, particularly through his contacts with Georges Florovsky, and came to see that theosis and justification are not incompatible with each other (Mosser, 2021a). Reformed theologians, in Mosser's view, are in some ways 'replicating the Orthodox recovery of *theosis* in the last century' (Mosser, 2021a: 150). Yet it is difficult to maintain that deification is embedded in the doctrinal outlook of more than a handful of Protestant theologians today. In the last century, Ben Drewery (a Methodist), despite a very clear understanding of theosis in the Greek patristic tradition, found it utterly repugnant (Drewery, 1975; cf. Louth, 2007: 33). There is still strong opposition to theosis from those who complain about 'the new orthodoxy of the twenty-first century', dismissing it as a fad of 'the divinization crowd' (Mosser, 2021a: 148). Nevertheless, scholars like Blackwell, Habets, and Mosser have made a start.[23]

'RELIANT ON THE CONCEPT OF PARTICIPATION'

Deification in its developed form is not, as we sometimes find in the Fathers, simply the acquisition of immortality and other divine attributes. It is entry, as Rowan Williams has shown, into 'a new form of relation to the divine Source' (2021: 111). This relation, initiated by baptism,

---

[23] Mosser notes my asking some years ago (in Russell, 2012) why Protestants are so interested in deification (Mosser, 2021a: 149). His recent articles have resolved my perplexity.

establishes a renewed human identity in Christ. The outcome of such an identity, the fruit of the recovery of the divine image, cannot be pursued as an individualistic goal, as one among a range of possibilities that we choose for ourselves. 'The person realizes the divine image precisely by abandoning the aspiration to be like God' (125).

Much of the thinking on this level (the maximalist or doctrinal level of theosis) has been done by Orthodox writers in their exploration of theological personalism. We have already examined, through Rowan Williams's eyes, the struggle of St Sophrony to participate in the Son's kenotic self-offering and thus in his 'being-toward' the Father. In Christos Yannaras, we have a sustained philosophical reflection on what such participation means in terms of attaining a new 'mode of existence'. Truth is personal relation, and knowledge is participation in truth. 'God is only known as personal disclosure, as a triadic communion of persons, as an ecstatic self-offering of erotic goodness' (Yannaras, 2007: 64). Our knowledge of God 'transcends every objective cognitive approach. It is an experiential fact of dynamic recognition and affirmation of God's erotic ecstasy – a fact of participation in another mode of existence, in the true life of the Uncreated' (64). Thus, theosis means to attain wholeness as persons, indeed to become 'all person' – 'all *prosōpon*' or 'all face' in the expression of St Macarius the Great – oriented towards the Father as our existential end (293). Such an attainment, far from being a private 'mystical' achievement, is the fruit of participation in the mysteries (the 'sacraments') of the Church. This last aspect has been studied at length by John Zizioulas, who develops the notion of 'ecclesial mysticism' in his *Communion and Otherness* (2006), where he repudiates a self-conscious introspective mysticism, saying that 'to know God as he knows himself is not to enter into the mechanism of divine self-consciousness, but to enter by grace into the sonship (υἱοθεσία) which is conveyed to us by the loving relationship between the Father, the Son and the Spirit, a relationship which allows each of these persons to emerge as utterly *other* while being utterly *one*' (Zizioulas, 2006: 306). Participation in the life of the Trinity – Yannaras's 'new mode of existence' – cannot be a chosen goal pursued individualistically and self-consciously.

AN ECUMENICAL CONSENSUS?

What emerges from the above survey of a selection of modern theologians is the key role of the ecumenical movement in the twentieth century's retrieval of the theme, as well as the doctrine, of deification. Without the ecumenical movement even Scheeben would have remained out on a limb. Within the ecumenical movement, long before the establishment of the World Council of Churches in 1948, a vital element was contributed by the work of the Russian émigré theologians living in Paris. Bulgakov, Florovsky, and later Lossky were the channels by which theological reflection on deification reached Anglicans through the Fellowship of St Alban and St Sergius. Along with Berdyaev and Lot-Borodine, these theologians, especially Lossky, were also in contact with Roman Catholic circles in Paris. Indeed, much of Lossky's work was produced at the request of his Catholic friends Henri de Lubac and Jean Daniélou, who were seeking to recover the teaching of the Fathers to counterbalance the Neo-Thomism then dominant in the Roman Catholic Church. Nor should we forget the work of the Paris YMCA. It was as a result of the ecumenical vision of YMCA's American Methodist leader, John Mott (1865–1955), that the Russian works of the Paris émigré theologians were published by the YMCA Press. Without Mott, it is doubtful whether the Russian works could have been published at all. By the time the WCC was founded, the Russian understanding of theosis, in its sophiological as well as its patristic form, was becoming widely known.

After the WCC's foundation, formal conversations between Protestant and Orthodox theologians led to greater familiarity with Orthodox teaching on deification. It was thus that Thomas Torrance came to a more favourable view of theosis and that the Finnish Lutherans of the Tuomo Mannermaa school were encouraged to take a fresh look at Luther. In 1968, shortly after the end of the Second Vatican Council, the Holy See sent a delegation to the Faith and Order Commission of the WCC, bringing the Roman Catholic Church into the debates. This consolidated the work of the *ressourcement* theologians, who had been very influential at the Vatican Council and for whom deification was central to a patristically based soteriology. When the new *Catechism of the Catholic Church* was promulgated in 1992, it seemed natural that references to deification should be made without any apologetic commentary.

BREAKING OUT OF THE ACADEMY

In 1992, however, the general public, at least in the Anglophone world, was less well prepared for talk about deification than was the community of professional theologians (Keating, 2007: 1–2). Despite the fact that the substance of deification, if not the word itself, is present in the Latin Liturgy (Ortiz, 2019a), the theme was as unfamiliar to Catholics as it was to Protestants. This began to change in the 1990s. In 1993, the year after the promulgation of the new Catholic *Catechism*, Olivier Clément's book, *The Roots of Christian Mysticism*, was published in an English translation by the press of the Focolare Movement, New City.[24] Olivier Clément (1921–2009) was perhaps, after Lossky, the best known lay Orthodox theologian of the twentieth century. Born in the south-west of France into a Socialist anti-Christian family, he was first drawn to Orthodoxy through acquaintance with Berdyaev's articles and then, on reading Lossky's *Mystical Theology of the Eastern Church* and seeking out the friendship of the author, was baptised at the age of thirty into the Russian Orthodox Church.[25] Although never ordained, he taught theology and church history at the Orthodox Institut Saint-Serge in Paris and also lectured at the Institut Catholique and the Institut Supérieur d'Études Œcuméniques. He was a public intellectual who reached out well beyond the academic community. At his funeral, Metropolitan Emmanuel of France rightly described him as 'a *deacon* of the Word' (Clément, 2021: xix).

Clément's *Roots of Christian Mysticism*, although first published in French forty years ago, is still a best seller. His discussion of deification comes in a section at the end of a chapter entitled 'Enstasy–Ecstasy', following sections with headings such as 'Into the Unknown', 'Love and Inebriation', 'Inward Birth', and 'The Embrace of the Infinite'. These headings seem to reflect something of Clément's own spiritual journey that starting from an atheist childhood passed through a period of fascination with esotericism, European and Oriental, to arrive in mature adulthood at Orthodox Christianity.[26] On deification, his chief guide is Maximus the Confessor. Maximus teaches us that the 'human being is truly human only in God' (Clément, 1993: 263), that this true humanity, while remaining completely human, is totally transfigured 'through grace and the divine brightness of the beatifying glory that permeates the whole

[24] The Focolare Movement was founded in Italy by Chiara Liubich (1920–2008), a remarkable Catholic laywoman who saw her life's vocation (according to New City's mission statement) as the promotion of 'dialogue, mutual understanding and unity in every sphere of human activity'. She was particularly concerned to bring together Christians of different traditions. During her last illness, she was visited in a Roman hospital by the Ecumenical Patriarch, Bartholomew I. The cause has been opened in Rome for her beatification.

[25] Clément's spiritual autobiography up to the moment of his baptism, first published in French in 1975, has recently been issued in an elegant English translation by Michael Donley (Clément, 2021). Later, Fr Sophrony became his spiritual father.

[26] On Clément's fascination with the Western esoteric tradition see Clément, 2012 (first published in 1994).

person' (267, citing Maximus, *Ambiguum* 7). This is the experience here and now of resurrection, which 'begins every time that a person, breaking free from conditionings, transfigures them' (268). Moreover, the transfiguration of humanity, understood not as a vague aspiration but as a work that begins with transforming oneself, points towards the transfiguration of the whole cosmos and indeed helps to bring it about.

'Transfiguration' is a key word for Clément. He admired the life of Taizé, a Catholic community in Burgundy, in eastern France, founded by a Swiss Reformed Protestant, Roger Schütz (1915–2005), where Catholics, Anglicans, and Protestants share a monastic life together, exercising a spiritual apostolate to vast numbers of young people who come on pilgrimage each year. 'Taizé', said Clément, 'is a small but deeply experienced foretaste of the reconciled and transfigured humanity towards which history is painfully groping' (Clément, 1997: 12). Clément's Maximian vision of the universal scope of theosis makes it a doctrine with a global reach.

THE WIDER RECEPTION OF THEOSIS

Archbishop Anastasios (Yannoulatos), Orthodox archbishop of Tirana and All Albania, has also written eloquently on deification as the goal of the whole of humanity: 'The call to embark on this journey is addressed to all human beings without exception, not only to those who are gifted or privileged. All human beings, as bearers of the divine image, are without exception "god-like." We are all "capable," according to Gregory [of Nazianzus], "of containing God within ourselves" [*Orat.* 30.6], and we are "all striving toward what lies before us" [*Orat.* 19.7]' (Anastasios, 2003: 174). Although deification is not 'possessed' by the Orthodox, it was developed *as a doctrine* in a particularly rich way within the Orthodox tradition. It is thus a treasure that Orthodoxy can share with the world, not in any spirit of proselytisation, for the archbishop is not calling on everybody to become Orthodox, but as a precious gift. In the twenty-first century, the world – at least the Christian world – is ready to accept such a gift.

The reason for this is that in the last century a distinction developed between 'religion' and 'spirituality'. Religion, as represented by the traditional churches, often came to be seen as patriarchal and masculinist, as hierarchical and elitist, as based on outmoded cosmological ideas, as transcendentalist and dogmatic or else as too fused with the social establishment, as sexually repressive – in short, as irrelevant to people's actual lives (Tacey, 2004: 36–37). In response to this situation, for humanity's spiritual yearnings cannot be suppressed indefinitely, there developed a personal quest for meaning in life, for what 'works for me', outside the restrictions of churches and dogmas. The 'New Age' movement is part of this, as is the 'Emerging' or 'Emergent' Church movement. In a fascinating study of the appropriation of the spirituality of the *Philokalia* and the *Way of a Pilgrim* by post-evangelical communities that now describe themselves as Emerging/Emergent Churches, Christopher Johnson shows how some originally Orthodox practices, such as the Jesus Prayer, along with an awareness of the goal of theosis, have become widely disseminated and reinterpreted in a totally new setting. This is not just a matter of subjectivisation but is the result of different understandings of tradition and authority (C. D. L. Johnson, 2010: 178). Drawing attention to the importance of blogs and other interactive internet sources in the transmission of such tradition, Johnson describes how 'a direct and reciprocal dialogue between listener and speaker' and 'the give-and-take of this apprenticeship' have replaced the traditional spiritual father-disciple relationship (179). In the context of an understanding of theosis, this dialogue has bypassed most of the work of academic scholars.

The personal quest for meaning and significance can also lead to an appropriation of 'theotic thinking', as Stephen Finlan calls it in a contribution to a recent collective volume, within the mainstream Christian traditions, because 'the foundational principle behind *theōsis* is spiritual growth' (Finlan, 2021: 213).[27] Another contributor to the same volume, Wyndy Corbin Reuschling, referring to deification as 'more than just a state of being in relationship and union with God' – 'more than just a state' presumably in a semantic rather than ontological sense – maintains that deification is not only a private relationship with God but 'also enables us to grow in integrity, where who we are, and who we are becoming, become reflected in how we live' (Reuschling, 2021: 230). Theosis, in the postmodern context, is to do with identity, growth, and personal transformation, yet as such can also become excessively individualistic. A third contributor, the Jesuit Bernie Owens, while accepting deification as personal transformation so that we live with the freedom of the risen Christ and yet at the same time become more fully our true self, also insists that we cannot be

---

[27] Finlan, 2019: 213. In his account of his spiritual journey, Finlan, an Evangelical pastor, speaks of the importance of his encounter with the works of Berdyaev and Soloviev. He also mentions the 2004 Drew Conference as playing a pivotal role in his theological development.

content with addressing deification simply in terms of what happens to us as individuals (Owens, 2019: 260). If our humanity is fully realised in the glorified Christ, when God will be all in all (cf. 1 Cor 15:28), it must be within a communal reality when we shall be completely receptive to the other – even to the non-human creation (261).

Owens's declaration resonates with a work on deification by an Orthodox theologian of Ukrainian descent, Job Getcha (b. 1974), which is subtitled 'Orthodox Spirituality in an Age of Secularisation'.[28] Like the American authors we have been considering, Getcha distinguishes between religion and spirituality, 'or more exactly faith', he adds (Getcha, 2020: 11). Spirituality for him is not a private matter but is expressed and transmitted most profoundly by the Liturgy, which he says is how he himself absorbed it as a child. Getcha is convinced that in the twenty-first century this spirituality/faith – 'a tradition profoundly anchored in the Bible and the writings of the Church Fathers and existentially expressed in liturgical worship and the life of prayer, a tradition which gathers together space, time, and eternity in astonishing manner' – has much to offer to today's secularised society (11). For Getcha, as for Clément, a key word is 'transfiguration'. As a Byzantine hymn for Matins of the Transfiguration (6 August) puts it, Christ's transfiguration on the mountain is 'a prefiguring of the radical transfiguration of the whole universe at the end of time' (256). It is not just the individual that will be transfigured but the entire material creation.

Transfiguration, Getcha maintains, is thus 'a Christian response to secularisation' (257). To transfigure the world is humanity's chief vocation. This requires first a personal transformation, the renouncing, as the great monastic Father, John Climacus, put it, of the world of pleasures and the world of sin, or, as we might say today, of a materialist and egotistical mode of existence, which is a transformation of our relation with the created world that brings with it a transformation of the world itself. The environmental crisis, Getcha reminds us, illustrates this truth. It is only by changing our relationship with creation that we can save it (260). Deification is thus a transfiguration that is first personal, then ecclesial, and ultimately universal, a resacralisation of our created world in order to save it. As the re-establishing of full communion between the creature and the Creator on all these levels – the personal, the ecclesial, and the universal – theosis is for every serious Christian.

---

[28] Getcha, 2020. Archbishop Job (Getcha) is now Metropolitan of Pisidia.

8

Afterword

Blank Pages

I had intended calling this chapter 'Concluding Reflections'. But an artist friend with whom I discussed the book as it was nearing its end said (with a nod to Derrida), 'No, there is no conclusion, there will always be blank pages.' I had told him that as I was composing the chapters I had left blank pages in order to jot down further thoughts on finally reviewing the text. He liked that, because what we were discussing under the rubric of theosis was in fact life itself as *epektasis* (to use Gregory of Nyssa's term), as movement without a 'conclusion'. I have attempted in this book a portrait of theosis in relation to different concepts of religion and no portrait, whether pictural or textual, is ever definitive. Or rather, what I have attempted is a translation of concepts and teachings concerning theosis from different contexts and epochs, and any translation is inevitably provisional, participating as it does 'in the necessities of the moment'.[1] So with the proviso that there are many blank pages and uncertainties in this work, I simply offer a summary of progress so far:

The theosis/religion binary is not a constant. In antiquity, religion (*religio*) is closely connected with cult and moral conduct. This is a sense we also find in Early Christianity (as *thrēskeia*) but with an increasing emphasis on 'reverence for God' (*theosebeia*) as the distinguishing characteristic of the Christian community. Theosis expresses this reverence for God both as a theological theme uniting creation with the eschatological fulfilment that has always been intended for it and also as the believer's practical orientation towards its fulfilment appropriated through baptism

---

[1] Personal communication from Étienne Leclercq dated 15 May 2022.

and participation in the Eucharist. In a philosophical context, theosis is also descriptive of spiritual ascent through moral development, always envisaged, at least implicitly, as taking place within the ecclesial community. In Byzantium, where religion (as *theosbeia* or *eusebeia*) is the Christian believer's orientation towards Orthodox piety in a society conceived as wholly Orthodox, theosis comes to be focused, under the pressure of controversy, on the implications of Christ's Transfiguration. The essence/energies distinction, adumbrated by the Cappadocians and elaborated by Maximus the Confessor, comes to be central to Gregory Palamas's explanation of how the Christian can share in the divine glory without compromising God's transcendence. Theosis, as a doctrine of transformation through participation in the divine energies, thus becomes an important mark of Orthodoxy. In the mediaeval West, where religion expressed the unity of the Christian community (either of Christendom as a whole, or of the narrower world of a monastic order), theosis, or rather, one of the equivalent Latin expressions, *glorificatio, deificatio, transformatio in deum*, could be union with the divinised humanity of Christ (John of Fécamp), or the ascent to God through love in ecstatic self-forgetfulness (Bernard), or the cessation of all intellectual activity and the transformation of the affective side of humanity into God (Bonaventure). A change takes place in the middle of the thirteenth century. With Albert the Great, the influence of Dionysius the Areopagite replaces that of Augustine. The intellective way of negation now becomes more important than the affective way of affirmation. God is not known through sensible or even intelligible objects. The soul can rise to knowledge of God (but not to comprehension of him) through being caught up in the light of glory. This change is intensified in Meister Eckhart, in whose sermons the focus is entirely on the interiority of the individual. External acts of devotion, such as pilgrimages and even the reception of the Eucharist, are only distracting. Religion, from having been a communal expression of Christianity, is now seen as a personal quest, one which, even though the word itself was not invented until the seventeenth century, may nevertheless be called 'mysticism'.

In the nineteenth and early twentieth centuries, many held that religion would fade away as scientific and technological advances came to satisfy the needs that had formerly been met by religion. But people like Scheler and Boutroux were convinced that humanity was 'hard-wired' for God, or in less anachronistic terms, that humanity was theomorphic because of the presence within it of the eternal – the *fünkelîn* of Meister Eckhart, or the *élan vital* of Henri Bergson. The esoteric movement also resurfaced and became important again, partly as a protest against the era's bleak scientific determinism. A universal human yearning for self-transcendence was widely recognised. Yet the emphasis was still resolutely on the individual. In the late twentieth century, it still seemed incontrovertible that 'Christian mysticism is primarily and essentially a matter of personal religion' (Knowles, 1975: 82).

In modernity, religion is 'a system of beliefs and practices relating to sacred things' (Durkheim, 1912: 65), with theosis occupying a place as an object of scientific study within a given belief system. A post-modern but still scientific way of looking at religion is as a cultural system (Geertz, 1973), in which theosis, as in Byzantium, is part of a symbolic pattern that gives meaning to life. The ecclesial aspect of religion, and with it of theosis as a relational category, receives attention again. Theosis, as Rowan Williams puts it, 'is a process of coming to inhabit divine relatedness' (2021: 97). In terms of religious practice this means that theosis 'is worship from beginning to end, for it is an active participation in Jesus Christ made possible by the Spirit' (Habets, 2009: 192).

Allowing for differences in emphasis, there is a remarkable consensus on theosis in the liberal ecumenical theology of modern faculties of theology, or – more often today – faculties of religious studies. This is not difficult to achieve when theosis is understood as one theological theme, albeit a leading one, among others. It carries scriptural and patristic authority and in the twentieth century has been found particularly helpful by both Roman Catholic and Anglican theologians (such as de Lubac and Milbank) in bridging the gulf that had arisen in scholastic theology between the natural and the supernatural, between nature and grace.[2] The maximalising Eastern version, which characterised Byzantine theology from the sixth century onwards and was defined doctrinally in the fourteenth century as a result of the Hesychast Controversy, has not been received so favourably by Western scholars. Encompassing as it does the whole of religion (and relying on a disputed understanding of the distinction between essence and energies), it cannot easily be accommodated alongside the different aspects of the *theme* of deification drawn from the earlier patristic tradition. Nevertheless, the Eastern version, largely through the modern ecumenical movement, has played a key role in the Western retrieval of the deification theme, not least through encouraging Protestants to go back behind the developments of nineteenth-

---

[2] In the twenty-first century, Hart, 2022, continues this argument from the Orthodox side.

century liberal theology and reassess their foundational documents in the light of the patristic tradition.

One of the new things I discovered (new to me, at least) when I was preparing my materials for this book was that the influence of esoteric traditions on mainstream Christian thinking, from the Hermetists and Kabbalists of fifteenth-century Rome to the Boehmians and Steinerians of Silver Age Russia, went much deeper than is often supposed. Jung thought that such movements derived their force from the fascination of the psyche. They also expressed the *Zeitgeist* of the early twentieth century. Berdyaev, while not according theosophy any intellectual value, understood its attraction ('temptation' is his expression) because of its promise to unite one with ancient cosmic wisdom and insert one's soul into 'the chain of divine cosmic evolution and divine cosmic hierarchy'. He therefore thought it useful as a bridge – the only bridge for many people – 'by which they can cross into the spiritual life, by which they can leave the soulless and meaningless life of the contemporary world' (Berdyaev, 2015: 144). Sherrard, too, speaking of the *Philokalia* in much the same vein, saw it as offering 'an itinerary through the labyrinth of time, a silent way of love and gnosis through the deserts and emptinesses of life' (Palmer, Sherrard, and Ware, 1979: 13).[3] New Age spirituality is widely derided by professional theologians as a matter of crystals and horoscopes and Wicca. But it has just as much to do with an understanding of the interconnectedness of the universe as a whole, a view of the world as a single living being, a sense of the imagination as giving access to different levels of reality. It finds expression today in the ecological movement, biodynamic agriculture, holistic medicine, and holistic education. Theosis as a theme ties in with this and could itself become a bridge to an authentic spiritual life in Christ for people who perhaps initially are repelled by the institutional church.

Theosis, clearly, is not simply of interest to academic theology. Through the dissemination of such texts as the sermons of Meister Eckhart, *The Philokalia*, and *The Way of a Pilgrim*, an awareness of theosis as a supreme spiritual goal has reached a popular audience. The widely read Trappist spiritual writer, Thomas Merton (1915–1968) was one of the first to bring Eckhart to the notice of a broad public. Since then, the immensely popular New Age teacher Eckhart Tolle (b. 1948) has used the Meister in conjunction with some of the spiritual traditions of non-

---

[3] The Introduction of the *Philokalia* is signed by all three editors, but this sentence was no doubt contributed by Sherrrard.

Christian religions to produce a powerful series of self-help books on the development of the inner life. *The Way of a Pilgrim*, together with the Jesus Prayer, was introduced to a large readership by J. D. Salinger's novel, *Franny and Zooey* (1961). Theosis is now much more than a theological theme studied by biblical and patristic scholars.

Tolle has done much to bring Christian mysticism to the notice of the general public. It is still, however, in Knowles's terms, 'essentially a matter of personal religion' (1975: 82). Admittedly, Western individualism has not left Orthodoxy untouched (Russell, 2017b). Nor is the Western tradition without eloquent advocates for the ecclesial context of theosis (Keating, 2007; Habets, 2009; Ortiz, 2021: 7–28). Nevertheless, it is in Orthodoxy that the ecclesial context of theosis has been most fully explored, not only in current scholarship (Nellas, 1987; Anastasios (Yannoulatos), 2003; Zizioulas, 2006; Yannaras, 2007; Loudovikos, 2010; Getcha, 2020; Asproulis, 2021), but also in older works of Russian theologians of the diaspora, particularly Bulgakov, which have only recently been translated (Bulgakov, 2002, 2004, 2008). The idiom of these Orthodox theologians, although still strange to many Western ears, has begun to resonate with Western concerns, particularly those relating to the environment, and has much to teach us. The Church is not an inward-looking coterie of pious believers. 'The Church is creation', says Nellas, 'grafted onto Christ and vivified by the Spirit' (1987: 142). Theosis, far from 'de-creating' us by a gnostic type of spiritualisation, brings the whole of creation to fulfilment. In the end – eschatologically – 'theosis and religion' encompasses the whole of reality.

Bibliography

Æ (1990). *The Candle of Vision: Inner Worlds of the Imagination*. Bridport: Prism Press (first published in 1918).

Alfeyev, H. (2000). *St Symeon the New Theologian and Orthodox Tradition*. Oxford: Oxford University Press.

Allchin, A. M. (1988). *Participation in God: A Forgotten Strand in Anglican Tradition*. Wilton, CT: Morehouse-Barlow.

Allen, P. (2015). Life and Times of Maximus the Confessor. In P. Allen and B. Neil, eds., *The Oxford Handbook of Maximus the Confessor*. Oxford: Oxford University Press, pp. 3–18.

Anastasios (Yannoulatos), Archbishop (2003). *Facing the World: Orthodox Christian Essays on Global Concerns*, trans. P. Gottfried. Crestwood, NY: St Vladimir's Seminary Press.

Andia, Y. de (1986). *L'Union à Dieu chez Denys l'Aréopagite*. Leiden: Brill.

(2006). *Consurge ignote ad unionem*. L'interpretation de Denys l'Aréopagite dans la *Théologie mystique* d'Hugues de Balma et 'les deux voies'. In Y. de Andia, ed. *Denys l'Aréopagite: Tradition et metamorphoses*. Paris: Vrin, pp. 213–56.

Arblaster, J., and Faesen, R. (2019). *Mystical Doctrines of Deification: Case Studies in the Christian Tradition*. London and New York: Routledge.

Asproulis, N. (2021). Eucharistic Personhood: Deification in the Orthodox Tradition. In J. Ortiz, ed., *With All the Fullness of God: Deification in Christian Tradition*. Lanham, MD: Lexington Press, pp. 29–57.

Ayres, L. (2005). Deification and the Dynamics of Nicene Theology: The Contribution of Gregory of Nyssa. *St Vladimir's Theological Quarterly*, 49/4, 375–94.

Barbet, J., and Ruello, F. (1995–96). *Hugues de Balma, Théologie mystique*. SC 408 and 409. Paris: Éditions du Cerf.

Bardy, G. (1957). Divinisation – chez les pères latins'. In M. Viller et al., eds., *Dictionnaire de spiritualité, ascétique et mystique*, vol. 3. Paris: Beauchesne, cols. 1390–98.

Barker, E. (1957). *Social and Political Thought in Byzantium: From Justinian I to the Last Palaeologus.* Oxford: Clarendon Press.

Barth, K. (2013). *On Religion: The Revelation of God as the Sublimation of Religion.* London: Bloomsbury.

Bartos, E. (1999). *Deification in Eastern Orthodox Theology: An Evaluation and Critique of the Theology of Dumitru Stăniloae.* Carlisle: Paternoster Press.

Berdyaev, N. (1939). *Spirit and Reality*, trans. G. Reavey. London: Geoffrey Bles.

  (1951). *Dream and Reality: An Essay in Autobiography*, trans. K. Lampert. New York: Macmillan.

  (2015). *The Brightest Lights of the Silver Age: Essays on Russian Religious Thinkers*, compiled and trans. B. Jakim. Kettering, OH: Semantron Press.

Bergson, H. (1932). *Les deux sources de la morale et de la religion.* Paris: Alcan (reprinted Paris: Presses Universitaires de France, 1990).

Bernhard, A. (2007). *Other Early Christian Gospels: A Critical Edition of the Surviving Greek Manuscripts.* London: T&T Clark.

Berthold, G. (1985). *Maximus the Confessor: Selected Writings.* CWS. Mahwah, NJ: Paulist Press.

Bihlmeyer, K. (1907), *Heinrich Seuse. Deutsche Schriften.* Stuttgart: Im Auftrag der Württembergischen Kommission für Landesgeshichte.

Billings, J. T. (2007). John Calvin: United to God through Christ. In M. J. Christensen and J. A. Wittung, eds., *Partakers of the Divine Nature: The History and Development of Deification in the Christian Traditions.* Madison, WI, and Teaneck, NJ: Fairleigh Dickinson University Press, pp. 200–18.

Blackwell, B. C. (2016). *Christosis: Engaging Paul's Soteriology with His Patristic Interpreters.* Grand Rapids, MI: Eerdmans (originally published Tübingen: Mohr Siebeck, 2011).

Blankenhorn, B. (2015). *The Mystery of Union with God: Dionysian Mysticism in Albert the Great and Thomas Aquinas.* Washington, DC: The Catholic University of America Press.

Blowers, P. M. (2016). *Maximus the Confessor: Jesus Christ and the Transfiguration of the World.* Oxford: Oxford University Press.

Blowers, P. M., and Wilken, R. L. (2003). *The Cosmic Mystery of Christ: Selected Writings from St. Maximus the Confessor.* Crestwood, NY: St Vladimir's Seminary Press.

Boersma, G. P. (2019). Aquinas and the Greek Fathers on the Vision of the Divine Essence. In M. Dauphinais, A. Hofer, OP, and Roger Nutt, eds., *Thomas Aquinas and the Greek Fathers.* Ave Maria, FL: Sapientia Press, pp. 130–50.

Bolshakoff, S. (1977). *Russian Mystics.* Cistercian Studies Series 26. Kalamazoo, MI: Cistercian.

Bonner, G. (1986). Augustine's Concept of Deification. *Journal of Theological Studies*, 37, 369–86.

  (1990) Deification, Divinization. In A. Fitzgerald, ed., *Augustine through the Ages: An Encyclopedia.* Grand Rapids, MI: Eerdmans, pp. 265–66.

Borysov, E. (2012). The Doctrine of Deification in the Works of Pavel Florensky and John Meyendorff: A Critical Examination. *Greek Orthodox Theological Review*, 57/1–4, 115–34.

Borysov. E. (2019). *Triadosis: Union with the Triune God*. Eugene, OR: Pickwick (reprinted Cambridge: James Clarke & Co., 2021).

Boutroux, É. (1925). *Morale et religion*. Paris: Flammarion.

(1926). *La nature et l'esprit*. Paris: Vrin (reprinted Paris: Hachette, 2018).

Bouyer, L. (1968). *The Spirituality of the New Testament and the Fathers*, trans. M. Ryan. Vol. 1 of *A History of Christian Spirituality*. London: Burns & Oates.

(1990). *The Christian Mystery: From Pagan Myth to Christian Mysticism*, trans. I. Trethowan. Edinburgh: T&T Clark.

Braaten, C. E., and Jenson, R. W. (1998). *Union with Christ: The New Finnish Interpretation of Luther*. Grand Rapids, MI: Eerdmans.

Bratsiotes, P. I. (1961). *Die Lehre der orthodoxen Kirche über die Theosis des Menschen*. Brussels: n.p.

Brock, S. (1973). An Early Syrian Life of Maximus the Confessor. *Analecta Bollandiana*, 91, 299–346.

Bulgakov, S. (2000). *Philosophy of Economy: The World as Household*, trans. and ed. C. Evtuhov. New Haven and London: Yale University Press.

(2002). *The Bride of the Lamb*, trans. B. Jakim. Grand Rapids, MI: Eerdmans and Edinburgh, UK: T&T Clark.

(2003). Dogma and Dogmatic Theology, trans. P. Bouteneff. In M. Plekon, ed., *Tradition Alive: On the Church and Christian Life in Our Time*. Lanham, MD: Sheed and Ward, pp. 67–80.

(2004). *The Comforter*, trans. B. Jakim. Grand Rapids, MI: Eerdmans.

(2008). *The Lamb of God*, trans. B. Jakim. Grand Rapids, MI: Eerdmans.

(2011). *Relics and Miracles: Two Theological Essays by Sergius Bulgakov*, trans. B. Jakim. Grand Rapids, MI: Eerdmans.

(2012). *Unfading Light: Contemplations and Speculations*, trans. T. A. Smith. Grand Rapids, MI: Eerdmans.

Byers, A. J. (2017). *Ecclesiology and Theosis in the Gospel of John*. Cambridge: Cambridge University Press.

Capánaga, V. (1954). La deificación en la soteriologia agustiniana. *Augustinus Magister*, 2, 745–54.

Caponi, F. J. (2007). Karl Rahner: Divinization in Roman Catholicism. In M. J. Christensen and J. A. Wittung, eds., *Partakers of the Divine Nature: The History and Development of Deification in the Christian Traditions*. Madison and Teaneck, NJ: Fairleigh Dickinson University Press, pp. 259–80.

Carrette, J., and King, R. (2005). *Selling Spirituality: The Silent Takeover of Religion*. London and New York: Routledge.

Carlson, M. (1993). *No Religion Higher than Truth: A History of the Theosophical Movement in Russia, 1875–1922*. Princeton, NJ: Princeton University Press.

(1996). Gnostic Elements in the Cosmogony of Vladimir Soloviev. In J. D. Kornblatt and R. F. Gustafson, eds., *Russian Religious Thought*. Madison: University of Wisconsin Press, pp. 49–67.

Casarella, P. (1995). Wer schreib die ex-Greco-Notizen im Codex Cusanus 44? *Mitteilungen und Forschungsbeitraege der Cusanus Gesellschaft*, 22, 123–32.

Cavarnos, C. (2008). *The Philokalia: Writings of the Most Holy Mystic Fathers in Which Is Explained How the Mind Is Purified, Illumined, and Perfected through Practical and Contemplative Ethical Philosophy.* Belmont, MA: Institute for Byzantine and Modern Greek Studies.

Chadwick, H. (2002). Note sur la divinisation chez saint Augustin. *Revue des sciences religieuses,* 76/2, 246–48.

Chouliaras, A. (2020). *The Anthropology of St Gregory Palamas: The Image of God, the Spiritual Senses, and the Human Body.* Studia Traditionis Theologiae. Turnhout: Brepols.

Christensen, M. J. (2007). The Problem, Promise, and Process of *Theosis.* In M. J. Christensen and J. A. Wittung, eds., *Partakers of the Divine Nature: The History and Development of Deification in the Christian Traditions.* Madison and Teaneck, NJ: Fairleigh Dickinson University Press, pp. 23–31.

(2021). The Royal Way of Love: Deification in the Wesleyan Tradition. In J. Ortiz, ed., *With All the Fullness of God: Deification in Christian Tradition.* Lanham, MD: Lexington Press, pp. 177–202.

Christensen, M. J., and Wittung, J. A. (2007). *Partakers of the Divine Nature: The History and Development of Deification in the Christian Traditions.* Madison and Teaneck, NJ: Fairleigh Dickinson University Press.

Ciraulo, J. M. (2019). Hans Urs von Balthasar's indifference to divinization. In J. Arblaster and R. Faesen, eds., *Mystical Doctrines of Deification: Case Studies in the Christian Tradition.* London and New York: Routledge, pp. 165–85.

Clément, O. (1993). *The Roots of Christian Mysticism,* trans. T. Berkeley and J. Hummerstone. London: New City.

(2012). *L'Œil de feu.* Clichy: Éditions de Corlevour.

(2021). *The Other Sun: A Spiritual Autobiography,* trans. with an Introduction and notes by M. Donley. Leominster, UK: Gracewing.

Coakley, S., and Stang, C. M. (2009). *Rethinking Dionysius the Areopagite.* Chichester: Wiley-Blackwell.

Coates, R. (2019). *Deification in Russian Religious Thought: Between the Revolutions, 1905–1917.* Oxford: Oxford University Press.

(2020). Theosis in Early Twentieth-Century Russian Religious Thought. In G. Pattison, C. Emerson, and R. A. Poole, eds., *The Oxford Handbook of Russian Religious Thought.* Oxford: Oxford University Press, pp. 240–54.

Combes, A. (1945–59). *Essai sur la critique de Ruysbroeck par Gerson,* 4 vols. Paris: Vrin.

(1958). *Ioannis Carlerii de Gerson De Mystica Theologia.* Lugano: Thesaurus Mundi.

Conticello, V., and Citterio, E. (2002). La Philocalie et ses versions. In C. G. Conticello and V. Conticello, eds., *La théologie byzantine et sa tradition. II. (XIIIe–XIXe s.).* Turnhout: Brepols, pp. 999–1021.

Coolman, B. T. (2009). The Medieval Affective Dionysian Tradition. In S. Coakley and C. M. Stang, eds., *Rethinking Dionysius the Areopagite.* Chichester: Wiley-Blackwell, pp. 85–102.

Cooper, P. R. (2019). The Abyss of Man, the Abyss of Love. In J. Arblaster and R. Faesen, eds., *Mystical Doctrines of Deification: Case Studies in the Christian Tradition.* London and New York: Routledge, pp. 98–115.

Copenhaver, B. P. (1992). *The Greek Corpus Hermeticum and the Latin Asclepius in a New English Translation, with Notes and Introduction.* Cambridge: Cambridge University Press.

Copleston, F. C. (1988). *Russian Religious Philosophy: Selected Aspects*. Notre Dame, IN: Search Press.

Cousins, E. (1978). *Bonaventure: The Soul's Journey into God, The Tree of Life, The Life of St Francis*. CWS. New York: Paulist Press and London: SPK.

Dagmawi, A. (2009). Some Ideas of Deification as Reflected throughout the Ethiopic Divine Liturgy. *Collectanea Christiana Orientalia*, 6, 45–66.

Dagron, G. (1996). *Empereur et prêtre. Étude sur le 'césaropapisme' byzantin*. Paris: Gallimard.

Dales, D. J. (2017). *Divine Remaking: St Bonaventure and the Gospel of Luke*. Cambridge: James Clarke & Co.

(2019a). *Way Back to God: The Spiritual Theology of St Bonaventure*. Cambridge: James Clarke & Co.

(2019b). 'In Thy Light Shall We See Light': The Spiritual Vision of St Bonaventure and St Gregory Palamas. *Sobornost*, 41/2, 22–38.

(2021). *Truth and Reality: The Wisdom of St Bonaventure*. Cambridge: James Clarke & Co.

Daley, B. E. (2013). *Light on the Mountain: Greek Patristic and Byzantine Homilies on the Transfiguration of the Lord*. Yonkers, NY: St. Vladimir's Seminary Press.

(2017). *Leontius of Byzantium: Complete Works*. Oxford Early Christian Texts. Oxford: Oxford University Press.

(2018). *God Visible: Patristic Christology Reconsidered*. Changing Paradigms in Historical and Systematic Theology. Oxford: Oxford University Press.

Darrouzès, J. (1957). *Syméon le Nouveau Théologien, Chapitres théologiques, gnostiques et pratiques*. SC 51. Paris: Cerf.

(1967). *Syméon le Nouveau Théologien, Traités théologiques et éthiques*. SC 129. Paris: Cerf.

Dauphinais, M., Hofer, A., and Nutt, R. (2019). *Thomas Aquinas and the Greek Fathers*. Ave Maria, FL: Sapientia Press.

Davies, B. (2002). *Aquinas*. Outstanding Christian Thinkers. London and New York: Continuum.

Davies, O. (2006). *God Within: The Mystical Tradition of Northern Europe*, rev. ed. with a foreword by R. Williams. Hyde Park, NY: New City Press.

Dell'Osso, C. (2006). Leonzio di Bisanzio e Leonzio di Gerusalemme: Una chiara distinzione. *Augustinianum*, 46, 231–59.

Derrida, J. (2002). Faith and Knowledge: The Two Sources of 'Religion' at the Limits of Reason Alone. In *Acts of Religion*, ed. G. Anidjar. London and New York: Routledge, pp. 40–101.

Dickey, L. (1993). Hegel on Religion and Philosophy. In F. C. Beiser, ed., *The Cambridge Companion to Hegel*. Cambridge and New York: Cambridge University Press, pp. 301–47.

Dodds, E. R. (1963). *Proclus. The Elements of Theology*. Oxford: The Clarendon Press.

Drewery, B. (1975). Deification. In P. Brooks, ed., *Christian Spirituality: Essays in Honour of Gordon Rupp*. London: SCM Press, pp. 33–62.

Dunkle, B. (2019). Beyond Carnal Cogitations: Deification in Ambrose of Milan. In J. Ortiz, ed., *Deification in the Latin Patristic Tradition*. Washington, DC: The Catholic University of America Press, pp. 132–52.

Dunlop, J. B. (1972). *Staretz Amvrosy: Model for Dostoevsky's Staretz Zossima*. Belmont, MA: Nordland.

Durkheim, É. (1912). *Les formes élémentaires de la vie religieuse: Le système totémique en Australie*. Paris: Alcan (trans. J. W. Swain as *The Elementary Forms of Religious Life*. London: George Allen & Unwin, 1915).

Edwards, M. J. (2002). *Origen against Plato*. Aldershot: Ashgate.

(2017a). Growing Like God: Some Thoughts on Irenaeus of Lyons. In M. Edwards and E. E. D-Vasilescu, eds, *Visions of God and Ideas on Deification in Patristic Thought*. London and New York: Routledge, pp. 37–51.

(2017b). Deification in the Alexandrian Tradition. In M. Edwards and E. E. D-Vasilescu, eds, *Visions of God and Ideas on Deification in Patristic Thought*. London and New York: Routledge, pp. 74–88.

Emerson, C., Pattison, G., and Poole, R. A. (2020). *The Oxford Handbook of Russian Religious Thought*. Oxford: Oxford University Press.

Erb, P. (1978). *Jacob Boehme, The Way to Christ*. CWS. New York and Mahwah, NJ: Paulist Press.

Evans, G. R. (2000). *Bernard of Clairvaux*. New York and Oxford: Oxford University Press.

Evlogy, Metropolitan (2014). *My Life's Journey: The Memoirs of Metropolitan Evlogy. As Put Together according to His Accounts by T. Manukhin*, trans. A. Lisenko. 2 vols. Yonkers, NY: St Vladimir's Seminary Press.

Evtuhov, C. (1997). *The Cross and the Sickel: Sergei Bulgakov and the Fate of Russian Religious Philosophy*. Ithaca and London: Cornell University Press.

Faesen, R. (2019). Ubi caro mea glorificatur, gloriosum me esse cognosco: Deification in John of Fécamp (c. 990–1078). In J. Arblaster and R. Faesen, eds., *Mystical Doctrines of Deification: Case Studies in the Christian Tradition*. London and New York: Routledge, pp. 89–97.

Faivre, A. (1998). Renaissance Hermetism and the Concept of Western Esotericism. In R. Van den Broek and W. J. Hanegraaf, eds., *Gnosis and Hermetism from Antiquity to Modern Times*. New York: State University of New York Press, pp. 109–23.

Feneuil, A. (2018). Becoming God or Becoming Yourself: Vladimir Lossky on Deification and Personal Identity. In J. Arblaster and R. Faesen, eds., *Theosis /Deification: Christian Doctrines of Divinization East and West*. Leuven: Peeters, pp. 49–63.

Ferentinou, V. (2016). Light from Within or Light from Above? Theosophical Appropriations in Early-Twentieth Century Greek Culture. In J. Chajes and B. Huss, eds., *Theosophical Appropriations: Esotericism, Kabbalah, and the Transformation of Traditions*. Beer Sheva: Ben Gurion University of the Negev Press, pp. 273–308.

Finlan, S. (2021). *Theōsis* That Means Something: My Journey. In J. Ortiz, ed., *With All the Fullness of God: Deification in Christian Tradition*. Lanham, MD: Lexington Press, pp. 205–22.

Fitzgerald, T. (2000). *The Ideology of Religious Studies*. Oxford: Oxford University Press.

Florensky, P. (1997). *The Pillar and Ground of the Truth: An Essay in Orthodox Theodicy in Twelve Letters*, trans. B. Jakim. Princeton and Oxford: Princeton University Press.

Fokin, A. (2014). The Doctrine of Deification in the Western Fathers of the Church: A Reconsideration. In T. Hainthaler, F. Mali, G. Emmenegger, and M. L. Ostermann, eds., *Für Uns und für unser Heil. Soteriologie in Ost und West*. Pro Oriente, Band XXXVII. Wiener Patristiche Tagungen VI. Innsbruck and Vienna: Tyrolia-Verlag, pp. 207–20.

(2015). Apocatastasis in the Syrian Christian Tradition: Evagrius and Isaac. In Metropolitan Hilarion (Alfeyev), ed., *Saint Isaac the Syrian and His Spiritual Legacy*. Yonkers, NY: St Vladimir's Seminary Press, pp. 123–34.

Fowden, G. (1993). *The Egyptian Hermes. A Historical Approach to the Late Pagan Mind*. Princeton, NJ: Princeton University Press.

Frank, S. L. (2001). *A Solovyov Anthology*, trans. N. Duddington. London: The Saint Austin Press (first published in 1950).

Gale, J. (2020). Angelus Silesius: Some Lesefrüchte on the Background to Lacan's Seminar. *European Journal of Psychoanalysis*, 7/1. www.journal-psychoanalysis.eu/angelus-silesius-some-lesefruchte-on-the-background-to-lacans-seminar/.

Gallacher, P. J. (1997). *The Cloud of Unknowing*. Kalamazoo: Western Michigan University Press.

Gavrilyuk, P. L. (2009). The Retrieval of Deification: How a Once-despised Archaism Became an Ecumenical Desideratum. *Modern Theology*, 25/4, 647–59.

Gavrilyuk, P. (2022). How Deification Was Rediscovered in Modern Orthodox Theology: The Contribution of Ivan Popov. *Modern Theology*, 38/1, 100–27.

Geertz, C. (1973). Religion as a Cultural System. In C. Geertz, *The Interpretation of Cultures: Selected Essays*. New York: Basic Books, pp. 87–125.

Getcha, J. (2020). *Participants de la nature divine: La spiritualité orthodoxe à l'âge de la secularisation*. Paris: Apostolia.

Golitzin, A. (1995–97). *St Symeon the New Theologian on the Mystical Life*. 3 vols. Crestwood, NY: St. Vladimir's Seminary Press.

(2013). *Mystagogy: A Monastic Reading of Dionysius Areopagita*, ed. B. G. Bucur. Collegeville, MN: Liturgical Press.

Gorodetzky, N. (1938). *The Humiliated Christ in Modern Russian Thought*. London: SPCK.

Gregorios, Hieromonk (2009). *The Divine Liturgy: A Commentary in the Light of the Fathers*, trans. E. Theokritoff. Koutloumousiou Monastery, Mount Athos. Columbia, MS: Newrome Press.

Grillaert, N. (2008). *What the God-seekers found in Nietzsche: The Reception of Nietzsche's Übermensch by the Philosophers of the Russian Religious Renaissance*. Amsterdam and New York: Rodopi.

Grillmeier, A., with T. Hainthaler (1995), *Christ in Christian Tradition*, vol. 2, part 2, *The Church of Constantinople in the Sixth Century*, trans. P. Allen and J. Cawte. London: Mowbray and Louisville, KY: Westminster John Knox Press.

Gross, J. (2002). *The Divinization of the Christian according to the Greek Fathers*, trans. P. A. Onica. Anaheim, CA: A&C Press (originally published as *La divinisation du chrétien d'après les pères grecs: Contribution historique à la doctrine de la grâce*. Paris: Gabalda, 1938).

Haas, A. M. (1987). Schools of Late Medieval Mysticism. In J. Raith, B. MGinn, and J. Meyendorff, eds., *Christian Spirituality: High Middle Ages and Reformation*. London: Routledge and Kegan Paul, pp. 140–75.

Habets, M. (2009). *Theosis in the Theology of Thomas Torrance*. Ashgate New Critical Thinking in Religion, Theology and Biblical Studies Series. London and New York: Routledge.

(2021). 'As Far as Our Capacity Allows': Deification in the Baptist Tradition. In J. Ortiz, ed., *With All the Fullness of God: Deification in Christian Tradition*. Lanham, MD: Lexington Press, pp. 155–76.

Haflidson, R. (2019), 'We Shall Be That Seventh Day': Deification in Augustine. In J. Ortiz, ed., *Deification in the Latin Patristic Tradition*. Washington, DC: The Catholic University of America Press, pp. 169–89.

Hallonsten, G. (2007) *Theosis* in Recent Research: A Renewal of Interest and a Need for Clarity. In M. J. Christensen and J. A. Wittung, eds., *Partakers of the Divine Nature: The History and Development of Deification in the Christian Traditions*. Madison and Teaneck, NJ: Fairleigh Dickinson University Press, pp. 281–93.

Harnack, A. (1958). *History of Dogma*, trans. N. Buchanan, 7 vols. New York: Russell and Russell.

Harrington, J. F. (2018). *Dangerous Mystic: Meister Eckhart's Path to the God Within*. New York: Penguin Press.

Hart, D. B. (2020). *That All Shall Be Saved: Heaven, Hell and Universal Salvation*. New Haven and London: Yale University Press.

(2022). *You Are Gods: On Nature and Supernature*. Notre Dame, IN: University of Notre Dame Press.

Hausherr, I., and Horn, G. (1928). Un grand mystique byzantin. Vie de Syméon le Nouveau Théologien. *Orientalia Christiana*, 12, 1–128.

Heil, G. (1991a). Dionysius Areopagita, De coelestia hierarchia, in *Corpus Dionysiacum II*. Berlin: De Gruyter.

(1991b). Dionysius Areopagita, De ecclesiastica hierarchia, in *Corpus Dionysiacum II*. Berlin: De Gruyter.

Hick, J. H. (1990). *Philosophy of Religion*, 4th ed. Englewood Cliffs, NJ: Prentice Hall.

Hladký, V. (2014). *The Philosophy of George Gemistos Plethon: Platonism in Late Byzantium, between Hellenism and Orthodoxy*. Farnham, UK and Burlington, VT: Ashgate.

Hobbins, D. (2009). *Authorship and Publicity before Print: Jean Gerson and the Transformation of Late Medieval Learning*. Philadelphia: University of Pennsylvania Press.

Hoffman, G. (1979). *Predigten: Vollständige Ausgabe/Johannes Tauler*. Einsielden-Trier: Johannes.

Hopkins, J. (1988). *Nicholas of Cusa's Debate with John Wenck. A Translation and Appraisal of De Ignota Litteratura and Apologia Doctae Ignorantiae.* Minneapolis, MN: The Arthur J. Banning Press. www.jasper-hopkins.info.

(1994). *A Miscellany on Nicholas of Cusa.* Minneapolis, MN: The Arthur J. Banning Press.

(2003). *Nicholas of Cusa's Early Sermons.* Loveland, CO: The Arthur J. Banning Press.

(2009). Nicholas of Cusa. In G. Oppy and N. N. Tratakis, eds., *Medieval Philosophy of Religion.* Durham: Acumen, pp. 235–49.

(website). 'Nicholas of Cusa's Last Sermons'. www.jasper-hopkins.info.

Hudson, N. (2007). *Becoming God: The Doctrine of Theosis in Nicholas of Cusa.* Washington, DC: The Catholic University of America Press.

Hügel, Baron F. von (1923). *The Mystical Element of Religion as Studied in St Catherine of Genoa and Her Friends.* London: Dent.

Idel, M. (2017). Kabbalah in Byzantium. In A. Kaldellis and N. Siniossoglou, eds., *The Cambridge Intellectual History of Byzantium.* Cambridge: Cambridge University Press, pp. 524–41.

James, W. (1902). *The Varieties of Religious Experience: A Study in Human Nature.* London: Longman, Green and Co.

Jankowiak, M., and Booth, P. (2015). A New Date-List of the Works of Maximus the Confessor. In P. Allen and B. Neil, eds., *The Oxford Handbook of Maximus the Confessor.* Oxford: Oxford University Press, pp. 19–83.

Johnson, C. D. L. (2010). *The Globalization of Hesychasm and the Jesus Prayer: Contesting Contemplation.* London: Continuum.

Johnson, T. J. (2012). *The Soul in Ascent: Bonaventure on Poverty, Prayer and Union with God.* New York: Franciscan Institute.

Jung, C. G. (1964). The Spiritual Problem of Modern Man. Vol. 10 of H. Read, et al., eds., R. F. C. Hull, trans., The Collected Works of C. G. Jung. Princeton, NJ: Princeton University Press.

Kadloubovsky, E., and Palmer, G. E. H. (1954). *Early Fathers from the Philokalia.* London and Boston: Faber and Faber.

Kärkkäinen, V.-M. (2004). *One with God: Salvation as Deification and Justification.* Collegeville, MN: Liturgical Press.

(2021). Justification as Union and Christ's Presence: Deification in the Lutheran Tradition. In J. Ortiz, ed., *With All the Fullness of God: Deification in Christian Tradition.* Lanham, MD: Lexington Press, pp. 59–81.

Karmiris, I. (1968). *Dogmatica et Symbolica Monumenta Orthodoxae Catholicae Ecclesiae.* Graz: Akademische Druck –u Verlagsanstalt.

Keating, D. A. (2004). *The Appropriation of Divine Life in Cyril of Alexandria.* Oxford: Oxford University Press.

(2007). *Deification and Grace.* Naples, FL: Sapientia Press.

(2015). Typologies of Deification. *International Journal of Systematic Theology,* 17/3, 267–83.

Kelly, T. (2016). 'An Activity of Special, Supernatural, and Extraordinary Beneficence and Love': Matthias Scheeben's Theology of Deification. In D. Meconi and C. E. Olson, eds., *Called to be Children of God: The Catholic Theology of Human Deification.* San Francisco: Ignatius Press, pp. 198–219.

Kenworthy, S. M. (2010). *The Heart of Russia: Trinity-Sergius, Monasticism, and Society after 1825*. New York: Oxford University Press.

Kern, K. (1950). *Antropologiia Sv. Gregoriia Palamy*. Paris: YMCA-Press (reprinted Moscow: Palomnik, 1996).

Kharlamov, V. (2012), ed. *Theōsis: Deification in Christian Theology*, vol. 2. Cambridge: James Clarke & Co.

Knowles, D. (1960). *The English Mystical Tradition*. London: Burnes and Oates.
    (1975). The Influence of Pseudo-Dionysius on Western Mysticism. In P. Brooks, ed., *Christian Spirituality: Essays in Honour of Gordon Rupp*. London: SCM Press, pp. 79–94.

Kornblatt, J. D. (2009). *Divine Wisdom: The Wisdom Writings of Vladimir Solovyov*. Ithaca, NY and London: Cornell University Press.

Kotter, B. (1973). *Die Schriften des Johannes von Damaskos II. Expositio fidei*. Berlin: De Gruyter.

Krausmüller, D. (2001). Leontius of Jerusalem, a Theologian of the Seventh Century. *Journal of Theological Studies*, n.s. 52, 637–57.

Krivochéine, B. (1964). *Syméon le Nouveau Théologien, Catéchèses 6–22*. SC 104. Paris: Cerf.

Krivocheine, B. (1986). *In the Light of Christ. St. Symeon the New Theologian (949–1022): Life – Spirituality – Doctrine*, trans. A. P. Gythiel. Crestwood, NY: St. Vladimir's Seminary Press.

Lachman, G. (2007). *Rudolf Steiner: An Introduction to His Life and Work*. Edinburgh: Floris Books.

Lamberz, E. (2008–16). *ACO series secunda III, 1–3. Concilium universale Nicaenum Secundum*. Berlin: De Gruyter.

Larchet, J.-C. (1996). *La divinisation de l'homme selon saint Maxime le Confesseur*. Paris: Cerf.
    (2015). The Mode of Deification. In P. Allen and B. Neil, eds., *The Oxford Handbook of Maximus the Confessor*. Oxford: Oxford University Press, pp. 341–59.

Laurant, J.-P. (1992). *L'ésotericisme chrétien en France au XIXe siècle*. Lausanne: L'age d'homme.

Layton, B. (1987). *The Gnostic Scriptures: A New Translation with Annotations and Introductions*. London: SCM Press.

Leff, G. (1967). *Heresy in the Later Middle Ages: The Relation of Heterodoxy to Dissent c. 1250–c. 1450*. Manchester: Manchester University Press.

Lefsrud, S. (2020). *Kenosis in Theosis: An Exploration of Balthasar's Theology of Deification*. Eugene, OR: Pickwick.

Leijenhorst, C. (1998). Francesco Patrizi's Hermetic Philosophy. In R. Van den Broek and W. J. Hanegraaf, eds., *Gnosis and Hermetism from Antiquity to Modern Times*. New York: State University of New York Press, pp. 125–46.

Libera, A. de (1984). *Introduction à la mystique rhénane d'Albert le Grand à Maître Eckhart*. Paris: OIEL.

Lindbeck, G. (2009). *The Nature of Doctrine: Religion and Theology in a Postliberal Age*. Philadelphia, PA: Westminster Press.

Linman, J. (2007). Martin Luther: 'Little Christs for the World': Faith and Sacraments as Means to *Theosis*. In M. J. Christensen and J. A. Wittung, eds., *Partakers of the Divine Nature: The History and Development of*

Deification in the Christian Traditions. Madison and Teaneck, NJ: Fairleigh Dickinson University Press, pp. 189–99.

Litwa, M. D. (2012). *We Are Being Transformed: Deification in Paul's Soteriology*. Berlin: Walter de Gruyter.

(2013). *Becoming Divine: An Introduction to Deification in Western Culture*. Eugene, OR: Cascade Books.

Lossky, V. (1957). *The Mystical Theology of the Eastern Church*, trans. members of the Fellowship of St Alban and St Sergius. London: James Clarke & Co.

(1963). *The Vision of God*, trans. A. Moorhouse. Leighton Buzzard, UK: The Faith Press.

(1974). *In the Image and Likeness of God*. Crestwood, NY: St. Vladimir's Seminary Press.

(1998). *Théologie négative et connaissance de Dieu chez Maître Eckhart*. Études de philosophie médiévale 48. Paris: Vrin.

(2012). *Seven Days on the Roads of France: June 1940*, ed. N. Lossky, trans. M. Donley. Yonkers, NY: St Vladimir's Seminary Press.

Lot-Borodine, M. (1970). *La déification de l'homme selon la doctrine des Pères grecs*. Paris: Cerf.

Loudovikos, N. (2010). *A Eucharistic Ontology: Maximus the Confessor's Eschatological Ontology of Being as Dialogical Reciprocity*, trans. E. Theokritoff. Brookline, MA: Holy Cross Orthodox Press.

Louth, A. (1983a). *Discerning the Mystery: An Essay on the Nature of Theology*. Oxford: Clarendon Press.

(1983b). Manhood into God: The Oxford Movement, the Fathers and the Deification of Man. In K. Leech and R. Williams, eds., *Essays Catholic and Radical*. London: Bowerdean Press, pp. 70–80.

(1996). *Maximus the Confessor*. The Early Church Fathers. London and New York: Routledge.

(2003). *St John of Damascus' Three Treatises on the Divine Images*. Crestwood, NY: St. Vladimir's Seminary Press.

(2007). The Place of *Theosis* in Orthodox Theology. In M. J. Christensen and J. A. Wittung, eds., *Partakers of the Divine Nature: The History and Development of Deification in the Christian Traditions*. Madison and Teaneck, NJ: Fairleigh Dickinson University Press, pp. 32–44.

(2009). The Reception of Dionysius up to Maximus the Confessor. In S. Coakley and C. M. Stang, eds., *Re-thinking Dionysius the Areopagite*. Chichester: Wiley Blackwell, pp. 43–53.

(2012). The Influence of the *Philokalia* in the Orthodox World. In B. Bingaman and B. Nassif, eds., *The Philokalia: A Classic Text of Orthodox Spirituality*. Oxford and New York: Oxford University Press, pp. 50–60.

(2015a). Maximus the Confessor's Influence and Reception in Byzantine and Modern Orthodoxy. In P. Allen and B. Neil, eds., *The Oxford Handbook of Maximus the Confessor*. Oxford: Oxford University Press, pp. 500–15.

(2015b). *Modern Orthodox Thinkers: From the Philokalia to the Present*. London: SPCK.

(2017). *The Way of a Pilgrim: Candid Tales of a Wanderer to His Spiritual Father*, trans. A. Zaranko. London: Penguin Random House.

(2018). The Slav *Philokalia* and *The Way of a Pilgrim*. In N. Fennell and G. Speake, eds., *Mount Athos and Russia 1016–2016*. Oxford: Peter Lang, pp. 99–116.

(2020). Review of J. Ortiz, *Deification in the Latin Patristic Tradition*. *Journal of Ecclesiastical History*, 71/4, 835–37.

McGinn, B. (1986). *Meister Eckhart: Teacher and Preacher*. CWS. New York, Mahwah, Toronto: Paulist Press.

McGuckin, J. (1996). Symeon the New Theologian (d. 1022) and Byzantine Monasticism. In A. Bryer and M. Cunningham, eds., *Mount Athos and Byzantine Monasticism*. Aldershot, UK: Variorum, pp. 17–35.

McInroy, M. (2021). How Deification Became Eastern: German Idealism, Liberal Protestantism, and the Modern Misconstruction of the Doctrine. *Modern Theology*, 37/4, 934–58.

Magnin, E. (1937). Religion. In A. Vacant, E. Mangenot and É. Amann, eds., *Dictionnaire de Théologie Catholique*, vol. 13, part 2. Paris: Letouzey, cols. 2182–306.

Mahn-Lot, M. (2004). Ma mère, Myrrha Lot-Borodine (1882–1954). Esquisse d'itinéraire spirituel. *Revue des sciences philosophiques et théologiques*, 88, 745–54. https://doi.org/10.3917/rspt.884.0745.

Mainoldi, E. S. (2018). *Dietro 'Dionigi l'Areopagita'. La genesi e gli scopi del Corpus Dionysiacum*. Rome: Città Nuova.

(2019). The Reception of the Greek Patristic Doctrine of Deification in the Medieval West: The Case of John Scottus Eriugena. In J. Arblaster and R. Faesen, eds., *Mystical Doctrines of Deification: Case Studies in the Christian Tradition*. London and New York: Routledge, pp. 60–71.

Mantzaridis, G. I. (1984). *The Deification of Man: St Gregory Palamas and the Orthodox Tradition*, trans. L. Sherrard. Crestwood, NY: St Vladimir's Seminary Press.

Marx, J. (1905). *Verzeichnis der Handschriften-sammlung des Hospitals zu Cues bei Bernkastel a./Mosel*. Trier: Selbstverlag des Hospitals.

Mascall, E. L. (1946). *Christ, the Christian and the Church: A Study of the Incarnation and Its Consequences*. London: Longman, Green and Co.

Meconi, D. V. (2013). *The One Christ: St. Augustine's Theology of Deification*. Washington, DC: The Catholic University of America Press.

Meconi, D. V., and Olson, C. E. (2016). *Called to be Children of God: The Catholic Theology of Human Deification*. San Francisco, CA: Ignatius Press.

Meyendorff, J. (1959). *Introduction à l'étude de Grégoire Palamas*. Paris: Seuil (trans. G. Lawrence, *A Study of Gregory Palamas*, Leighton Buzzard, UK: Faith Press, 1984).

Meyer, M. (2007). *The Nag Hammadi Scriptures: International Edition*. New York: HarperOne.

Milbank, J. (2005). *The Suspended Middle. Henri de Lubac and the Debate concerning the Supernatural*. London: SCM Press.

(2009). Sophiology and Theurgy: The New Theological Horizon. In A. Pabst and C. Schneider, eds., *Encounter between Eastern Orthodoxy and Radical Orthodoxy : Transfiguring the World through the Word*. Farnham, UK and Burlington, VT: Ashgate, pp. 45–85.

Miller, C. L. (2017). Cusanus, Nicolaus [Nicolas of Cusa]. In E. N. Zalta, ed., *The Stanford Encyclopedia of Philosophy*, https://plato.stanford.edu/archives/sum2017/entries/cusanus.

Moreschini, C. (2000). *Gregorio di Nazianzo, Tutte le orazioni.* Milan: Bompiani Il Pensiero Occidentale.

Mosser, C. (2020). Recovering the Reformation's Ecumenical Vision of Redemption as Deification and Beatific Vision. *Perichoresis*, 18/1, 3–24.

(2021a). Orthodox–Reformed Dialogue and the Ecumenical Recovery of Theosis. *The Ecumenical Review*, 73/1, 131–51.

(2021b). The Gospel's End and Our Highest Good: Deification in the Reformed Tradition. In J. Ortiz, ed., *With All the Fullness of God: Deification in Christian Tradition.* Lanham, MD: Lexington Press, pp. 83–108.

Nault, F. (1998). Qu'appelle-t-on promettre? Jacques Derrida et la religion. *Théologiques*, 6/2, 119–44.

Neil, B., and Allen. P. (2003). *The [Greek] Life of Maximus the Confessor: Recension 3.* Strathfield, NSW: St Paul's Press.

Nellas, P. (1987). *Deification in Christ: The Nature of the Human Person*, trans. N. Russell. Crestwood, NY: St Vladimir's Seminary Press.

Niqueux, M. (1996). Lev Karsavin 'Dans le ventre de la baleine': L'épreuve du camp (1950–1952). *Revue des Études Slaves*, 68/3, 375–84. Persée: persee.fr/doc/slave_0080-2557_1996_num_68_3_6348.

Olson, R. E. (2007). Deification in Contemporary Theology. *Theology Today*, 64, 186–200.

Ortiz, J. (2016). Deification in the Latin Fathers. In D. Meconi and C. Olson, eds., *Called to be Children of God: The Catholic Theology of Human Deification.* San Francisco, CA: Ignatius Press, pp. 59–81.

(2019a). Making Worshipers into Gods: Deification in the Latin Liturgy. In J. Ortiz, ed., *Deification in the Latin Patristic Tradition.* Washington, DC: The Catholic University of America Press, pp. 9–29.

(2019b). *Deification in the Latin Patristic Tradition.* Washington, DC: The Catholic University of America Press.

(2021). *With All the Fullness of God: Deification in Christian Tradition.* Lanham, MD: Lexington Books.

Owens, B. (2021). More Than You Could Ever Imagine: A Catholic Pastoral Perspective on Deification. In J. Ortiz, ed., *With All the Fullness of God: Deification in Christian Tradition.* Lanham, MD: Lexington Press, pp. 241–63.

Palmer, G. E. H., Sherrard, P., and Ware, K. (1979). *The Philokalia: The Complete Text Compiled by St Nikodimos of the Holy Mountain and St Makarios of Corinth*, vol. 1. London: Faber and Faber.

Peters, J. S. (2019). *Quidam Graecus*: Theophylact of Ochrid in the *Catena Aurea In Ioannem* and the *Lectura Super Ioannem*. In M. Dauphinais, A. Hofer, OP, and Roger Nutt, eds., *Thomas Aquinas and the Greek Fathers.* Ave Maria, FL: Sapientia Press, pp. 244–73.

Pilch, J. (2018). *'Breathing the Spirit with Both Lungs': Deification in the Work of Vladimir Solov'ev.* Eastern Christian Studies 25. Leuven: Peeters.

Plested, M. (2012). *Orthodox Readings of Aquinas*. Oxford: Oxford University Press.

Popov, I. V. (2012). The Idea of Deification in the Early Eastern Church, trans. B. Jakim. In V. Kharlamov, ed., *Theōsis: Deification in Christian Theology*, vol. 2. Cambridge: James Clarke & Co., pp. 42–82.

Price, R. (2020). *The Acts of the Second Council of Nicaea*. TTH. Liverpool: Liverpool University Press.

Pyman, A. (2010). *Pavel Florensky: A Quiet Genius. The Tragic and Extraordinary Life of Russia's Unknown Da Vinci*. New York and London: Continuum.

Quint, J. (1977). *Meister Eckhart: Deutsche Predigten und Traktaten*. Munich: C. Hanser.

Rahner, K. (1966). Christianity and the Non-Christian Religions. In K. Rahner, *Theological Investigations*, vol. 5, trans. K.-H. Kruger. Baltimore, MD: Helicon Press and London: Darton, Longman and Todd, pp. 115–34.

Raines, J. (2002). *Marx on Religion*. Philadelphia, PA: Temple University Press.

Raschke, C. A. (2005). Derrida and the Return of Religion: Religious Theory after Postmodernism. *Journal for Cultural and Religious Theory*, 6/2, 1–16.

Reuschling, W. C. (2021). Living into the Fullness of God: A Protestant Pastoral Perspective on Deification. In J. Ortiz, ed., *With All the Fullness of God: Deification in Christian Tradition*. Lanham, MD: Lexington Press, pp. 223–39.

Richmond, S. (1995). Deconstruction. In T. Honderich, ed., *The Oxford Companion to Philosophy*. Oxford and New York: Oxford University Press, pp. 180–1.

Ricoeur, P. (1967). *The Symbolism of Evil*, trans. E. Buchanan. New York: Harper and Row.

Rigo, A. (2021). Le séjour de Grégoire Palamas au monastère de saint-Michel de Sosthénion (octobre 1341–24 mars 1342). In M.-H. Blanchet and R. E. Gómez, eds., *Le monde byzantine du XIIIe au XVe siècle. Anciennes ou nouvelles formes d'impérialité*. Travaux et Mémoires 25/1. Paris: Association des Amis du Centre d'Histoire et Civilisation de Byzance, pp. 667–94.

(2022). Dionysius from Niketas Stethatos to Gregory the Sinaite (and Gregory Palamas). In M. Edwards, D. Pallis, and G. Steiris, eds, *The Oxford Handbook of Dionysius the Areopagite*. Oxford: Oxford University Press, pp. 269–87.

Robinson, J. M. (1988). *The Nag Hammadi Library in English*. Leiden: E. J. Brill.

Rorem, P. (2009). The Early Latin Dionysius: Eriugena and Hugh of St Victor. In S. Coakley and C. M. Stang, eds., *Rethinking Dionysius the Areopagite*. Chichester: Wiley Blackwell, pp. 71–84.

Rudavsky, T. M. (1997). Medieval Jewish Neoplatonism. In D. H. Frank and O. Leaman, eds, *History of Jewish Philosophy*. Routledge History of World Philosophies, vol. 2. London and New York: Routledge, pp. 149–87.

Russell, N. (2004). *The Doctrine of Deification in the Greek Patristic Tradition*. Oxford: Oxford University Press.

(2006). Modern Greek Theologians and the Greek Fathers. *Philosophy and Theology*, 18/1, 77–92.

(2009). *Fellow Workers with God: Orthodox Thinking on Theosis.* Crestwood, NY: St Vladimir's Seminary Press.

(2012). Why Does Theosis Fascinate Western Christians? *Sobornost*, 34/1, 5–15.

(2015). The Christological Context of Palamas' Approach to Participation in God. In C. Athanasopoulos, ed., *Triune God: Incomprehensible but Knowable – The Philosophical and Theological Significance of St Gregory Palamas for Contemporary Philosophy and Theology.* Newcastle upon Tyne: Cambridge Scholars, pp. 190–98.

(2016). Cyril of Alexandria's *Mia-physis* Formula in the Christological Debates of the Fifth and Sixth Centuries. In C. Chaillot, ed., *The Dialogue between the Eastern Orthodox and Oriental Orthodox Churches.* Volos: Volos Academy, pp. 94–112.

(2017a). Orthodoxy. In J. Rasmussen, J. Wolfe, and J. Zachhuber, eds., *The Oxford Handbook of Nineteenth-Century Christian Thought.* Oxford: Oxford University Press, pp. 540–54.

(2017b). St Nikodemos the Hagiorite and the Spirituality of the Catholic Reformation. *The Way*, 56/4, 83–95.

(2017c). The Hesychast Controversy. In A. Kaldellis and N. Siniossoglou, eds., *The Cambridge Intellectual History of Byzantium.* Cambridge: Cambridge University Press, pp. 494–508.

(2018). Christian Identity, Sharia Law and Voluntary Martyrdom in the Ottoman Empire. *International Journal for the Study of the Christian Church*, 18/2–3, 158–72.

(2019a). A Common Christian Tradition: Deification in the Greek and Latin Fathers. In J. Ortiz, ed., *Deification in the Latin Patristic Tradition.* Washington, DC: The Catholic University of America Press, pp. 272–93.

(2019b). *Gregory Palamas and the Making of Palamism in the Modern Age.* Oxford: Oxford University Press.

(2020). *Gregory Palamas, the Hesychast Controversy and the Debate with Islam: Documents Relating to Gregory Palamas.* TTB. Liverpool: Liverpool University Press.

(2022). *Saint John of Damascus. An Exact Exposition of the Orthodox Faith.* Yonkers, NY: St Vladimir's Seminary Press.

(forthcoming). St Symeon the New Theologian and the Byzantine Monastic Tradition. In A. Hofer, M. Levering, and P. Gavrilyuk, eds, *The Oxford Handbook of Deification.* Oxford: Oxford University Press.

Sakharov, N. V. (2015). *I Love Therefore I Am: The Theological Legacy of Archimandrite Sophrony.* Crestwood, NY: St. Vladimir's Seminary Press.

Salladin, J. (2021). From Offspring of God to Sons of God; Deification in the Anglican Tradition. In J. Ortiz, ed., *With All the Fullness of God: Deification in Christian Tradition.* Lanham, MD: Lexington Press, pp. 129–54.

Sannino, A. (2000). Berthold of Moosberg's Hermetic Sources. *Journal of the Warburg and Courtauld Institutes*, 63, 243–58.

(2003). Il concetto ermetico di natura in Bertoldo di Moosberg. In P. Lucentini, I. Parri, and V. Perrone Compagni, eds., *Hermetism from Late Antiquity to Humanism.* Turnhout: Brepols, pp. 203–21.

Schiavoni, V. (2018). *Corpus Hermeticum*. Milan: Mondadori (reprint of A. D. Nock and A.-J. Festugière, *Corpus Hermeticum*, 2 vols. Paris: Belles Lettres, 1992, with an Italian translation).

Schmidt, K. L. (1965). θρησκεία, θρῆσκος, ἐθελοθρησκεία. In G. Kittel, ed., *Theological Dictionary of the New Testament*, trans. G. W. Bromily, vol. 3. Grand Rapids, MI: Eerdmans, pp. 155–59.

Scholem, G. (1988). *Kabbalah*. Jerusalem: Keter.

Sergent, F. T. (2015). *Unitas Spiritus* and the Originality of William of Saint-Thierry. In F. T. Sergent, A. Rydstrøm-Poulsen, and M. L. Dutton, eds, *Unity of Spirit. Studies on William of Saint-Thierry in Honor of E. Rozanne Elder*. Collegeville, MN: Liturgical Press, pp. 144–70.

Sidaway, J. (2016). *The Human Factor: 'Deification' as Transformation in the Theology of Hilary of Poitiers*. Leuven: Peeters.

(2019). Making Man Manifest: Deification in Hilary of Poitiers. In J. Ortiz, ed., *Deification in the Latin Patristic Tradition*. Washington, DC: The Catholic University of America Press, pp. 111–31.

Sinkewicz, R. E. (2002). Gregory Palamas. In C. G. Conticello and V. Conticello, eds., *La théologie byzantine et sa tradition*, vol. 2 (XIIIe–XIXe s.). Turnhout: Brepols, pp. 131–88.

Sinnet, A. P. (1883). *Esoteric Buddhism*. London: Trübner & Co.

Smith, O. (2014). The Russian Boehme. In A. Hessayon and S. Apetrei, eds., *An Introduction to Jacob Boehme: Four Centuries of Thought and Reception*. London and New York: Routledge, pp. 196–223.

Smith, T. A. (2012). Elders of Optina Pustyn'. In A. Casiday, ed., *The Orthodox Christian World*. London and New York: Routledge, pp. 332–37.

Soloviev, V. (1996). *The Crisis of Western Philosophy (Against the Positivists)*, trans. and ed. B. Jakim. Hudson, NY: Lindisfarne Press.

Solovyev, V. (1948). *Lectures on Godmanhood*, trans. with an intro. by P. P. Zouboff. London: Dennis Dobson; 2nd (facsimile) ed., San Rafael, CA: Semantron Press, 2007. Revised trans. ed. B. Jakim, *Lectures on Divine Humanity*. Hudson, NY: Lindisfarne Press, 1995.

Sophrony (Sakharov), Archimandrite (1988). *We Shall See Him as He Is*, trans. R. Edmonds. Tolleshunt Knights by Maldon, Essex: Stavropegic Monastery of St John the Baptist.

Souter, A. (1949). *A Glossary of Later Latin to 600 A.D.* Oxford: Clarendon Press.

Southern, R. W. (1970). *Western Society and the Church in the Middle Ages*. The Pelican History of the Church, vol. 2. Harmondsworth, UK: Penguin Books.

Spezzano, D. (2015). *The Glory of God's Grace: Deification according to St Thomas Aquinas*. Ave Maria, FL: Sapientia Press.

Stewart, D. (1993). Theosophy and Abstraction in the Victorian Era: The Paintings of G. F. Watts. *Apollo*, 139/381, 298–302.

Stroumsa, G. (1996). *Hidden Wisdom: Esoteric Traditions and the Roots of Christian Mysticism*. Leiden and New York: E. J. Brill.

Sturlese, L. (1980). Saints et magiciens: Albert le Grand en face d'Hermès Trismégiste. *Archives de philosophie*, 43, 615–34.

Swinburne, R. (2013) A Response to Christos Yannaras' *Against Religion*. *Oxbridge Philokalic Review*, 2, 54–60.

Tacey, D. (2004). *The Spirituality Revolution: The Emergence of Contemporary Spirituality*. London and New York: Routledge.

Tachiaos, A.-E. (1995). La creazione della 'Filocalia' e il suo influsso spirituale nel mondo greco e slavo. In A. Mainardi, ed., *Nil Sorskij e l'esicasmo*. Magnano: Edizioni Qiqajon, pp. 227–49.

Taylor, C. (2003). *Varieties of Religion Today: William James Revisited*. Cambridge, MA: Harvard University Press.

Theissen, G. (1999). *A Theory of Primitive Christian Religion*, trans. J. Bowden. London: SCM Press.

Theodorou, A. (1956). Ἡ περὶ θεώσεως τοῦ ἀνθρώπου διδασκαλία τῶν Ἑλλήνων πατέρων τῆς Ἐκκλησίας μέχρις Ἰωάννου τοῦ Δαμασκηνοῦ. Athens: n.p.

Théry, G. (1926). Édition critique des pièces relatives au procès d'Eckhart contenues dans le manuscrit 33b de la Bibliothèque de Soest. *Archives d'histoire doctrinale et littéraire du moyen âge*, 1, 129–268.

Thomas, S. (2007). *Deification in the Eastern Orthodox Tradition: A Biblical Perspective*. Piscataway, NJ: Gorgias Press.

Titus, A. (2022). The Reception of the Dionysian Corpus in the *Triads* of St. Gregory Palamas. Unpublished doctoral dissertation, Princeton Theological Seminary.

Tollefsen, T. T. (2012). *Activity and Participation in Late Antique and Early Christian Thought*. Oxford: Oxford University Press.

Turner, D. (2009). Dionysius and Some Late Medieval Mystical Theologians of Northern Europe. In S. Coakley and C. M. Stang, eds., *Rethinking Dionysius the Areopagite*. Chichester: Wiley-Blackwell, pp. 121–34.

Turner, H. J. M. (1990). *St Symeon the New Theologian and Spiritual Fatherhood*. Oxford: Oxford University Press.

(2009). *The Epistles of St Symeon the New Theologian*. Oxford: Oxford University Press.

Uro, R. (2003). *Thomas: Seeking the Historical Context of the Gospel of Thomas*. London: T&T Clark.

Valliere, P. (2000). *Modern Russian Theology: Bukharev, Soloviev, Bulgakov – Orthodox Theology in a New Key*. Edinburgh: T&T Clark.

Van Egmond, D. (1998). Western Esoteric Schools in the Late Nineteenth and Early Twentieth Centuries. In R. Van den Broek and W. J. Hanegraaf, eds., *Gnosis and Hermetism from Antiquity to Modern Times*. New York: State University of New York Press, pp. 311–46.

Van Nieuwenhove, R. (2003). *Jan van Ruusbroec, Mystical Theologian of the Trinity*. Notre Dame, IN: University of Notre Dame Press.

Vannini, M. (1992). *Jean Gerson, Teologia Mistica*. Milan: Edizioni Paolini.

Versluis, A. (1998). Christian Theosophic Literature of the Seventeenth and Eighteenth Centuries. In R. Van den Broek and W. J. Hanegraaf, eds., *Gnosis and Hermetism from Antiquity to Modern Times*. New York: State University of New York Press, pp. 217–36.

Vial, M. (2009). Le Viae Sion Lugent de Hugues de Balma et l'évolution de la compréhension Gersonienne de la théologie mystique. *Revue d'histoire et de philosophie religieuse*, 89, 347–65.

Walshe, M. O'C. (2009). *The Complete Mystical Works of Meister Eckhart*, rev. with a foreword by B. McGinn. New York: Crossroads.

Ware, K. (1971). Review of *Panagiotis N. Trembelas: Dogmatique de l'Eglise Orthodoxe Catholique*. *Eastern Churches Review*, 3/4, 477–80.

(1991). The spirituality of the *Philokalia*. *Sobornost*, 13/1, 6–24.

(2003). Deification in Symeon the New Theologian. *Sobornost*, 25/2, 7–29.

(2012). St. Nikodimos and the *Philokalia*. In B. Bingaman and B. Nassif, eds., *The Philokalia: A Classic Text of Orthodox Spirituality*. Oxford and New York: Oxford University Press, pp. 9–35.

Warner, G. (2007). *Ruusbroec: Literature and Mysticism in the Fourteenth Century*, trans. D. Webb. Leiden and Boston: Brill.

Weber, M. (1920), Die Protestantische Ethik und der 'Geist' des Kapitalismus (originally published in Tübingen journal *Archiv für soziale Gesetzgebung und Statistik*, 20/1 and 21/1 [1904–5] of the *Gesammelte Aufsätze zur Religionssoziologie von Max Weber*, vol. 1, part 1. Tübingen: Paul Siebeck; trans. T. Parsons, *The Protestant Ethic and the Spirit of Capitalism*. London: Allen and Unwin, 1930).

Wild, P. T. (1950). *The Divinization of Man according to Saint Hilary of Poitiers*. Mundelein, IL: Saint Mary of the Lake Seminary.

Williams, A. N. (1999). *The Ground of Union: Deification in Aquinas and Palamas*. New York and Oxford: Oxford University Press.

Williams, M. A. (1996). *Rethinking 'Gnosticism': An Argument for Dismantling a Dubious Category*. Princeton, NJ: Princeton University Press.

Williams, R. (2021). *Looking East in Winter: Contemporary Thought and the Eastern Christian Tradition*. London: Bloomsbury Continuum.

Wiseman, J. A. (1985). *John Ruusbroec: The Spiritual Espousals and Other Works*. CWS. New York: Paulist Press.

Wolfson, E. R. (1997). Jewish Mysticism: A Philosophical Overview. In D. H. Frank and Oliver Leaman, eds, *History of Jewish Philosophy*. Routledge History of World Philosophies, vol. 2. London and New York: Routledge, pp. 450–98.

Wolters, C. (1978). *The Cloud of Unknowing and Other Works*. Harmondsworth, UK: Penguin Books.

Yangazoglou, S. (2001). Κοινωνία θεώσεως. Ἡ σύνθεση Χριστολογίας καὶ Πνευματολογίας στὸ ἔργο τοῦ ἁγίου Γρηγορίου τοῦ Παλαμᾶ. Athens: Domos.

Yannaras, C. (1991). *Elements of Faith. An Introduction to Orthodox Theology*, trans. K. Schram. Edinburgh: T&T Clark.

(2007). *Person and Eros*, trans. N. Russell. Brookline, MA: Holy Cross Orthodox Press.

(2013). *Against Religion: The Alienation of the Ecclesial Event*, trans. N. Russell. Brookline, MA: Holy Cross Orthodox Press.

Yates, F. (2002). *Giordano Bruno and the Hermetic Tradition*. London and New York: Routledge (first published in 1964).

Zdenk, V. D. (1962). The influence of Jacob Boehme on Russian Religious Thought. *Slavic Review*, 21/1, 43–64.

Zernov, N. (1963). *The Russian Religious Renaissance of the Twentieth Century*. London: Darton, Longman & Todd.

Zizioulas, J. (2006). *Communion and Otherness*, ed. P. McPartlan. London: T&T Clark.

Index

Abelard, Peter, 88
Abhängigheitsgefühl (sense of dependence), 15, 146
Abraham, 51
Abul Farag, Samuel ben Nissim, 102, 113
Abulafia, R. Abraham, 108
Adam, 53, 151, 165, 172, 181
Adyar, India, 119
Æ. *See* Russell, George William
Agapetos, deacon, 35
Aimeric, Cardinal, 67
Akindynos, Gregory, 58–60
Albert the Great, 65, 69–71, 74–75, 90, 94, 100, 111, 157
Albrecht of Lauingen. *See* Albert the Great
Aleksii, Bishop, 150
Alexander VI, pope, 113
all-unity. *See* pan-unity
Ambrose of Milan, 30, 65
Amvrosii of Optina, 129
analogy
    distinguished from reality, 158
    of union with the divine, 48, 77, 81, 83, 93, 99
Anastasios (Yannoulatos), archbishop, 196, 203
Anastasius Bibliothecarius, 64
Anastasius I, emperor, 35
Anastasius of Sinai, 133
Andrew of Crete, 145
Andronikos II, emperor, 57
Andronikos III, emperor, 57
Androutsos, Ch., 179

Angela of Foligno, 155, 173
Angelic Brethren, the, 118
Anselm of Canterbury, 168
Anthroposophical Society, 24
Anthroposophy, 136–38
Apollo, 134
apophasis, 52, 73, 77, 82
Aquinas. *See* Thomas Aquinas
Arianism, 12
Aristeus, Frixos, 123
Aristotle, 67, 70, 77, 80
Arnobius of Sicca, 10
Arnold, Gottfried, 118
ascent, spiritual, 1, 18, 26–29, 43–44, 49–50, 66, 72, 74, 84, 87, 97–98, 108, 114, 142, 159, 174, 177, 200
Asclepius, 111–12
Asproulis, N., 183, 203
Athanasios Parios, 62
Athanasius of Alexandria, 12, 28, 50, 104, 140, 145, 158, 164
Athos, Mount, 57, 62, 148
Augustine, 1, 10, 12, 19, 30, 33, 64, 66–67, 70, 77, 88–89, 95, 112, 133, 150, 156–57, 164, 170, 175, 188, 200
auras, 169
Avicenna, 77

Balfour, David, 172
Balliol College, Oxford, 111
Balthasar, Hans Urs von, 3, 156, 180, 186–87, 191
Bañez, Domingo, 185

Neoplatonism, 80, 108, 187
New Age, 1, 125, 197, 202
Newman, John Henry, 189
Nicaea, Second Council of (787), 31, 39, 42, 61
Nicholas of Cusa, 65, 93–100, 117, 156, 184
Nicholas of Methone, 111
Nicholas V, pope, 95
Nietzsche, Friedrich, 133, 152
Nikodemos the Hagiorite, 4, 32, 62, 127–29, 131
Niqueux, M., 155
Noah, 48
Nock, A. D., 106
nous, 107
Novoselov group, 147
Novoselov, Mikhail, 147

obozhenie (deification), 1, 129–31, 134, 141–42
occultism, 137–38
Olcott, Henry Steel, 119
Old Lavra, 46
Olson, C. E., 188
Olson, R., 2
On First Principles (Origen), 28, 132
On Mystical Theology (Gerson), 89
Onica, P., 177
Optina Pustyn, 129, 144
Oration on the Dignity of Man (Pico della Mirandola), 113
Oriental Orthodox, 36
Origen of Alexandria, 27–28, 30, 103, 132, 147, 162, 178, 184
Orlov, Anatoly, 143
Orsini, Giordano, 94
Orthodoxy, interiorisation of, 63
Ortiz, J., 188
Osiris, 134
Otto of Ziegenhain, 94
Otto, Rudolf, 16
overforminghe (deiformity), 86
Owens, B., 197
Oxford Movement, 189

Pachymeres, George, 69
Palamas, Gregory. *See* Gregory Palamas
Palamas, Konstantinos, 57
Palamas, Kostis, 123
Palmer, Gerald, 124
Palmer, William, 3
pantheism, 99, 110
pan-unity, 134

Paphlagon, Niketas David, 94
Paracelsus. *See* Hochenheim, Theophrastus von
Paris
   and the Russian émigré theologians, 151, 153–54, 160, 166, 170, 180, 189, 194
   'School' of, xi, 3, 32
   University of, 69, 71, 75, 88–89
   and the YMCA, 194
partakers of the divine nature, 29, 73
participation
   in Christ, 45, 61, 85, 97–98, 191, 201
   in Christ's incorruption, 27
   definitions of, 48
   in the divine attributes, 29, 43
   in divine glory, 174
   in the divine life, xi, 4, 42, 49, 73–74, 124, 167, 178, 182
   in the divine nature, 185–86
   in divine power, 97
   in divine unity, 68
   in ecclesial life, 29, 192–93
   and essence/energies, 2, 7, 57, 74, 121, 177, 182, 200
   in the Eucharist, 5, 27–29, 61, 83, 99, 193, 200
   in God, 2, 5, 33, 52, 59, 87, 172, 183, 186
   inclusive of the body, 56
   in the new humanity, 134
   as a philosophical notion, 27, 41, 112, 150, 177–78, 193
   productive of modal change, 97, 193
   in the relations of the Trinity, 2, 28–29, 182, 189, 193
   as sharing in grace, 58
   in Sophia, 150
   through symbols, 45, 52
   as used by Cyril of Alexandria, 29
   as used by Gregory Palamas, 58
   as used by Matthias Scheeben, 185–86
   as used by Maximus the Confessor, 52
   as used by Nicholas of Cusa, 97–98
   as used by Thomas Aquinas, 73
Patmos, monastery of, 62
Patrizi, Francesco, 114
Paul, Apostle, 178–79
perennialism, 23–24, 103, 114–15, 121, 124
perichoresis, 105, 161, 167
Peter the Fuller, 132
Peter the Iberian, 42
Petrizi, Joane, 111

For EU product safety concerns, contact us at Calle de José Abascal, 56–1°,
28003 Madrid, Spain or eugpsr@cambridge.org.

www.ingramcontent.com/pod-product-compliance
Ingram Content Group UK Ltd.
Pitfield, Milton Keynes, MK11 3LW, UK
UKHW020354140625
459647UK00020B/2457